EFFECTIVE LETTERS IN BUSINESS

ROBERT L. SHURTER

SECOND EDITION

McGRAW-HILL BOOK COMPANY, INC.
NEW YORK   TORONTO   LONDON

Library of Congress Catalog Card Number 53-12437

11121314151617 MUMU 7654321

ISBN 07-057340-9
ISBN 07-057339-5

Acknowledgments

In preparing this revised edition of *Effective Letters in Business,* I have been most conscious of the debt I owe to a great many businessmen, teachers, and editors. Their help in supplying me with material and in offering suggestions affords tangible evidence of the importance they attach to the subject of writing in business. But beyond that, their assistance also testifies to their own generosity for which I here, inadequately, express my gratitude.

In the six years since the first edition appeared, I have had the privilege of serving as a consultant for such companies as the American Steel and Wire Division, United States Steel Corporation; the Central National Bank of Cleveland; The Chesapeake and Ohio Railway Company; The Cleveland Electric Illuminating Company; and Standard Oil of Ohio. I am especially grateful to these companies for permitting me to use certain materials and situations which arise in the practical, everyday communication of American business.

For contructive suggestions and permission to reprint materials, I am indebted to Professor C. A. Brown of The General Motors Institute; Professor C. R. Anderson, editor of the *Bulletin* of the American Business Writing Association; Henry Hoke, editor of *The Reporter of Direct Mail Advertising;* H. Jack Lang, editor of *The Wolf Magazine of Letters;* C. B. Larrabee, president and publisher of *Printers' Ink;* Kermit Rolland of the New York Life Insurance Company; Professor John B. Lord of Washington State College; Professor Mary L. Lynott of Long Beach City College; Professor Donald G. Wilson of Nichols Junior College; R. M. Severa, executive manager of the Credit Bureau of Greater New York, Paul Griswold of the Strathmore Paper Company; William G. Werner of the Procter and Gamble Company; John D. Yeck of Yeck and Yeck; Arnold W. Lehman of Richard T. Brandt Inc.; the editors of *Fortune;* the National Office Management Association; and more than thirty-five personnel men from various American businesses who took time to read and comment upon the chapter on "The Application Letter" during their visits to the Case campus.

I am particularly grateful for the numerous suggestions made by two of my colleagues—Professor Howard Barton and Professor David M. Rein, and to Mrs. Margaret C. Garretson, for her untiring and efficient help in preparing the manuscript.

ROBERT L. SHURTER

Contents

Read not to contradict and refute, nor to believe and take for granted, nor to find talk and discourse, but to weigh and consider.
Francis Bacon, *Of Studies*

CHAPTER I

Introduction

It would be almost impossible to find better advice for reading this—or any other—book of instruction than the well-known words of Sir Francis Bacon. Presumably, you are reading or studying these pages because you want to learn how to write business letters or to improve the letters you are now writing. This introductory chapter is, therefore, intended to tell you how to read this book so that you can best achieve your goal of writing better letters.

Before you "weigh and consider" the chapters which follow, you ought to expect answers to these three questions:

1. What does this book attempt to do?
2. Why is its subject—the business letter—important?
3. What is the author's point of view in treating this subject?

The answers to these questions should be important to you as a student or as a general reader. Quite obviously, you shouldn't spend your time reading this book if your major interest lies in learning about raising wire-haired terriers. Nor should you read it unless you are convinced that the techniques of writing business letters are important to your career. Finally, you will need to know the point of view from which this book is written so that you can pass critical judgments on the principles and ideas it contains. In brief, you need answers to three questions—What? Why? and How?—and then you can read with understanding, motivation, and judgment, for the reader who sees the usefulness of what he is learning while he learns it will read to better purpose.

WHAT THIS BOOK ATTEMPTS TO DO

This book is intended to present the fundamental principles of the major types of business letters and to assist the student or the correspondent in learning these principles by numerous examples and exercises. It grew out of a conviction that there is a need for a comparatively brief text whose scope would be halfway between the sketchy handbook with its Do's and Dont's and the encyclopedic volumes of six or seven hundred pages covering every conceivable problem in business correspondence. Since conciseness is one of the most desirable qualities in business letters, we ought in all fairness to expect the same desirable quality in the books on the subject. The major emphasis in this book is on the fundamental principles of effective letter writing, with sufficient practice in the application of these principles to teach the reader to apply them to the various business situations which arise from day to day. Wherever possible, the examples used are taken from actual business letters to give the reader an understanding of the day-to-day problems correspondents face and the specific methods and techniques they use to solve them.

WHY THE BUSINESS LETTER IS IMPORTANT

It seems almost trite to say that the business letter is one of the most widely used forms of writing in the twentieth century. Yet that fact needs emphasis, for, paradoxically enough, our schools and colleges devote more time to such types of writing as the research paper, complete with the scholarly paraphernalia of footnotes and bibliographies and knee-deep in *ibids.* and *op. cits.*, than to more widely used forms of writing. The research paper certainly has its place, but for every person who will find occasion to write a research paper, there are probably a thousand who will be required to produce effective business letters. For that reason, this book stresses the conviction that learning to write good business letters is a highly important aspect of a student's education.

We can make this point clear in another way—by showing the size of the investment modern American business has in its correspondence. This is, at best, an "educated guess," because no one can be sure of the statistical information available—and even statistics lead to some strange conclusions. Remember the mining town with a hundred men and two women? When two inhabitants married, a reporter sent out a story that "1 per cent of the men married 50 per cent of the women!"

To get even an approximation of the total annual investment in business letters, we need two factors: the average cost of a letter and the total number of letters sent. Estimates of the average cost of a letter written in the past two years vary from a low of 70 cents to a high of $1.25; a realistic figure would probably fix the cost at about $1.00. This includes the dictator's and the stenographer's time and the cost of overhead, postage, printing, and paper and envelopes.

The Postmaster General's Annual Report for 1951 shows the following number of pieces of mail for all classes:

First class	25,626,462,000
Second class	5,979,552,000
Third class	10,387,000,000
Fourth class	1,240,592,000

Since business letters go chiefly as first- and third-class mail—most so-called "form letters" are sent third class—we are concerned with a total of 36,013,462,000 pieces of mail. If we assume that only one out of five of these letters is a business letter—a very conservative estimate—at a cost of a dollar, the total cost runs over 7 billion dollars a year. Even if we take a very low average cost for letters—75 cents—the total cost is more than 5 billion dollars annually. In view of the magnitude of this investment in the art of "putting words down on paper," is it any wonder that modern business puts a high premium on writers who can express themselves concisely and effectively? The simple fact is that the student or employee who can apply the principles of effective letters has learned a skill which can prove invaluable to him in his career.

This skill can be rated even more highly when it is compared to the quality of much writing in business today. Students who have had no business experience are inclined to be skeptical of the statement that the quality of many of the letters produced in the modern business world is poor. By way of instruction on this point, therefore, the following article by Gordon Cobbledick, columnist of the *Cleveland Plain Dealer,* underscores the need for improvement in letter writing:

A publicity release discloses that the Dartnell Corp. of Chicago has embarked upon an enterprise so worthy as to merit the support and encouragement of all the English-speaking, and more especially the English-writing peoples. It purposes to teach businessmen the art of writing business letters, using as a starting point the revolutionary thesis that anything which needs saying in commerce can be said in words and phrases in common use among ordinary people.

According to the release, when the average businessman sits down to write a letter he completely changes his personality. Instead of being friendly and cheerful, he usually becomes as cold as an oyster and as formal as the king's butler. He fusses and fumes, "ums" and "ahs," then finally comes out with something like this:

> We beg to advise and wish to state
> That yours has arrived of recent date.
> We have it before us, its contents noted,
> And herewith enclose the prices we quoted.
> Attached please find as per your request
> The samples you wanted, and we would suggest,
> Regarding the matter and due to the fact
> That up until now your order we've lacked,
> We hope you will not delay it unduly,
> And beg to remain yours very truly.

This style of composition is known as "goozling," and anyone who has had occasion to carry on any considerable amount of business correspondence is aware that many executives who dictate America's business letters are confirmed goozlers.

Nor has this strange variety of English come about through accident or by a process of evolution rooted in necessity. I seem to remember being taught the "enclosed please find" brand of writing in school, where teachers begged to advise that it gave a businesslike tone to our letters, as did "yours of even date" and "yours of the 19th inst."

In conjunction with its assault on goozling, the Dartnell Corp. has launched a campaign against an interesting kind of double talk peculiar to business correspondence. And it quotes:

"Dear Sir: We refuse and decline to write more letters. We take the position and are most convinced that you have been unfair and unjust. Therefore be advised and informed that we expect a check at once and immediately. We demand and insist that you send us this check with no further cost or expense. We beg to remain—"

By way of contrast, the crusading corporation submits a letter similar in purpose which, it says, brought from a reluctant debtor a check by return mail:

"Dear Sir: Can you give us the name of a good attorney in your town? We may have to sue you. Cordially—"

It quotes as a horrible example a letter sent by a girl correspondent in a mail-order house to a farmer's wife who had bought a set of chess men and asked for instruction in their use:

"Dear Madam: In regard to your letter I would suggest that you take one chess and move it from the bottom to the center, following the game through to the finer points. The first party that fills in the top of the board wins the game. We assure you that if you follow these instructions you will have every satisfaction. We beg to remain—"

If this appraisal seems exaggerated, let's look at a more sober and thoughtful analysis. Here are *Fortune's* comments in an excellent article on "The Language of Business":

Not so long ago, the businessman used to take his language pretty much for granted. He could afford to. His place was respected and his authority unquestioned. And so he bought, he sold, he collected his bills, made an occasional speech perhaps—and if the public, the workers, or the government didn't quite understand what he was up to, well, so much the better for all concerned.

But no longer. Acknowledging the fact—and the necessity—of others' scrutiny, he has made the interchange of facts and ideas with them one of his principal jobs. The house organ, the interoffice memo, the press release, the press conference, the annual report—the range of his efforts has grown enormous. So widespread, indeed, that business has become almost as extensive a publisher as the government itself.

Is the language of business up to the job? The news—and refreshing news it is—is that the American businessman himself has begun to conclude that it is not. Some, in fact, have gone so far as to assert that the pomposity of management prose is the "root ill of our communication troubles." While that may be an overexcited judgment, management's surveys have demonstrated that a large amount of its language has been not only incomprehensible to the people it is trying to reach, but enormously expensive in money, time, and misunderstanding as well. "It is high time the American businessman discovered the English language—it would be very useful to him" . . . . "We've turned our offices into paper mills" . . . . "We love curt clear correspondence—but damned few of us know how to write it." Everywhere the chorus of self-criticism is growing.

. . . By the use of regular English the cost of the average letter—commonly estimated at 75 cents to $1—can be cut by about 20 cents. For a firm emitting a million letters a year, this could mean an annual saving of $200,000. Probably it would be even greater; for, by the calculations of correspondence specialist Richard Morris, roughly 15 per cent of the letters currently being written wouldn't be necessary at all if the preceding correspondence had been in regular English in the first place.

The positive results of such examinations of writing in business have been numerous. Many companies are putting their employees into correspondence-improvement courses, hiring correspondence supervisors and experts in communications, and holding "clinics" on letters. At Long Beach City College, Professor M. L. Lynott's class in business letters wrote to firms asking if they published a manual on letter writing for their employees; twenty-six companies sent such manuals. Among them were names that belong in the "Blue Book" of American industry—Remington Rand, Royal Typewriter, Armstrong Cork, Prudential Insurance, Goodyear, International Harvester, Minneapolis Honeywell, Esso, Swift, Borden, L. C. Smith and Corona, Johns-Manville, The American Rolling Mill, U.S. Rubber, Procter and Gamble, New York Central, and others too numerous to mention.

Is the art of writing letters important in business? Obviously business and industry think so. The annual dollars-and-cents investment in letter writing makes it one of our most important enterprises. And the general quality of today's letters, which might be described as not-as-good-as-it-should-be but improving, adds additional incentive for the individual who wants to learn to write effective letters in business.

THE POINT OF VIEW OF THIS BOOK

Now that you know what this book is about and why letters are important, you should understand the convictions that color its writing. First, there is no mention in these pages of something called "business English"; this strange concept, which results in the production of books on engineering English, legal English, medical English, the English of business, and eventually—if the trend continues to its logical conclusion—mortician's English, finds no support in these pages. In the last analysis, there are only two types: good English, well adapted to its purpose and occasion, and poor English. The person who can write good English will soon find that the same basic principles apply in business, engineering, and other fields. There is no escaping the inexorable connection between clear thinking and clear writing, and breaking the use of English into separate compartments is merely a delusion. What is needed is a knowledge of the purposes, points of view, methods, and forms which are most acceptable in the correspondence of modern business. This book attempts to provide that knowledge.

Second, it stresses the belief that the business letter offers as much opportunity for originality, good organization, and creative ability as any other form of writing. Many of the examples have been particularly selected to illustrate this belief. Inevitably the writer who thinks business correspondence is a routine, unimaginative form of communication will write routine, unimaginative, and ineffective letters.

Finally, it aims at simplicity in its presentation. Perhaps this constitutes a minor revolt from longer, more involved treatments which leave the reader feeling that a combination Shakespeare-Dickens-Hemingway could not possibly measure up to the task of writing a business letter. No one should underestimate the fact that writing in any form is hard work, and the old saw that "easy reading means hard writing" still holds good. Nevertheless, the basic premise behind this book is that the letter is a comparatively simple form of writing and should be treated so. And that very fact should serve as the greatest possible source of encouragement to those who start the following pages with a desire to write effective letters in business.

One of the earliest comments made on the subject of letter writing is contained in a collection of papers in the British Museum. Under the highly undescriptive title of *Ms. Sloane 459*, there is catalogued an exercise book which an unknown medieval student used for translating English letters into Latin. On one of these letters, someone—probably a tutor—has inscribed a quaint marginal note: "Thou hast bestowed paynes in thy composition." This is a comment which would gratify almost any writer of letters; and if this book helps its readers to gain similar plaudits from their instructors or supervisors, it will indeed have served its purpose.

The difficulty is not to write, but to write what you mean, not to affect your reader, but to affect him precisely as you wish.
Robert Louis Stevenson

CHAPTER II

What Is an Effective Letter?

To be effective, every kind of writing must be preceded by thought and analysis. Too much of the communication in modern business is essentially "thought-less," and therefore a great deal of it is stereotyped and unoriginal. The letters of many correspondents are almost automatic, like the response of a muscle to a nerve impulse. This failure to think about the fundamental aspects of a letter situation results inevitably in muddled expression or vague and inadequate phraseology. Such thoughtlessness also results in wasted time and money since the "automatic response" usually leaves questions unanswered, fails to supply sufficient information, or makes the reader feel that he is receiving routine treatment. *Think before you write,* for in business wasted words mean wasted time and money.

Anyone who hopes to write effectively in business should first have a general understanding of what the business letter is, and then, before he writes any letter, he should think specifically about answering the following questions:

1. What am I trying to accomplish in this letter?
2. How can I best accomplish this purpose?

Considered in its most fundamental terms, *the business letter may be defined as a message that attempts to influence its recipient to take some action or attitude desired by the sender.* In other words, the correspondent tries to get his reader to agree with him; this attempt at agreement should always be part of the letter, whether the desired result is of immediate importance, such as the collecting of a bill, or whether it is an intangible attitude like good will. Any type of letter can be judged in terms of how successfully it gains agreement from the reader. The successful sales message gets its reader to agree that a product or service is worth buying; the collection letter to be effective should convince the debtor that payment of his bill is the wisest policy; the application letter attempts to win agreement from the prospective employer that the applicant is well qualified to get the job for which he applies.

In fact, it is comparatively simple to list the general purposes for which all the letters of the modern business world are written. They fall into these three categories:

1. To get action
2. To build good will
3. To furnish information

Within the framework of these primary purposes are set all the types of letters which are customarily labeled as sales, application, collection, credit, adjustment, and answers to inquiries. It is, therefore, helpful for the letter writer to keep these major purposes in mind as a functional approach to his writing. But he must also know the specific goal of each letter and the best method of attaining it—or, to paraphrase Robert Louis Stevenson, he must know precisely how he wishes to affect his reader.

1. What Am I Trying to Accomplish in This Letter?

If this discussion of the letter is correct—and there is no other way of explaining its purpose—the first question to be answered by anyone confronted with the task of writing a business letter is, "What am I trying to accomplish in this letter?" If, before writing, he does not think clearly about his purpose, his letter will be ineffectual. This necessity for thinking before writing would seem so obvious as to require no emphasis, yet time and again business letters reveal the writer's lack of thought about the action or attitude the letter is designed to prompt.

Consider the following two letters, dealing with the same situation. Which message gives evidence of careful thought? Which writer has made up his mind about what he wants his letter to accomplish?

Dear Sir:

We are sorry that we cannot fill your order of November 5 for 12 dozen men's shirts to retail at $2.25 because we are no longer manufacturing them.

We have gone into the production of more expensive shirts for men. In the event that you need any of these, we will be glad to serve you.

Yours truly,

Dear Mr. Wiley:

We regret that we cannot fill your order of November 5 for 12 dozen men's shirts to retail at $2.25.

We have found that men are demanding a shirt that will wear longer and look better than those that can be made to sell at $2.25.

In order to meet this demand, we have designed "The Monitor," a genuine broadcloth, preshrunk shirt to sell at $3.50. These shirts will give you, the dealer, a larger margin of profit; they will enable you to take advantage of our national advertising campaign which features "The Monitor"; they will help to convince your customers that your store carries quality merchandise.

The enclosed post card lists the wholesale prices for "The Monitor." If you will sign and mail it today, a supply of these high-quality shirts will reach you within a week to bring you added profit and satisfied customers.

Sincerely yours,

The fundamental difference between these two letters lies in the thought and analysis by the correspondent before putting a word on paper. The first writer shows not the slightest indication of thinking in advance about what his letter ought to do. His is the automatic, the "thought-less" response. A routine brain working in routine fashion simply stops with the refusal of the order. The second writer has analyzed what he wants his letter to do; for him it is not enough merely to refuse the order for $2.25 shirts; he has considered the question, "What am I trying to do in this letter?" very specifically. His letter's task is to sell higher priced shirts, and everything in it after the first paragraph is directed toward that purpose. Its success comes from thought and analysis.

2. How Can I Best Accomplish This Purpose?

Having determined what he wants his letter to do, the writer's next problem is, obviously, how best to do it. What technique or characteristics will make the letter most effective as a message to influence its reader to do what the writer wants him to do? Certainly, qualities like courtesy, friendliness, and helpfulness are the minimum essentials of any effective letter, if only because these characteristics help us to persuade others to do what we want them to do. This is putting a low premium indeed upon these personal traits, but where such qualities are naturally a part of the correspondent's personality, he will need no conscious effort to inject them into his letters.

As the most effective method of answering our second question —"How can I best accomplish this purpose?"—the rest of this chapter discusses three major qualities all business letters should have: the "you attitude," a tone adapted to the reader, and personality.

THE "YOU ATTITUDE"

Much has been written about such subjects as the psychology of selling, the correct attitude of the letter writer, and the use of psychology in his letters. Actually, there is just one fact that the letter writer must keep constantly in mind; he must remember that we can most readily persuade others to do what we want them to by demonstrating that it is to their advantage to do it. Nothing related to business correspondence is more important than this point of view, known usually as the "you attitude." The letter writer accomplishes his purpose most effectively by adopting the reader's viewpoint, by writing not in terms of "how much we should like to have your order," but of "when you order this merchandise, you will benefit by increased profit and utility." Human beings must be shown not just that they should agree but that it is to their advantage to agree. The first requisite of a successful letter is that it should have the you attitude, that is, *it should take the reader's point of view.*

Notice how different these two letters are in their point of view although they both aim at the same result:

Dear Sir:

Enclosed is a questionnaire we are sending to all our retail stores in this area.

Will you please answer as soon as possible? It's essential that we have an immediate reply because we are delaying plans for this year's sales training program until we get replies.

I know that questionnaires are often a nuisance, but I hope you will recognize the need for this one.

Very truly yours,

Dear Mr. Flemming:

The enclosed questionnaire was designed to give us information so that we can make this year's sales training program most useful to you and your sales force.

Your opinions about past programs and our tentative plans for this year will help us to serve your needs. If you will fill out and return the questionnaire as soon as possible, we can let you and our other dealers know promptly about the changes recommended.

We will greatly appreciate your assistance in this important phase of our training program.

Sincerely yours,

The you attitude can be used to good effect in any letter-writing situation, however difficult. To the inexperienced correspondent, the you attitude appears ill-adapted to such a situation as collecting past-due accounts; nevertheless, thousands of collection letters are written daily whose chief effectiveness lies in their argument that it is to the debtor's own advantage to pay his bills. The following paragraph from one such letter shows how this may be done.

As a businessman, you must realize that your most valuable asset is your credit reputation. Without it, you cannot long remain in business. We know that you would not willingly lose this priceless possession for a mere $70.12, the amount of our bill. By placing your check in the mail today, you will help to keep your business on that firmest of foundations—a sound credit rating.

Anyone who sees many application letters knows how sadly they lack the you attitude. Perhaps getting the right job *is* the most difficult job in the world, but the task could be much simplified if the applicant in his letter or interview would constantly keep in mind the prospective employer's point of view. Imagine yourself, for a moment, to be a personnel director. Which of the following opening paragraphs would interest you more?

I happened to see your advertisement for a junior chemist in this morning's paper, and I should like to have you consider me as an applicant for the position. I am very much interested in working for your company because I have heard of its liberal attitude toward employees.

My four years' education in chemical engineering at the University of Michigan and two summers working as chemist's assistant at the Dow Chemical Company should prove to be valuable in the position of junior chemist, which you advertised in this morning's *Daily News.*

The you attitude in letter writing is not merely a matter of phraseology but is also one of attitude. Nothing can improve your letter writing more than constantly keeping in mind the interests and desires of your reader and designing your letter to appeal to him. Point out qualities related to the reader's advantage—concrete things like profit, pleasure, utility, appearance, or enjoyment. A glance through the advertising pages of any magazine will show how effectively copy writers do this. Their appeal is always to the reader's interests, such as pleasure ("A trip through the great West will give you endless hours of sheer delight, hours spent in riding, swimming, hiking, or in just gazing at the magnificent views spread out before you.") or profit ("A small investment in tires now will bring you great economy and the secure knowledge that your family is safe on Firestones.") or utility ("You relax, have fun, never worry about tire trouble when you equip your car with world-famous, quick-stopping, longer mileage U.S. Royal Masters!").

All of us are tempted to write about what we ourselves are doing or hoping to do. We delude ourselves by thinking that everyone is interested in *our* problems, *our* products, *our* wishes. In letter writing, it is a good principle to forget yourself. Think about the person to whom you are writing. He probably will not be interested in your affairs unless you show him that he should be by appealing to *his* interests. If you do that, your letter will be effective because it will have the you attitude.

One last word of caution should be added to the concept of the you attitude as a means of insuring good human relations in correspondence. There is a danger that inexperienced correspondents will think of it merely as a "pose" or a "gimmick" which offers them a short cut to achieving their purposes. Nothing could be further from the truth. In the term "you attitude," the emphasis should be placed on *attitude*, something which directly reflects our feelings, moods, or convictions. What are the attitudes which we ought ideally to reflect in our relations with others? Sincerity, truthfulness, and integrity should rank high on the list—and unless we use the you attitude sincerely and in good faith, we shall pervert its intent and defeat its purpose. Readers of letters are quicker to detect insincerity than any other quality; and effective writers have learned that the essence of good human relations in letters is the avoidance of superficial cordiality and exaggerated claims. Properly used, the you attitude tells the reader in an honest, tactful, truthful manner the benefits he obtains from an action or attitude implicit in your letter.

A TONE ADAPTED TO THE READER

The you attitude is also important because it automatically eliminates a fault present in too many letters—a tone that is too technical or too specialized or otherwise inappropriate for the general reader. As we have defined it, the you attitude involves putting yourself in your reader's place and taking his point of view. If you do, you will find yourself "talking his language" and writing to him as if he were a human being instead of a name. By learning to do this, you will avoid one of the worst faults of writing in modern business.

Here, for instance, is a horrible example of what not to do:

Dear Mr. Blane:

Surrender of the policy is permissible only within the days attendant the grace period on compliance with the citation relevant options accruing to the policy so we are estopped from acquiescing to a surrender prior to the policy's anniversary date. We are confident that an investigation relevant to the incorporation of this feature will substantiate that the policy is not at variance with policies of other companies.

Yours truly,

This is how the policy holder replied to that letter:

Dear Mister:

I am sorry but I don't understand your letter. If you will explain what you mean, I will try to do what you ask.

Yours truly,

Henry Blane

Commenting on this exchange of correspondence, H. T. Heggen, Jr., speaking at the annual conference of the Life Office Management Association, said, "As long as any letter like that one comes out of any insurance office, we have a job to do."

One cannot always know exactly what kind of person the reader is, but it is a mistake to assume that he will be interested in highly technical language or specialized nomenclature. Letters sent to engineers, lawyers, doctors, or dentists should naturally differ in tone and phraseology from those sent to a cross section of the public. Certain appeals to various groups have been found by experienced correspondents to be most effective. A letter sent to dealers or retailers can use the profit motive as an excellent means of adaptation to its readers' interests. Letters to women may well stress an emotional appeal by discussing a product's beauty, attractive design, or modern styling. Letters to men are usually made more effective by a reasoned appeal stressing utility, efficiency, economy, or the details of construction and materials. The problem of selecting the right appeal for selling highly technical products or services to the general public is a difficult one, over which advertising men and letter writers have labored long. It involves adapting a highly specialized product or service to the general point of view. How one salesman successfully tackled this problem is shown in the following letter:

Dear Mr. Barnes:

Just a brief note to thank you for your courteous attention to my sales story when I called on you last Wednesday.

It will be a pleasure to work with you in producing literature (letterpress or offset) to sell air conditioners.

Remember the three men in the lower right-hand corner of the American League official score cards? They don't pitch. They don't bat worth a hoot. But they perform a very useful service—coaching. Our twenty-five years of "coaching" experience is available to aid you in producing literature that will sell your products.

I'll be listening for that telephone bell!

Sincerely yours,

Among letters written to special groups, the following sent to children urging them to renew subscriptions is successful in adopting the proper appeal:

Dear Friend:

Remember the circus Dad took you to and how that fellow at the side show hollered, "Hurry! Hurry! Hurry! See the best show in town!"

Well, we feel just like that fellow at the circus. We want to holler, "Hurry! Hurry! Hurry! Send in your renewal order to *Boys' Life* today!" We can guarantee you that it's the best "show" in town when it comes to giving you twelve months of swell fun and entertainment!

It isn't necessary to tell you all about the exciting serials and adventure stories and news pictures and all the other entertaining, exciting features in every issue, because you've been enjoying them for a whole year now and you know what's there. But golly! We do have to tell you that you'll be missing all that swell fun if you don't renew your subscription, NOW!

Your subscription expires with the December issue, and since we have already written you once before, and time is getting short for you to get your renewal in, we're just sending this "hurry-up" message so that you won't be disappointed.

Tell you what you do—take this letter and show it to Mom or Dad, and, you know, I've got a hunch they'll see to it that you have *Boys' Life* for another year! That sounds like a good idea, doesn't it?

Here's a subscription blank and a postage-free envelope. Get Mom or Dad to help you fill it out and send it to us TODAY. You'll be glad you did when those copies of *Boys' Life* come along each month!

REMEMBER . . .

"Hurry! Hurry! Hurry!"

Your friend,

The importance of remembering that the reader is a human being has never been more aptly illustrated than in the following letter from Yeck and Yeck, of Dayton, Ohio. For all letter writers, it points up a moral that the best technique for correspondents is nothing more or less than good human relations.

QUEEN VICTORIA
WAS A TOUGH CUSTOMER:

If you think Congress doesn't like the President because he vetoes some of their bills, you should have talked to Prime Minister W. E. Gladstone back in Queen Victoria's day.

Every time he went in to see her on a matter of State he came out looking vetoed. He didn't seem able to convince her of anything. She was proud and haughty and dignified. She loved to say "no."

Now, when Disraeli was prime minister, things were different.

"The Queen was pleased"; "The Queen agreed"; "The Queen commended." Everything was peaches and cream for Dizzy.

One day someone asked the Queen, "Why?"

She thought a moment, pushed her crown back on her head, cleared the room and her throat, and said softly, "It's this way . . . "

"When Mr. Gladstone talks to us, he talks as though we were a public meeting; but when Mr. Disraeli talks to us, he talks as though we were a woman."

The Queen had something there.

When *you* want conviction, remember Queen Victoria of Great Britain, her possessions beyond the seas and Empress, if you please, of India . . . it paid to talk to her "man to man"—like a human being.

Yes, in advertising; in public relations . . . it helps to be human. Writing that is friendly, interesting, pleasant, is writing

to a Queen's taste.

John & Bill.

Yeck and Yeck

PERSONALITY

Finally, the effective letter should have another quality, an indefinable tone called personality. Contrary to the opinion of many letter writers—an opinion glaringly reflected in their letters—personality does not mean peculiarity or freakishness. Your letters should reflect you at your best; they should be natural, unaffected, direct. If a stranger, reading one of your letters, can gain an impression that you are the sort of person he would like to know, your letter has successfully avoided the two extremes of complete impersonality or outlandish freakishness. Notice how effectively the following letter, addressed to the Square D Company of Detroit, makes its appeal:

Gentlemen:

We have a Westinghouse Pump with one of your switches on it. Since we live out in the country on very low land and depend completely on your switch to keep water out of our cellar, you can imagine our predicament when I say that without this pump we have *four feet of water* in our cellar and this, of course, puts our fire out!

We bought the pump only last March, but, although it is not a year old, the switch has gone berserk and we are at our wits' end. We cannot get another switch here or get this one repaired. Please send us another switch quickly before everything floats out the cellar windows.

We have to set the alarm every hour all night long to get us up to turn the pump on and off by hand besides staying home all day to do it. And I'm going to have a baby soon. Here's hoping we get that switch quickly or I'll have my baby in the cellar.

Yours sincerely,

Rosemary La Reau

The best letters are those that convey a tone of friendly interest or a sense of humor; they reflect definite personalities and avoid a cold, impersonal tone. The following letters show how this may be accomplished:

Dear Mr. Foster:

As I write this letter, I'm reminded of an old Norwegian proverb which says:

> "On the path between the homes of
> friends . . . grass does not grow!"

In a manner of speaking, the grass seems to have grown somewhat lush between your doorstep and our store during the past year. Frankly, I am a little concerned because you have not used your charge account for so long a time. I am concerned because your absence from our store may indicate some dissatisfaction.

Perhaps we unwittingly have done something to displease you. If so, won't you write to me so that I may make amends?

Cordially,

Dear Mr. and Mrs. Edwards:

Although the telephone book calls us landscape architects, we much prefer to be known simply as people who for over eighty years have been helping folks with THEIR ideas and THEIR schemes in making their grounds more useful and attractive.

If you will visualize a capable friend working with you, that's mostly what it's like . . . and that's somewhat the manner in which we should like to' be of assistance to you.

I wonder whether you feel that we could be of service.

Sincerely yours,

Thus far, we have been discussing the thinking or the mental attitude that precedes letter writing. Before going on, in the next chapter, to the actual form and writing of the letter, let us summarize this important process of analysis. If you think before you write—and you cannot write a good letter otherwise—you will formulate clear-cut answers to the following questions before a word is dictated or put on paper:

1. What am I trying to accomplish in this letter?
2. How can I best accomplish that purpose?
   a. How can I show my reader that it is to his advantage to do what I want him to do? (you attitude)
   b. How can I adapt my letter to my reader's interests?
   c. How can I make this letter sound like me? (personality)

EXERCISES

1. What is wrong with the point of view of the following letters? Has the writer clearly made up his mind about what he wants his letter to do? Has he accomplished his purpose in the most effective way or can you improve on the technique?

Dear Mr. James:

Referring to your letter of July 16, we appreciate your need of credit to open your new factory, but we cannot grant it to you.

We are operating on a very narrow margin of profit and we dare not take the risk involved in assuming credit losses. Since we are now manufacturing the finest home furnishings at what we can guarantee to be the lowest prices in the country, we know you will want to buy from us on a cash basis and will find some way of doing so.

We hope to have your cash order soon.

Sincerely yours,

Dear Mr. Stauffer:

We find it difficult to believe your complaint of October 22 regarding the failure of our portable radio, Model X, to receive stations only 40 miles away.

All of our other customers report excellent reception of stations much farther away than that. We want you to know that our engineering staff has put the most modern design and best materials into this portable, and such a failure as you report seems incredible.

We suggest that you take the radio back to your dealer to let him see what is wrong.

Yours truly,

Gentlemen:

I can't understand why my gas bill is always so high. My gas furnace has been checked over carefully by my son who is a sophomore in an engineering college, and he says it is very efficient. Yet, regardless of the weather, my bills are always too high.

Utility companies like yours take advantage of the public and put in meters that always read the same. I get tired of you big companies squeezing us small customers. I want some action and smaller bills.

Yours truly,

2. What action or attitude should each of the above letters attempt to produce?

3. Rewrite the letters using the you attitude to influence your reader to take this action.

4. Criticize the point of view in each of the following paragraphs from actual letters. Rewrite them to make them more effective in influencing the reader to take the action desired.

    a. I should like to be considered for a position with the New York Standard Products Company because I particularly want to be located in New York City. While I haven't had any experience with the type of work your company does, I am so anxious to be in New York, where most of my college friends are working, that I know I can make up for my lack of experience.

    b. We hope that you will send us your check for $73.19 as soon as possible. It is expensive for us to send out monthly statements on past-due accounts, and furthermore, we have bills of our own to meet. You can help us greatly, therefore, by forwarding your remittance promptly.

    c. I am sorry that I cannot send you any information concerning the method of using our photo exposure meter in enlarging. All such inquiries are handled by the sales department in Chicago; we are merely subcontractors for various parts in the meter. It will be appreciated if you will write direct to our sales office in the future.

d. I regret that we cannot accept your application for admission to Alpha College. We have so many applications from very excellent students that we cannot accept yours. If there is any way in which I can be of further assistance to you, please let me know.

5. As the secretary for your organization, you have been authorized by unanimous vote of the membership to secure as speaker for your annual meeting Mr. John C. Collins, a prominent industrialist and formerly a member of your organization. Since your group has no funds with which to pay speakers, you must obtain without charge Mr. Collins' services as speaker for your 225 members. Write an appropriate letter to Mr. Collins.

6. Rewrite these paragraphs using the reader's point of view:

a. We are surprised and disappointed that we have not yet received your order for display space at this year's Office Equipment Convention. We want to emphasize that more than 8,000 people attended this convention last year, and we feel that you are missing a great opportunity to display your new models. We, of course, make no profit on the sale of space; we merely offer space as a service to our members. A booth 15 feet square, for instance, costs only $150 for four days, and on a total investment of $20,000, last year's displayers received orders totaling almost $3,000,000.

b. May we take the liberty of notifying you that we have entered the business of servicing office equipment in this city? Perhaps you will at some time in the future need repairs for your typewriters, adding machines, and duplicating equipment. If so, we would be pleased to hear from you and to estimate the costs of servicing your equipment on an annual basis.

c. We were puzzled by the paragraph in your recent letter which claimed that we had not shipped your order promptly. As a matter of fact, we maintain a policy of shipping all orders the day they are received. However, we are taking the trouble to see what happened in your case.

d. For many years we have followed a policy of sending a wrist watch to customers we have served for ten years. Since you have now purchased from us for that period of time, we are sending your watch by parcel post. If you do not receive it within the next five days, please let me know.

e. We could hardly understand why the valves which we sent you on March 24 did not fit your boiler. Upon investigation, we found that you had specified the wrong size in your order. The boiler you purchased from us in 1951 requires 2-inch valves; that is why the 1½-inch valves did not fit. If you want us to send the larger valves, please let us know.

7. Criticize the point of view of the following paragraphs. Using the same situations with which they deal, write paragraphs incorporating the you attitude.

a. We hope that you will soon send us your check for $37.19. After all, we have bills of our own to meet, and we can pay them only by collecting our own bills. The first of the year is a time when our own obligations are especially heavy, and, for that reason, we are urging you to send us your remittance.

b. I especially hope that you will give favorable consideration to this application. I am very anxious to work for your company since it enjoys a reputation for treating its employees fairly and generously. In addition, I need employment badly because I incurred a debt of $1,200 in order to acquire my college education. I hope you will consider these facts when you examine my qualifications.

c. In asking for an adjustment on the overcoat which you purchased from us, you seem to lose sight of the fact that, if we granted such claims, we should be unable to stay in business very long. We purchase these garments from a wholesale clothing company, and we certainly do not expect them to grant such adjustments to us.

d. We hope that you will send us the answers we ask for in this questionnaire because this information is of vital importance to us. We are deferring the whole plan of our new sales program pending the answers to these questionnaires. Since you can realize how important this matter is to us, won't you help us by sending your answer today?

e. This new radio is our greatest engineering triumph. We developed it in our own laboratories, and we are going to distribute it through our own exclusive dealers. You will know why we are so proud of this instrument when you hear it at your dealer's.

8. Prepare a brief outline or notation of the main points you would use to incorporate the you attitude in letters dealing with the following situations:

a. A letter to be sent to your classmates in which you attempt to get them to subscribe to your favorite magazine.

b. As vocational guidance or placement official for your school, you want to obtain information from 50 large companies concerning the possibilities of employment for your graduates, the methods of orientation for new employees, and the starting salary range for recent graduates. The results will be tabulated and sent to all those who return your questionnaire.

c. You are organizing an evening course in the great books (or any other subject you prefer) to be given at your local community center. A registration fee of $5 will be used to pay the instructor. Your letter will be sent to 46 persons who expressed an interest in such a course in a preliminary survey.

d. A letter to be sent to dealers to persuade them to become exclusive agents in their territory for a new line of men's or women's clothing.

9. As a class project, select two members of your group to interview a correspondent in your community on the general subject "The Three Most Important Qualities in Business Letters." They are to question him on the methods he uses in taking the reader's viewpoint in his letters and, if possible, to bring back several examples of letters he regards as effective. They are to make an oral report to the class on their findings.

10. A prominent businessman has set up an award in your school for the best letter on "The Responsibility of the Letter Writer." His motive in arranging this award was to counteract charges in a business magazine that today's business suffers from the exaggerated claims and insincere appeals in many letters. Address your letter to The Board of Judges, The Blank Prize Award, at your school. The judges are a banker, an advertising executive, and the writer of the critical article in the magazine.

Be not the first by whom the new is tried,
Nor yet the last to lay the old aside.

Alexander Pope

CHAPTER III

The Form of the Letter

No one can say authoritatively that one specific form for a letter is "the correct form." Instead, there are certain practices which are widely used in today's correspondence but which are constantly changing. Ten or fifteen years ago, for example, the indented form of letter was widely used, with what was known as closed punctuation. The inside address of such a letter looked like this:

```
Mr. Jason Edwards,
    219 St. James Parkway,
        Baltimore 8, Maryland.
```

Today, the indented form is practically obsolete because it requires unnecessary stenographic time for margins and punctuation.

We would be mistaken, however, if we made efficiency the sole criterion for letter make-up. To do so would ignore the intangible but, nonetheless, powerful effect of custom, which dictates many current uses in the business letter as well as in every other aspect of our daily lives. It is interesting to speculate about the changes that would take place in the form of the business letter if an efficiency expert were given absolute power to set it up in its most logical, efficient, and functional pattern. He would doubtless issue a decree making it mandatory for all letters to incorporate these changes:

1. All envelopes to be addressed as follows to save postal employees' time by presenting information in the logical order in which it is used in distribution of mail:

```
Mass., Boston 17
The Caxton Bldg.   207
Jones, Thomas R.
```

2. All women to be addressed as Ms. to resolve the endless confusion about marital status.
3. All useless appendages of the letter such as salutations like "Dear Mr. Jones:" and complimentary closes like "Sincerely yours," to be eliminated to save typing.

Our efficiency expert could undoubtedly save hundreds of millions of dollars annually by these and other changes he would recommend. What stands in the way of such savings? Custom, with its concepts of tradition, courtesy, and "the proper thing to do." It is the same force that prevents reform in English spelling, which Mario Pei calls "the world's most awesome mess." Let those who would minimize the importance of custom look around them at the men in business offices on hot summer days with uncomfortable neckties around their throats, at the men walking on the curb side of their ladies, at our political campaigns, and at the thousand-and-one other outmoded habits which somehow persist.

These same forces—sometimes unconscious, sometimes organized to achieve specific results—swirl around the form of the modern business letter. Conservatives are reluctant to change for fear of being charged with freakishness; liberals argue that waste and inefficiency are inherent in the traditional pattern. In this respect, as W. S. Gilbert said in *Iolanthe,* our attitudes fall into one or the other category:

> I often think it's comical
> > How nature always does contrive
> That every boy and every gal
> > That's born into the world alive,
> Is either a little Liberal,
> > Or else a little Conservative!

The sanest advice for business writers to follow in selecting a letter form is contained in Pope's words at the head of this chapter—though it should not be taken too literally, for no change would be made if everyone refused to be first! In the constant struggle between custom and efficiency, the correspondent ought to know that there are styles in letter writing as well as in dress; if he is a student, he ought to try the several modes which he can use to "clothe" his ideas and select the one which is most appropriate. His choice will be governed in most instances, by the

practice of the company he will work for and the type of reader
to whom his letter is addressed. But since a selection of a suitable
garb for his thoughts can be made intelligently only if he knows
the practices now in effect, he ought to consider the following
patterns.

1. The Block Form

This is a widely used form today (see the illustration on p. 27).
It takes its name from the fact that the inside address, the salutation, and the paragraphs of the letter are arranged in blocks
without indention. Divisions between the inside address and the
salutation, between the salutation and the body of the letter, and
between the paragraphs in the body of the letter are indicated by
spacing, with double spaces *between* the units (*i.e.*, between the
inside address, the salutation, and the body of the letter) and
single spacing *within* the units (*i.e.*, within the inside address
and the individual paragraphs). The open form of punctuation
should always accompany the block form (see the illustration on
page 37).

The block form offers two definite advantages: it saves stenographic time because each part of the letter except the date, the
complimentary close, and the signature is aligned with the left
margin so that no time is consumed by indention, and, second, its
wide acceptance at the present time offers assurance that the letter arranged in block form is correct and modern.

2. The Semiblock Form

A compromise between the block form and the indented form,
the semiblock employs the block form with open punctuation in
all parts, except that the first word of each paragraph is indented
5 spaces (see illustration on page 28).

This form may appeal to those who like the efficiency of the
block form but who also feel that the paragraphs of a letter should
be indented just as in any other form of typing or printing.

3. The Complete-block Form

Another variation of the block form is the complete or full
block (see the illustration on page 30). The basic principle of this

[EXAMPLE OF BLOCK FORM OF LETTER]

March 5, 1954

Mr. J. C. Cummings
347 East Oak Street
Council Bluffs 10, Iowa

Dear Mr. Cummings:

This letter illustrates the block form of
letter dress, which has become one of the most
widely used methods of arranging letters.

It takes its name from the fact that the inside address, the salutation, and the paragraphs of the letter itself are arranged in
blocks without indention. The block form
offers two distinct advantages: it saves
stenographic time and reduces the number of
margins. Its wide acceptance at the present
time offers assurance that the letter arranged in block form is correct and modern.

If you desire your letters to be attractive
in appearance, modern, and economical with
regard to stenographic time, I heartily recommend the block form as the most suitable
for the needs of your office.

Sincerely yours,

Geraldine A. Fisher
Correspondence Supervisor

GAF:GWC

[EXAMPLE OF SEMIBLOCK FORM OF LETTER]

March 5, 1954

Mr. Robert C. Vanderlyn
2202 Middlebury Road
Winchester 4, Maine

Dear Mr. Vanderlyn:

　　I appreciate your interest in my reasons for recommending the type of letter arrangement which our company uses in its correspondence.

　　After careful consideration, I recommended the semiblock form as the most effective for our company. This recommendation was based on my belief that this form combined most of the advantages of the block and the indented forms.

　　The block arrangement of the inside address appeals to me as symmetrical and economical of secretarial time; furthermore, open punctuation is modern and efficient. Perhaps it is no more than a whim on my part, but I prefer to have the paragraphs of the actual message indented as they are in books, newspapers, and magazines.

　　The semiblock form meets all these requirements; it has proved effective and is well liked by our staff of correspondents and secretaries after six years of use.

Sincerely yours,

John H. Porter
Correspondence Supervisor

JHP:CPA

letter consists of bringing all the elements of the letter out to the left-hand margin. Hence no changes of margin are required of the typist. This form of letter is regarded by many as somewhat ultra-modern, and some correspondents object to it because its appearance gives the impression of being unbalanced and "heavy" on the left side. Nevertheless, it does carry the basic premises of the block form to their logical conclusion.

4. The Hanging-indention Form

This form has not come into wide acceptance except in sales letters (see illustration on page 31). The block form with open punctuation is used in the inside address; within the body of the letter, the first line of each paragraph is brought out to the left margin, but every other line in each paragraph is indented five spaces.

This form is effective in attracting attention because of its difference from the more common letter arrangements, but that very difference is a disadvantage for those who want to adopt the more widely accepted forms of letter dress. Furthermore, because of its numerous indentions, the hanging-indention arrangement requires more stenographic time.

5. The Simplified Letter

Perhaps the most controversial of all the modern letter forms is the Simplified Letter advocated by the National Office Management Association, from whose initials it has come to be popularly known as the "NOMA Letter" (see the illustration on page 32). According to NOMA's literature, this letter is "a protest against the prosaic and a reminder that we can progress through change." They ask, "Why follow a beaten path from dateline to signature in writing your business letters? NOMA's Simplified Letter is a highroad to more forceful and efficient correspondence."

The chief characteristics of the Simplified Letter's form are the complete elimination of the salutation and complimentary close and the left-hand block format, which is in general like that of the complete-block form already discussed. According to NOMA, a basic unit analysis of the typing alone on a 96-word letter proves that the Simplified Letter saves 10.7 per cent. They believe that reduction in key strokes, reduction in motion for positioning the

March 5, 1954

Mr. Donald E. Woodbury
3126 Westview Road
Seattle 5, Washington

Dear Mr. Woodbury:

Your comments about the form of our letters interested me greatly. As you pointed out, letters do reflect the personality of the firm which sends them, and that fact played a large part in our decision to adopt the complete or, as it is sometimes called, the full-block form.

As management consultants, we felt that our letters should exemplify the same standards of efficiency and the modern methods we advocate in industry. For that reason, we saw no sound reason for retaining a letter form which requires changes of margins and unnecessary stenographic time.

The salient features of the full-block form are illustrated in this letter. You will be interested to know that we have received a number of favorable comments about our letter form and that our Stenographic Department likes it very much.

Sincerely yours,

E. J. Baumgartner
Partner

EJB:mo

[EXAMPLE OF HANGING-INDENTION FORM OF LETTER]

March 5, 1954

Mr. Howard C. Mathews
3794 Maple Street
West Newton 6, Massachusetts

Dear Mr. Mathews:

Since the first impression that the reader forms
    concerning a letter is of the arrangement
    of text on the page, we try to make our
    sales letters as distinctive as possible.

To achieve this result, our company has adopted
    the hanging-indention form as the standard
    setup for all sales correspondence. We feel
    that it is sufficiently unusual to attract
    the reader's attention, a factor of espe-
    cial significance in selling by mail.

You will notice that the effect of this type of
    letter is to emphasize the first words of
    each paragraph. In a carefully planned
    sales message this device can be used to
    good advantage by headlining the salient
    facts concerning the product sold.

Very truly yours,

Edward H. DuBois
Sales Manager

EHD:ELM

[EXAMPLE OF SIMPLIFIED-LETTER FORM]

March 5, 1954

Miss Office Secretary
Better Business Letters, Inc.
1 Main Street
Busytown, U.S.A.

HAD YOU HEARD?

There's a new movement under way to take some of
the monotony out of letters given you to type.
The movement is symbolized by the Simplified
Letter being sponsored by NOMA.

What is it? You're reading a sample.

Notice the left block format and the general
positioning of the letter. We didn't write
"Dear Miss ____," nor will we write "Yours
truly" or "Sincerely yours." Are they really important? We feel just as friendly to you without
them.

Notice the following points:

1 Date location
2 The address
3 The subject
4 The name of the writer

Now take a look at the Suggestions prepared for
you. Talk them over with your boss. But don't
form a final opinion until you've really tried
out The Letter. That's what our Secretary did.
As a matter of fact, she finally wrote most of
the Suggestions herself.

She says she's sold—and hopes you'll have good
luck with better (Simplified) letters.

VAUGHN FRY

letter, and improved typist's morale add up to more production when the Simplified Letter is used.

These are highly logical reasons for the adoption of the Simplified Letter. As we said at the start of this chapter, if efficiency in letters were the sole criterion, this letter form would be universally adopted. But since custom and tradition still carry a heavy weight, each reader can best make his own decision about this letter form in terms of his own reaction. Does the NOMA letter strike him as too unusual, too different? If so, he had better stick to more conventional forms, for *his* reader may react in much the same way.

ARRANGEMENT OF THE LETTER ON THE PAGE

Whichever letter form is used, the correspondent should remember that the first impression of a letter results from the arrangement of text on the page. The arrangement is the most noticeable feature of the letter and can interest or prejudice the reader at a glance. A letter's first appeal is to the reader's eye by means of attractive display, balance, and proportion. Lopsided letters, top-heavy letters, or letters running off the bottoms of pages indicate inefficiency and carelessness which reflect unfavorably on the sender. The text should be centered on the page with wide margins on both sides and top and bottom. The usual procedure is to leave a margin of 20 spaces at the left. If the message is very brief, double spacing may be used. The letter should be symmetrical and balanced in appearance; if it is unattractively arranged, it should be rewritten unless the correspondent is willing to have his reader conclude that he is careless and inefficient.

STATIONERY AND LETTERHEAD

Businessmen are becoming increasingly conscious of stationery and letterheads, partly because manufacturers have educated them to appraise other companies by their letterheads and stationery. Whether rightly or wrongly, a snap judgment may be passed on a company as the result of the impression made by its letterhead and stationery. Those who use cheap stationery run the risk of being judged parsimonious and careless. While undue importance should not be placed on the physical appearance of the letterhead and stationery, an attractive letterhead certainly possesses great value. Like a well-tailored suit, it makes a good impression; and since the cost of this "suit" is a very minor part of letter costs—current estimates show that stationery and envelopes constitute between 2½ and 5 per cent of the total cost of a letter—it should be custom-tailored to your needs.

A standard size and good quality of stationery is, therefore, a good investment. Although there has been a trend to various colors of stationery, white or some conservative color is preferable to anything that might give an impression of gaudiness. The letterhead should be as simple as possible, but it may be considered inadequate unless it answers the following questions:

1. Does it tell who you are?
2. Does it tell what you do? When the company name is not sufficiently descriptive of the type of business, a line should be added to do this.
3. Does it tell where you are located and how you may be reached by telephone, cable, or both?
4. Can it be read easily at a glance?
5. Does it represent your company in the same way your best salesmen do?

Any symbol or emblem associated with a business may be included as a part of the letterhead. Many companies include the date of their founding and names of company officials, but long lists of agencies, products, or personnel ought never to be a part of the letterhead because they give the whole letter a cluttered appearance. In fact, a recent survey shows that the worst fault of most letterheads is the attempt to pack too much information in them, with a resulting complexity and cluttered appearance.

If simplicity of design and quality are the criteria used in selecting the letterhead and stationery, the result will be in good taste. Unfortunately, many letterheads used today do not measure up to these standards because of a tendency to cling to forms that were used forty or fifty years ago. We could use a "Society to Retire Tired and Worn-out Letterheads." For its motto, nothing would be quite so appropriate as Henry David Thoreau's admonition about leading the good life—"Simplify, simplify, simplify!"

GOOD ENGLISH IN LETTERS

In business letters, as in any other form of writing, there is an inseparable relationship between clear thinking and clear writing. Vague, unorganized thought inevitably produces such writing as, "In this case, we have been working along these lines, and it is our hope that we shall produce something definite in the near future." Grammatically, this sentence is correct, but the writer has not sharpened his thought to produce an exact, concise statement, such as, "We have been working on the problem of spoilage in shipping citrus fruits, and we expect that our research department will soon have a solution." The first essential of good writing in any form is that the writer should have a clear conception in his own mind of what he wants to say; otherwise, he must fall back on meaningless words and vague generalities.

As a minimum requirement for any letter, we can certainly expect correctness in grammar, spelling, and punctuation. Athough errors in grammar do not always result in a lack of clarity—for example, so far as clearness is concerned, it makes no difference whether a writer says, "It don't matter to us" or "It doesn't matter to us"—yet students should remember that the grammatical rules of our language generally incorporate the most logical means of expression. Grammar involves not an artificial and an arbitrary set of rules but a logical system of expressing our thoughts clearly and exactly. We should follow these rules not—as so many students seem to think—because they are the annoying whims of English teachers but because good grammar is the easiest, most logical form of construction.

Our use of English is the standard by which we are judged more often than any other; especially is this true of our written English, as in the business letter where all who read may see our errors preserved in black and white. Furthermore, such errors in grammar and spelling call attention to themselves and thus distract the reader's mind from the message. And in that moment of distraction, he will probably make this harsh comment about the writer, "He doesn't know any better."

The best way to avoid such comments is by taking the time and effort to learn the rules and to see that every letter conforms to the best usage in grammar, spelling, and punctuation. Careful proofreading and a willingness to consult any of the numerous handbooks of English will aid greatly in eliminating errors in business letters.

To the letter writer, a knowledge of correct English usage is a basic and minimum skill. Not only do grammatical errors distract his reader, but ignorance of correct usage interferes constantly with the task of writing. For if the writer has to stop continually to think about whether his verb should be singular or plural or whether his pronouns should be subjective or objective case, he cannot concentrate his whole attention on his message. Effective writers have learned to use correct language in the same way that good drivers instinctively use the mechanical equipment of their cars without stopping to decide whether they should step on the accelerator or the brake. And as a final word of warning, the writer who does not use his "mechanical equipment" almost instinctively will, at best, be a "traffic hazard" because of his over-cautiousness and, at worst, be responsible for some "fatal accidents."

PUNCTUATING THE LETTER

Over the years, a marked decrease has occurred in the amount of punctuation used in the business letter as well as in all other forms of writing. One survey of the punctuation used in the editorial pages of *The New York Times* shows that the number of commas decreased almost 50 per cent in sixty years. In letters, closed punctuation, which puts commas at the end of the lines and a period at the conclusion of the inside address, is now practically obsolete. It has been replaced by what is known as the open form of punctuation. The modern trend is to omit punctuation wherever it is not necessary for clarity; from that principle, open punctuation may be considered as the most up-to-date method. How far to extend this functional approach to punctuating business letters still constitutes a problem, however, since usage has not completely crystallized. A number of companies, for example, have stopped using the colon after the salutation and the comma after the complimentary close, although the vast majority of letters still carry these nonfunctional marks of punctuation. Writers, therefore, have to choose how far they want to go toward an absolute minimum in punctuating the major parts of the letter; if they follow the most widespread practice now used, the date, salutation, and complimentary close will be punctuated as shown in these examples.

September 15, 1953

Mr. John McDowell
15 East Main Street
Ann Arbor, Michigan

Dear Mr. McDowell:

Sincerely yours,

The Eastside Corporation
2900 Amsterdam Avenue
New York 47, N.Y.

Gentlemen:

Yours truly,

Within the letter itself, the accepted rules of punctuation should, of course, be followed. Particularly pertinent to business letters are the following:

1. The Most Frequent Uses of the Comma

a. To separate two independent clauses connected by a co-ordinating conjunction (*and, but, for, or, nor*).

We greatly appreciate the interest you have shown in our methods, and we certainly wish we could comply with your request of October 15.

The fact that the users of our products take the time to write us of their experiences is a source of gratification to us, for through such reports we get a valuable indication of how our appliances perform under conditions of everyday use.

We had hoped that our sales representative would arrive at your store in time for your spring sale, but he was delayed by the floods in southern Ohio.

When the two clauses are short and closely connected, the comma may be omitted.

This is your responsibility and you must accept it as such.

b. To separate words, phrases, or clauses in series.

This plan is designed to give you more profit, easier payments, and wider selection of merchandise.

You will find him to be cooperative, likable, and intelligent.

Increasing acceptance is now given to omitting the last comma between the next to the last and the last elements in such series.

We have it available in cotton, wool and silk.

c. To set off lengthy dependent elements preceding the main subject and verb.

When you have seen all the features of this latest model, you will certainly want one.

To be one of our dealers, you must take our three-week sales course.

Since our offer of an adjustment did not seem satisfactory to you, we should like you to tell us just what you would regard as a fair settlement.

Where the elements are brief and closely connected to the rest of the sentence, the comma may be omitted.

Naturally you should expect better mileage.

d. To set off nonrestrictive clauses, introduced usually by *who, which, that,* or *where.*

Mr. Gray, who has been with us many years, has earned an enviable reputation in our personnel department.

Our largest plant, which is located in Columbus, will be open for inspection this spring.

Our annual convention is held in New York City, where our sales offices are located.

Notice that the following clauses require no punctuation because they are clearly restrictive:

Any tire that goes 25,000 miles is a good tire.

The man who sold me this merchandise is no longer associated with your company.

The order that we received on October 15 was shipped on October 17.

e. To set off parenthetical expressions and appositives.

We are sending Mr. James Hanson, our chief engineer, to assist you.

We knew, of course, that these prices would not prevail for a long time.

Our latest model, the finest that we have ever produced, will be available shortly after June 1.

2. The Most Frequent Uses of the Semicolon

a. To separate two independent clauses not connected by a coordinating conjunction.

We shall send your merchandise on March 24; this should arrive in ample time for your Easter sale.

This new camera is not intended for novices; it was designed primarily for those whose knowledge and experience enable them to appreciate its greater versatility and finer craftsmanship.

b. To separate two independent clauses connected by conjunctive adverbs, such as *however, thus, hence, therefore,* and similar words.

We know that you will like this new design; however, you may return any of this merchandise within 30 days.

By placing your order now, you can be certain of delivery within 30 days; thus, you can assure your customers of an adequate supply of antifreeze this winter.

3. The Use of the Apostrophe

The only other punctuation mark likely to cause difficulty in business correspondence is the apostrophe. It is required in two situations: to show possession and to indicate the omission of letters in contractions like *can't, aren't, don't,* and *doesn't.*

The real problem in using the apostrophe with possessives lies in placing it properly. The following rules should be strictly observed:

a. Add an *'s* to form the possessive singular.

A child's book. A company's location. A customer's statement.

b. Add an *'s* to form the possessive plural of words which *do not* end in *s* in their plural form.

Women's clothes. Children's books. Men's suits.

c. Add only the apostrophe to plural nouns ending in *s.*

The creditors' meeting. The directors' report. Three days' pay.

d. Personal pronouns require no apostrophe in the possessive. It should be noted, however, that the form *it's* is a contraction for *it is.*

The book is hers (yours, theirs, ours, etc.).

e. Proper names ending in *s* or *z* add *'s* if the name is of one syllable; if it is a two-syllable name ending in *s* or *z*, only the apostrophe is required.

One-syllable names ending in *s* or *z:*

Keats's poems. Schwartz's clothes. Jones's report.

Two-syllable names ending in *s* or *z:*

Dickens' novels. Landis' ideas. Hopkins' appointment.

CAPITALIZATION

In the business letter, difficulties in capitalization occur in the salutation and the complimentary close.

1. Except for proper names and titles (President, Mr., Sir., Dr., etc.) capitalize only the first letter of the first word of the salutation.

```
Dear Mr. Davidson:
My dear Mr. Davidson:
My dear Sir:
```

2. Capitalize only the first letter of the first word of the complimentary close.

```
Yours very truly,
Very truly yours,
Sincerely yours,
Cordially yours,
```

AGREEMENT BETWEEN THE SALUTATION AND THE COMPLIMENTARY CLOSE

As we have seen, much of the verbiage of business letters is now somewhat meaningless as the result of outworn tradition; however, certain degrees of formality or acquaintanceship can be expressed in the choice of the salutation and the complimentary close. These two parts should agree in tone since it is obviously inconsistent to begin with a highly formal salutation and to close in an informal or even friendly fashion. The following groups show the various salutations and closes that may appropriately be used together.

RATHER FORMAL

```
My dear Mr. Smith:}          {Yours very truly,
My dear Sir:      }          {Very sincerely yours,
```

LESS FORMAL

```
Dear Sir:         }          {Sincerely yours,
Dear Mr. Smith:   }          {Yours truly,
Gentlemen:        }          {Sincerely,
```

"Cordially yours" usually implies acquaintanceship or long business relationship; "Respectfully yours" is generally used in letters to those older or of higher rank than the letter writer. "Dear Sirs" as a salutation is practically obsolete.

THE SIGNATURE

The signature of the letter should be several spaces directly below the complimentary close; the stenographer customarily leaves sufficient space between the typed name and the title of the writer for his actual signature, as in the following example:

Sincerely yours,

James Adams

James Adams
Sales Manager
The Green Company

Company policy will determine whether letters should be signed with the typed name of the company and the individual's signature, as in this example, or whether the company name comes first as in the following example:

Sincerely yours,

THE GREEN COMPANY

James Adams

Sales Manager

There is no hard and fast rule on whether the individual's signature or the typed company name is the better practice. A survey by *Printer's Ink* indicates that the use of the company name is somewhat affected by the subject of the letter. Where the message tends to be more personal in tone or is addressed to an individual known to the writer, the great majority of letters surveyed carried the personal signature followed by the typed name and title. On the other hand, when the subject is more general or the correspondents do not know one another, the company name is likely to be used as part of the signature. Recent interpretations of the legal implications of these signature arrangements indicate no difference in legal liability in the two arrangements. This interpretation stems from the obvious fact that when a man signs his name, with his title appearing immediately beneath it, he is speaking for the company or corporation whose name appears on the letterhead.

Another guide as to whether the company or individual form of signature should be used is whether the letter is written in terms of "I" or "we." The use of "we" exclusively in such expressions as "We have looked into the record" and "We want to extend our best wishes for a prosperous year" often gives the letter a rather pompous air. On the other hand, frequent shifts from "I" to "we" within one letter are likely to confuse the reader. Here again practice is not fixed; many companies set up their own policies governing this phase of letter style.

Two final comments pertain to the signature: if the correspondent is a woman that fact and her marital status should be clearly indicated, and the signature should be legible. With the increased number of women in business, the need for a standard technique for their signatures is evident, as anyone will realize who has addressed a letter to "Mr. A. Winters" and found later that his correspondent is Agatha Winters. Such situations can be readily eliminated by having women sign their first name in full instead of using initials. But where initials are used, "Miss" in parentheses should be included. A married woman signs her full name with her married name below it in parentheses:

> Alberta Potter Webb
> (Mrs. Robert J. Webb)

The widespread use of the typewriter has fortunately decreased the need for handwriting. This boon to the business world has not altered the fact that too many correspondents still sign their names in indecipherable scrawls and too many typists fail to type the correspondent's name beneath his signature. Particularly in companies that deal with the handwritten letters from the general public the cry is still heard, "Why on earth don't you sign your name so I can read it?" People who have received such letters will enjoy the opinions expressed by Thomas Bailey Aldrich in the following letter to Professor Edward S. Morse:

It was very pleasant to me to get a letter from you the other day. Perhaps I should have found it pleasanter if I had been able to decipher it.

I don't think I have mastered anything beyond the date (which I knew) and the signature (which I guessed at). There's a singular and a perpetual charm in a letter of.yours; it never grows old, it never loses its novelty.

Other letters are read and thrown away and forgotten, but yours are kept forever—unread. One of them will last a reasonable man a lifetime.

Since the signature is an integral and important part of the business letter, it should be legible, placed correctly in the space provided for it, and put on an even keel. Many correspondents erroneously think that a distinctive touch is added by slanting the signature or, what is worse, by writing over the typed name.

MISCELLANEOUS SITUATIONS THAT CAUSE DIFFICULTY

1. Placing the Date

Unless specific arrangement is made for it on or directly below the letterhead, the date should be placed in the upper right-hand section of the letter and at least two spaces above the first line of the inside address. The day of the month should always be set off from the year by a comma:

```
February 24, 1953
December 5, 1953
```

Such abbreviations as 6/7/53 should be avoided because they cause confusion; there is no necessity for writing *th, nd, rd* after numerals in the date (September 15th, May 2nd, July 3rd). Write September 15, May 2, July 3.

2. The Address

The correct address to use in writing to any company or individual is exactly the same form as the company or individual uses on its stationery or advertising. When street names using numerals, such as Fifth Avenue, East 116th Street, Second Avenue, are part of the address, the best procedure is to write them out if they can be expressed in one word; if they are more complex, use numerals:

```
79 Fifth Avenue
2719 East 116th Street
3019 102nd Street
```

3. Choosing the Salutation

The salutation should always agree with the first line of the inside address; if that line is plural (a partnership, a company, a firm name), the salutation should be plural. If the first line is feminine (a firm composed entirely of women), the salutation should be feminine. Even though the letter is directed to the attention of an individual, if the first line of the address is the company name, the salutation should be plural. The following examples illustrate these points:

```
Williams, Clement, Constant, and Williams, Inc.
1410 Broadway Building
Cleveland 6, Ohio

Gentlemen:


The Three Sisters Dress Shop
3914 East Third Street
Seattle 5, Washington

Mesdames:

    or

Ladies:


Mr. Arnold Lehman, Sales Manager
The Viking Air Conditioning Company
3133 Constitution Avenue
Omaha 17, Nebraska

Dear Mr. Lehman:
```

but

```
The Viking Air Conditioning Company
3133 Constitution Avenue
Omaha 17, Nebraska
```

Attention of: Mr. Arnold Lehman, Sales Manager

Gentlemen:

When addressing a post-office box, a newspaper number, or a reader whose identity is unknown, use "Gentlemen" as the proper salutation:

```
B 14978, The New York Times
Times Square
New York 36, New York
```

Gentlemen:

4. Directing the Letter to the Attention of an Individual within the Company

Frequently it is desirable to direct letters which concern the business of a whole firm or corporation to the attention of an individual within the company with whom one has had previous correspondence or who is familiar with the specific problem at hand. The attention device may be placed in either of the following ways:

```
The Black Company
1419 Broad Street
Winchester 3, Massachusetts
```

Attention: Mr. Michael Cunningham

Gentlemen:

or

```
The Black Company
1419 Broad Street
Winchester 3, Massachusetts
            Attention of Mr. Michael Cunningham
```

Gentlemen:

Mention of file numbers, policy numbers, or other aids in identifying the business at hand may be made in a similar manner.

```
The Worthy and White Company
2789 Canal Street
Kingston 9, New York
                                    Your file No. 71698
```

Gentlemen:

5. The Second Page of the Letter

When letters are more than one page in length, the additional pages should be on stationery to match the first sheet but without the letterhead. These pages may be headed in any of the following ways:

```
Mr: Cunningham:   2
```

–2–

```
Page 2
Mr. Cunningham
```

6. Indicating the Dictator and the Stenographer

Numerous methods of indicating the initials of the dictator of the letter and the stenographer are in common use. This information should be placed at the left margin of the letter and at least two spaces lower on the paper than the last line of the signature.

```
FJP/KRS
```

```
FLT:CMJ
```

```
W:m
```

```
RLS:mcg
```

Whenever enclosures are to be made, notation of that fact should be made as follows:

```
FJP/KRS
Encl.
```

Enclosures should be arranged in back of the letter in the order of their importance or in the sequence in which they are mentioned in the letter. With the exception of checks or drafts, enclosures should never be placed on top of a letter.

7. Envelopes

Small envelopes should be used for single-page letters without enclosures; larger envelopes for all other letters. The complete address should always be given even though the company or the individual is well known; the address on the envelope should agree exactly with the inside address on the letter, and, as many correspondents have discovered to their chagrin, a great deal of confusion and embarrassment can be avoided by placing the proper letter in the proper envelope!

A GUIDE TO CURRENT PRACTICE

In this chapter, we have outlined the common practices in business today regarding the form, punctuation, and parts of the business letter. Inevitably, the question arises about what is the most general practice.

While no exhaustive survey of today's letter forms and styles has been made, enough evidence is available to provide a tentative answer to this question. Interestingly, this evidence results from a classroom project carried on by students in a course in business correspondence such as many of the readers of this book are taking. Under the supervision of Professor Donald G. Wilson, a group of students at Nichols Junior College sent inquiry letters to approximately 1,250 well-known companies and received 934 answers. While the object of these inquiries was to find out about current practices, this purpose was disguised in the actual inquiry letters on the theory that if questions were asked about English in letters, for instance, every effort would be made by the answering correspondent to have his letter perfect in that respect. The group, therefore, sent letters inquiring about training programs, employee benefits, company products, and possible employment. Replies to these letters, from company presidents, vice-presidents, personnel directors, public-relations officers, training directors, production and sales managers, and secretaries, were then studied for form and actual practice.

The results showed the following as the most customary usage in American business:

1. The semiblock style used in 519 letters as compared to 388 block style, 23 full block, and 4 indented form.
2. Single spacing. In many instances, spacing had no plan except to suit the typist; in others, the inside address was single-spaced and the letter double-spaced.
3. A mixture of punctuation methods.
4. A salutation of "Dear Mr. Jones:" or "Dear Sir:" or "Gentlemen:".

5. A complimentary close of "Very truly yours," (454) as compared to "Sincerely yours," (182) "Yours very truly," (177) and "Cordially yours," (62).
6. An evenly divided practice of typing the company name immediately after the complimentary close (449 letters) or not at all (463 letters).
7. The initials of the dictator typed in capitals and those of the typist in small letters.

The most frequent errors revealed in this survey were trite expressions, participles at the beginning or end of the letters, lack of consistent or correct punctuation, telegraphic style, excessive abbreviations, and frequent strikeovers or erasures.

Professor Wilson regarded only 91 of the 934 replies as perfect letters—but let no one use this as justification for his errors. Instead, it points up the need for properly trained correspondents and typists in American business.

While such a survey makes no pretense of being conclusive, it does show today's trends and the chief errors to be avoided. It should be regarded as only a general guide rather than a rigid formula, for, as we said at the opening of this chapter, there is no one correct form for the letter.

ON BECOMING LETTER-PERFECT

Since the finished letter is, in a very real sense, *your* representative, take care to make it correct in every detail. In today's business world, the best letters are those which are the result of careful thought by *both* dictator and transcriber. Ultimately, the final responsibility for every aspect of the letter rests completely on the person who signs it, but the best results occur when the dictator and transcriber work as a team. The transcriber should proofread carefully for errors in spelling, punctuation, grammar, or typing. She should see that all initials, names, dates, and addresses are accurate. The correspondent should then read the letter carefully for the same purposes and to see that it effectively does what it is intended to do. When he signs the letter without reading it—as too many correspondents do—he is shirking his fundamental obligation to see that every letter he writes is as nearly perfect as he and his typist can make it.

EXERCISES

1. Punctuate the following letter:

June 6 1953

Mr James Lloyd President
Black Black and Black Inc
231 First Street
Warren Pa

Dear Mr Lloyd

Mr Robert Eastman who was formerly a clerk in your firm has given your name as a reference and has indicated that you can tell of his education his experience and his character

We should appreciate your answers to the following questions

How long was Mr. Eastman connected with your firm

What was his highest salary

What were his specific duties

We shall of course keep this information in the strictest confidence and we shall be grateful for any other material that might bear on our consideration of Mr Eastman as a prospective employee

Sincerely yours

If this letter were arranged in complete-block form, what changes should be made in its form and punctuation?

2. What salutation and complimentary close would be used appropriately for each of the following inside addresses?

   a. P.O. Box 76394
   Binghamton, New York

   b. The John C. Meade Company
   371 East 50th Street
   Canton 5, Ohio

   c. The Honorable Thomas E. Dewey
   Governor of the State of New York
   Albany, New York

   d. The Registrar
   Amherst College
   Amherst, Massachusetts

3. Arrange the following letter in semi-block form and add the necessary punctuation:

June 22 1953
The C F Thomas Mfg Co East Liverpool Ohio
Attention M F Ely Sales Manager
Gentlemen
We appreciate your thoughtfulness in calling our attention to the article on Air Conditioning in South Africas Largest City in the June 6 issue of Im-

port-Export Magazine. Since we shall be able to use excerpts from the article in a sales letter you have done us a real service for none of the members of our organization had seen the article before you called it to our attention

Sincerely yours   George C Delaney   President

4. What errors are made in the form, grammar, and spelling of the following letters?

> *a.* Box 2Z 3719   6–7–53
> The New York Herald-Tribune
> New York 47, N.Y.
>
> Dear Sir:
>
> I was reading the advertisements in this morning's Herald-Tribune and I happened to see your ad. for a secretary.
>
> I am a high school graduate with one year of business college and two years of experience as secretary to the sales manager of the Brown Novelty Corporation, manufacturer of children's toys.
>
> I hope you will consider my qualifications which I am giving in some detail on the enclosed personal record sheet, because I dislike my present position and I want very much to work in New York City.
>
> In the event that you are interested, I shall hope to hear from you.
>
> > Sincerely Yours,
> >
> > Ruth Smith.

> *b.* The A. B. Bradley Co.   July 17th, '53
> 241 East One Hundred Sixth Street,
> Birmingham 10, Ala.
>
> Attention: Mr. C. E. Black
>
> My Dear Mr. Black,
>
> We have recieved your request for our booklet "Principles of Selling" which we are glad to send you. This booklet has had excellent affects in aiding numerous companies to increase their sales.
>
> We hope you will find it useful.
>
> > Yours Truly

    c. Mr. D. H. Hale   6/21/53
       3179–16th Street
       Bangor 8, Maine.

       Gentlemen:

       Referring to your letter of June 18th, the matter you wrote us of has interested us greatly.

       We cannot however send you the samples like you suggested, if we did we would be violating the principals of our trade association. They would object to us sending samples even to an old customer like you.

       Everyone of us in this company are trying to cooperate in each and every way with the National Trade Association. We are determined that we shall comply with everyone of their rules. We hope our refusal will not effect our pleasant relations.

                      Most cordially yours,

5. Punctuate the following sentences from business letters:
    a. Our records show that on January 3 1953 he ordered the following models No 25 $126 No 27 $139 No 29 $152
    b. The cost of the repairs on your machine is slight however we must have your approval before we can proceed
    c. The camera has been dropped or damaged in some way and its lens must be replaced
    d. This model which is our best seller at present will give you the dealer a 20 per cent margin of profit
    e. This catalogue was not written for the public it was designed especially for executives like you
    f. Since you have made no reply to our letters of December 15 January 2 and January 15 we must conclude that you do not wish to assume the responsibility which you must realize is yours
    g. We shall be forced therefore to turn this bill over to our attorney we are of course reluctant to do this
    h. The letter which closes with a specific request for action is better than the one with a vague indefinite or participial ending
    i. Our graduates have their choice of three different fields production sales or research
    j. Does this interest you you can double your profits within three weeks if you will devote your spare time to our proposal
    k. Before signing an important letter you should read it over very carefully and ask yourself how would this sound in court if suit were brought

l. Our representative Mr. Gray has told you of this newest model of ours which has broken all sales records within the first six months of 1953

m. Make your letters sound like you then you need never worry about their impersonality

n. We are grateful to you for telling us of your experience with our heater in your letter of February 12 but we believe that the fuel not the heater is causing your difficulty

o. When you buy Blank products you know you are getting the best

p. At the directors meeting on June 30 1953 Mr. Jones Annual Report to the stockholders was approved and the yearly dividend was increased

q. A refrigerator such as yours that has given ten years of service should have a thorough reconditioning

r. During these many months of material shortages weve had to write so many letters refusing orders that it is a pleasure to tell you that we can now fill your order in 30 days

s. When we extended credit to you we expected that you would meet your obligations promptly however we are forced to the conclusion that we were wrong

t. The applicant is a man of fine character and good habits and I am sure that upon investigation you will find he possesses the qualifications which are necessary for the position he seeks

u. This product which resulted from three years work in our research laboratory will be on the market in three weeks

v. According to authoritative reports from the coat and suit industry there will be a shortage of mens suits and childrens clothes which will last until August 1953

w. This plan a product of our intense market research will give you greater information wider choice of markets and increased protection against price fluctuation

x. Our credit arrangements with the company which you mentioned in your letter have proved rather unsatisfactory however with the greater demand for childrens books they may show some improvement in the future

y. Thank you for your interest in our sales methods we are delighted naturally that you have selected us for inclusion in your report

6. To be effective, business letters must be correct. Although grammatical construction and correct spelling do not fall within the province of this book, it is essential that students heed their importance. This exercise and the one following are, therefore, included as a general review. The following sentences from business letters contain grammatical errors. State the rule that is violated and correct the sentence in accordance with the rule:

a. Referring to your letter of April 29, our representative, Mr. J. W. Watt, will call on you on May 3.

b. Included in this remarkable offer is a set of drawing instruments, a drawing board, and a scientifically designed lamp.

c. Everybody will be happy to learn that neither the depression nor two world wars has affected their investments in life insurance.

d. The suggestion that our sales force should devote all their time to our lowest priced models have proved sound.

e. When Mr. Jones reported the discrepancy to the sales manager, he told him that some adjustment would have to be made.

f. We are sending this inquiry because we believe that either your treasurer or the members of your auditing department has had experience with this kind of problem.

g. This fine radio may be obtained in a variety of attractive models. Each of which carries an unconditional guarantee for one year.

h. None of our salesmen are more competent than him.

i. The possibility of you winning this contest is greater than ever.

j. Answering your inquiry of May 4, past experience shows that our largest model is the most efficient of the two you suggested for installation in a hotel.

k. I regret that I cannot recommend Mr. Raymond for the position you suggested; when he was with us, he acted like he knew everything and was difficult to get along with.

l. A thorough knowledge of the product, the market, and of the buyers are all that is necessary.

m. Our company is devoting all their efforts to this work.

n. Whom shall I tell him you are?

o. I can give you the assurance of three of us, Mr. Brown, Mr. Black, and I, that costs of production will surely rise.

p. I should like to direct this inquiry to whomever is in charge of your research department.

q. The award which was presented to my partner and I is a symbol of this company's part in the project.

r. One customer tells a friend that his heating costs are the lowest in years, and then our sales increase.

s. The salesman together with two men from our research department are to demonstrate this new model in your territory on January 4.

t. Neither of the applicants you recommended were fitted for this position.

u. If I was in your place, I would consult the Blank Marketing Service for advice.

v. Everybody must be at their desk at 9 o'clock.

w. The first ones to take advantage of your offer were my associates and me.

x. Who did you talk to the last time you visited our organization?

y. Referring to your inquiry of August 15, the information you requested cannot be divulged.

7. Rewrite the following sentences to correct any grammatical errors:

a. Every member of the department have to do their share of the work.

    b. Included in the set was a ledger, a journal, and a cash book.

    c. An illustrated booklet together with samples of the materials were sent to you this morning.

    d. We are not a big company, but everyone of us are doing our best to increase our business.

    e. The exchange of raw materials, manufactured goods, and grain exist between these European countries and the United States.

    f. In this book is recorded the name and address of every employee.

    g. The cashier, whom we thought was an honest man, embezzled the money.

    h. Please cross off the names of those whom you think will not be interested.

    i. They are writing to a man whom I am told is very capable.

    j. Our letter of November 10, as well as two previous ones, have been ignored.

    k. A comparison of their resources show a marked improvement.

    l. With all signs pointing toward a recession, every merchant should do their buying with caution and cut their orders to a minimum.

    m. We do not approve of him buying on the installment plan.

    n. He has never objected to us using the telephone during office hours.

    o. We regret that we were not aware of you being in the city.

    p. Since the first of this month, he sold only two automobiles.

    q. If the machine does not work satisfactory after these adjustments are made, please return it to us.

    r. It was him who told you to answer that letter.

    s. Our sales department loses a lot of valuable time in sending out letters to people which could be used much more profitably.

    t. If our labor supply was more abundant, we could produce more of these parts.

    u. Having so many debts and creditors seeking payment, the court was forced to appoint a referee in bankruptcy for the company.

    v. Which of the two methods recommended by the committee was best?

    w. If he was in a different type of job where he didn't have to work with people, he would be better off.

    x. The goods were already shipped when we received your cancellation notice.

    y. In performing this assignment, the worker must fix his eyes on the instrument board to keep them under control.

8. The following list includes 200 words frequently misspelled in business correspondence. Use the list to check the accuracy of your own spelling:

acceptable	accommodate	adjustment
accessories	accustom	advisable
accidentally	addressed	allotted

all ready
all right
already
analysis
apologize
assurance
authorize

balance
believing
beneficial
benefited
bookkeeper
bureau

calendar
changeable
chargeable
Cincinnati
clientele
collectible
column
commission
commitment
committee
commodities
comparative
concede
concession
confer
conference
congratulate
conscientious
controlled
convenience
corroborate
courteous
creditor
criticize

decision
deductible
deferred
deficit

depreciation
description
desirable
development
disappointment
discrepancy
dissatisfied
distributor

eligible
embarrass
enforceable
equipped
equitable
equivalent
evidently
exaggerate
exceed
exchangeable
exorbitant
experience
extension

feasible
February
financial
financier
forcible
foreign
forfeit
formally
formerly
forty
fulfill
fundamental

government
grievance
guarantee
guaranty

hesitancy

inaugurate
incidentally
independent
indispensable
inducement
insolvency
intercede
interchangeable

jeopardize
judgment
justifiable

laboratory
liable
license
liquidation

maintain
maintenance
manageable
manufacturer
mercantile
merchandise
miniature
miscellaneous
mortgage

necessary
negligible
nineteenth
ninety
ninth
noticeable

occasionally
occur
occurred
occurrence
omission
omitted
opportunity
optimistic

pamphlet
parallel
permanent
permissible
persistence
personal
personnel
planned
possession
precede
precedence
preference
preferred
prejudice
preparation
prevalent
principal
principle
privilege
procedure
proceedings
profited
promissory
proportionate
purchasing

quantity
questionnaire

readjustment
receipt
receivable
receive
recipient
recommend
reducible
reference
referred
reimbursement
remittance
repetition
representative
requisition
retroactive

salable
schedule
seize
separate
serviceable
similar
stationary
stationery
statute
subsidiary
succeeds
successful

superintendent
supersede
supervisor
supplementary

tendency
transferable
transferred
treasurer
typical

undoubtedly
unforeseen
unnecessary
until
usage
using
usually

vacancy

warehouse
Wednesday
welfare

9. Select 10 members of your group to write to different companies asking their reasons for deciding upon the particular form of letter which they use. Appoint three of your classmates to report on the replies in a panel discussion on "Letter Styles in Use Today."

10. You have been asked to write an answer to a letter inquiring why your company has adopted the Simplified Letter Form of the National Office Management Association. Assume that you have used this letter form for two years, that you have received a number of letters praising your use of it, and that your typists prefer it to any other letter style.

Except ye utter by the tongue words easy to be understood,
how shall it be known what is spoken? For ye shall speak into the air.

I Cor. 14:9

CHAPTER IV

Business Jargon

"A specter haunts our culture," writes Lionel Trilling in the *American Quarterly.* "It is that people will eventually be unable to say 'We fell in love and married' . . . but will, as a matter of course, say, 'Their libidinal impulses being reciprocal, they integrated their individual erotic drives and brought them within the same frame of reference.'" The specter is Jargon; its practitioners, the Jargoneers. The Jargoneer loves to show off, to cloak a simple idea in elaborate language, to impress his reader by trying to make him think it is really a profound idea. By learning to use pompous, trite, abstract expressions, Jargoneers earn the right to wear the fraternal garb—the stuffed shirt—and sing their anthem to the tune of Rudolph Friml's "March of the Musketeers":

> We are the Jargoneers,
> Trite, pompous Jargoneers,
> Stuffed-shirted Jargoneers,
> Bound to write worn-out words, old and tired.

For his language, the Jargoneer has many choices; when he uses language in his occupation or profession, he may select from commercialese, federalese, journalese, legalese, pedagese, medicalese, or an endless variety of tongues. For more general purposes, his language is called Gobbledygook (the sound a turkey gobbler makes when it struts) or Bafflegab ("multiloquence characterized by consummate interfusion of circumlocution"). The present Grand Jargoneer, a lawyer, attained office by submitting the best translation of "Jack and the Bean Stalk," beginning, "Once upon or in or about a period of the historical development of our planet, there was a minor named, or with the appellation of, John or 'Jack'

57

as he will be hereinafter designated, addressed, or noted, his other name or names to your relator unknown."

Fortunately, a great deal of progress has been made recently in reducing the number of Jargoneers. The very fact that business has become conscious of jargon is a hopeful sign. But much remains to be done. In business, particularly, an amazing collection of strange, meaningless, trite, and pompous expressions has persisted, chiefly because untrained correspondents sit down to write letters with only the incoming correspondence and the hackneyed letters in the files to guide them. Executives who pride themselves on their efficiency and on the forcefulness of their speaking lapse in writing into the stilted style known as "Business Jargon." The same man who would phone a business friend and say in a natural way, "I'm sending a check for $110.15 along to you today. Thanks for being so patient about this," is all too likely to write a letter dealing with the same situation in a formal, pompous tone:

Dear Sir:

With reference to your letter of November 21, addressed to our Treasurer, in connection with our account, we are remitting·herewith our check as per your statement in the amount of $110.15. Please be advised that according to our records our account with you is paid to date. We also wish to express our appreciation for your consideration in this matter.

Yours truly,

To those unacquainted with business, this letter may sound like an absurd exaggeration; actually, it is all too typical. Here's what C. B. Larrabee, president and publisher of *Printer's Ink,* said in a recent editorial:

Far too little has been written about communication in business. Use the term "business writing," and the chances are 1000 to 1 that you are talking about articles in the business press or perhaps about business books. Use the word "writer" in front of the average business man and he thinks immediately about a professional writer. He never stops to think that the average business executive in the course of his career writes as many words as the average novelist.

It is impossible to figure out how many millions of dollars are wasted each year because of poor, fuzzy, incoherent business communication. Orders are lost because the executive cannot write a clear letter of explanation. Executive directives are not carried out properly because the man who makes them has not explained himself well enough so that his associates understand his wishes clearly.

Stilted, overdone, outworn phrases continue to crop up in business correspondence. Business executives at the end of busy days find themselves drowsing over memoranda of the greatest importance because the men who wrote the memoranda express themselves with a dull ponderousness that can be found only in business communication.

As we have seen, the average cost of the business letter is about one dollar. Even small companies with comparatively few letters have a large proportional investment in their correspondence. The important fact that every letter writer should remember is this: *It is less expensive to write a good letter than a poor one.* The vague or ambiguous letter requires further correspondence to clarify the situation; the wordy letter, with meaningless phrases and hackneyed expressions, requires more time and marks the writer as a stuffed shirt. It is, therefore, both good business and good human relations to eliminate all useless phrases and unnecessary words from letters. How may this be done?

The wide use of such hackneyed phrases as "attached herewith," "please be advised that," and "enclosed herewith is our check in the amount of" stems only from a refusal by many letter writers to think originally. These trite expressions always reflect a willingness to let business communications fall into the same pattern that other writers use, without any critical examination. Two criteria would eliminate all Business Jargon from letters; the letter writer should ask himself:

1. Have I phrased this as directly and concisely as possible?
2. Would I say it this way if I were talking instead of writing?

This second question is perhaps the clue to the whole situation. Most of us have developed a vague dislike for writing letters—a dislike which usually arises from a feeling that letter writing is an unnatural and strange means of communication. As a result, our letters sound unnatural and strange. By contrast, conversation seems to us more natural, easier; it reflects our personalities directly without requiring the medium of cold words on the printed page. If this analysis is correct, the correspondent can eliminate almost all the pompous jargon that surrounds letters by asking himself, "Would I say it this way if I were talking?" There is a remote possibility that he may be that hitherto-undiscovered person who greets a friend in Business Jargon at its flowery worst, "Mr. Brown, with reference to your phone call of recent date, my wife and I beg to acknowledge your kind favor of an invitation to bridge, as per our previous conversations, and we beg to state that we thank you in advance for a happy evening." There is a greater probability, if he keeps this criterion in mind, that his letters will take on the natural tone of his speech, "Thanks for the invitation, Bill. We are looking forward to a pleasant evening with you and Mrs. Brown." Business Jargon belongs to the age of the quill pen; it has no place in the era of the typewriter.

TRITE AND OUTWORN EXPRESSIONS TO AVOID

The following is a list of the more common expressions included in Business Jargon. Beginning students should consider them as warnings of bad habits that writers may fall into; experienced letter writers may use them as a yardstick against which they can measure the effectiveness of their diction.

According to our records—Why drag in the way you get your information? Say "We find."

Acknowledge receipt of—as in "We wish to acknowledge receipt of your letter." Forget it; say "Thank you for your letter."

Advise—as in "In answer to your letter of August 7, we wish to advise that shipment has been made." "Advise" is a perfectly good word, but it means "to give advice"; in general, it should be replaced by "inform" when information is being conveyed.

Allow me to—as in "Allow me to express our appreciation for." A pompous method of saying "Thank you for."

Along these lines—as in "We are carrying on research along these lines." A meaningless phrase. Make it specific.

As a matter of fact—Five unnecessary words with the implication that other statements in the letter are not matters of fact.

As per—as in "As per our records," "As per your letter," etc. Another barbaric mixture; say "According to."

As stated above, as indicated below—Charles Lamb, the English essayist, called users of these expressions "the above boys" and "the below boys." Say "from these facts" or "as we have shown" or "for the following reasons."

Attached please find—No hunting is necessary if your check or order is attached. Say " We are attaching" or "We enclose our check" and let it go at that.

At an early date, at the earliest possible moment—Say "soon" and save yourself some words.

At hand—as in "I have your letter of May 9 at hand." Omit it entirely since "at hand" adds nothing. "Thank you for your letter of May 9" or better "Your letter of May 9 . . . ."

At the present writing, at this time—Overworked and roundabout jargon for "now."

At your earliest convenience—Say "soon" and save yourself some words.

Awaiting your favor—This might make a song title, but you probably mean "We hope to hear from you soon" or "Please let us hear from you."

Beg—as in "Beg to inform," "Beg to acknowledge," "Beg to state," "Beg to remain," etc. Omit "beg" entirely. Go ahead and inform, acknowledge, state, or remain; it is absurd for perfectly solvent firms to go around begging in their business letters.

Contents duly noted—as in "Your favor received and contents duly noted." Say "Thank you for your letter" and let it go at that.

Dictated but not read—Of all the insulting notations on letters, this is the worst. Readers who receive them should immediately write back "Received but not read."

Each and every—as in "Each and every one of us appreciates this." Why say the same thing twice? Say "Every one of us" or "Each one of us."

Enclosed please find—as in "Enclosed please find our check for $25." He won't have to hunt for your check if it *is* enclosed; simply say "We enclose" or "We are enclosing."

Even date, current date, recent date—as in "Your letter of even date." Give the specific date. "Your letter of January 12."

Favor—as in "Thank you for your favor of October 22" or "In response to your favor of July 10." Never call a letter a "favor"; call it what it is—a letter.

For your information—Tactless. Everything in the letter is for his information. Omit it.

Hand you—as in "We herewith hand you our check for $37.10." A meaningless and outworn expression—and what long arms you have, Grandma! Say "We enclose our check for $37.10."

Hoping, waiting, referring, thanking, etc.—When these are used in beginning or ending a letter, as in "Referring to your letter," the chances are good that this construction will result in a dangling participle. Avoid all participial constructions in beginning and ending letters; recast the sentence to get rid of the participle.

I have your letter, I have received your letter—A thoughtless warm-up for starting letters. Since you are answering, he knows you have the letter. Say "Thank you for your letter" or "We appreciate your letter of February 15."

In receipt of—as in "We are in receipt of your check." Say "We have received your check" or "Thank you for your check."

In (or to or for) the amount of—as in "We enclose our check in the amount of $33.16." Simply say "for" as in "We enclose our check for $33.16."

In the near future—Be specific, or save words with "soon."

Permit me to say—Go on and say it; no permission is needed.

Replying to yours of December 12—a sure way of showing your reader that you want to avoid thinking. Omit it and refer to the date of his letter indirectly.

Same—as in "In answer to same." "Same" should be used as an adjective; it is correctly used as a pronoun only in legal terminology.

Thanking you in advance—as in "Thanking you in advance for any information you may send." Poor psychology because it antagonizes the reader by too obviously assuming that he is going to do what you want him to. Say "We shall be grateful for any information you may care to send."

Thank you again—Once is usually enough.

Thank you kindly—An absurd statement. Why are you being kind in thanking him? Just say "Thank you."

The writer—as in "The writer believes" or "It is the opinion of the writer." An obvious and pompous attempt to give the impression of modesty by avoiding the use of "I" or "we." Don't be afraid to use "I believe" or "We think."

This letter is for the purpose of requesting—Why all this preliminary? Go ahead and ask. When you write effective letters, their purpose is clear.

This will acknowledge receipt of your letter—Another wasted warm-up.

Under separate cover—as in "We are sending under separate cover." This should be used very sparingly; wherever possible be specific. "We are sending by parcel post" (or express or air mail).

The undersigned—See comments on "the writer." Say "I."

Up to this writing—Say "Up to now."

We regret to inform you that we are in error—Wordy and hackneyed. Say "We are sorry for our mistake."

You claim, you state, you say—Avoid these wherever possible because they antagonize the reader by implying that his statement is not true. Recast the sentence to eliminate them.

Yours—as in "Yours of recent date." Say "Your letter" or "Your order."

These are the specters that haunt business correspondence. But the Jargoneer has other devices to assure pompousness. Above all else, he enjoys using several words where one or two are necessary, and he likes to say the same thing twice by using what are known as "doublets." Just as he prefers "in the amount of" to "for," he selects the following wordy expressions in the left-hand column rather than those in the right, which effective writers use.

Agreeable to your wishes in this matter	"like"
Along these lines	be specific
Answer in the affirmative	say "Yes"
At a later date	"later"
At the present time	"now"
Despite the fact that	"though," "although"
Due to the fact that	"since," "because"
For the purpose of	"to," "for"
For the reason that	"since," "because"
In accordance with your request	"as you requested"
In addition	"also"
Inasmuch as	"since"
In order that	"so"

In order to	"to"
In the event that	"if"
In the nature of	"like"
In the neighborhood of	"about"
In the normal course of our procedure	"normally"
In the very near future	"soon"
In this connection	omit
In this day and age	"today"
In view of the fact that	"since," "because"
Of the order of magnitude of	"about"
On the grounds that	"because"
On the occasion of	"when," "on"
Prior to	"before"
Pursuant to our agreement	"as we agreed"
Subsequent to	"after"
The reason is due to	"because"
Under date of	"on"
We are not in a position to	"we cannot"
Will you be kind enough to	"please"
With a view to	"to"
Without further delay	"now," "immediately"
With reference to	"about"
With regard to	"about"
With respect to	"about"
With the result that	"so that"

Equally dear to the hearts of Jargoneers are the doublets and the redundant phrases in which several words bloom where one or two are necessary. Here are a few examples.

Absolutely complete	"complete"
Agreeable and satisfactory	just one
Anxious and eager	one or the other
Basic fundamentals	"fundamentals," being "basic," will suffice
Consensus of opinion	"consensus" can't be anything but opinion; say just "consensus"

Courteous and polite	one or the other, not both
Each and every one of us	"each of us," "every one of us," "all of us"
Exactly identical	"identical"
First and foremost	either one, not both
Full and complete	just one
Hope and trust	"hope"
If and when	either one
Insist and demand	choose one
My personal opinion	"my opinion"; it can't be anything but personal
Right and proper	don't say the same thing twice
Sincere and earnèst	select one
Thought and consideration	only one
True facts	since facts are true, omit the adjective
Unique—as "the most unique," "very unique," etc.	"unique" cannot be qualified; it means one of a kind, without equal

Fortunately, as we have seen, greater attention is being paid to eliminating jargon from today's business letters. As more correspondents grow conscious of hackneyed phrases, doublets, and redundant expressions, business writing becomes direct and forceful. Too many correspondents are still saying, "It is my own personal opinion" instead of "I think"; and too many dictators, at a loss for words with which to begin, clutch at that last straw of the routine mind, "This is to acknowledge receipt of your letter of April 20." The overstuffed expressions of Business Jargon will fall into the class of dead languages only when writers become sensitive to its waste, when they are willing to revise their letters, and when they ask themselves, "Would I *say* it this way if I were talking instead of writing?" Only then will they follow the best advice on becoming a Jargoneer—*don't!* "Blessed is the man," says George Eliot, "who, having nothing to say, abstains from giving in words evidence of the fact."

EXERCISES

1. Correct any errors in the form and diction of the following letters:

June 21st, 1953

    a. The Green Manufacturing Co.,
2742 — 9th Street
Cincinnati 11, Ohio.

Att: of Mr. James Whitney

My Dear Mr. Whitney:

Referring to yours of the 16th. We beg to advise you that shipment of your order was made yesterday, June 20.

As per our records, shipment was to have been made on June 15, and the - writer wishes to state that we regret exceedingly any inconvenience you may have experienced as the result of this delay. In reference to your suggestion that shipments be made by truck rather than by train, we are taking this matter under advisement. We are of the opinion, however, that shipment by rail is generally preferable because our plant has direct connections by rail.

Regretting the inconvenience caused and hoping that it will not affect our amicable relations, I am.

Cordially yours

Robert Clark

    b. Dear Sir:

In reply to yours of October 29 would state that the undersigned cannot give out the information requested.

Unfortunately our company policy is such as to make it impossible for me to help you in your research on plastic cases for portable radios. I would respectfully suggest that you consult some consulting engineer in your section on the problem raised.

Trusting we may continue to solicit your business in the future, I remain,

Sincerely yours,

    c. Dear Mr. Oliver:

Yours of 14th received and contents duly noted.

Enclosed please find our booklet "Air Conditioning for Tomorrow's Home." Should there be other questions do not hesitate to write in the near future; a willingness to serve customers is the very backbone of our entire sales policy.

Along that line, our Mr. Lamppert will be in your vicinity in a month or two. Advise us if you want him to call on you.

Yours very truly,

d. Dear Sir:

Your esteemed favor of even date has been given due consideration. In reply we wish to state that in view of the stated facts we are remitting herewith our check No 31764 to the amount of $16.23 for the balance due.

Kindly be advised that as per our records of this date our account with you is paid. We would beg to remain,

Yours very truly,

2. Rewrite the following sentences to eliminate jargon and to make them direct and forceful:

a. We are in receipt of yours of the 19th and in reply would state that we regret exceedingly our mistake in sending you a collection letter for a bill which you had already paid.

b. Referring to your communication of recent date, we wish to take this opportunity to state that the merchandise about which you inquired was shipped as per your instructions on January 9.

c. Your letter of 7—11—53 addressed to the undersigned was received and in due course was referred to our shipping department. You will hear from them in the near future relative to the reasons for the delay in the shipment of the merchandise you ordered.

d. Answering your favor of August 21 which we appreciate very much. In response would say that we were gratified to learn that our meters have given you such good service.

e. Yours of the 2nd received and in reply permit me to say that we regret we cannot send you the samples you asked for because of material shortages.

f. Due to the fact that our shipping department has been undergoing a reorganization, it is my personal opinion that your request has been delayed until sometime in the near future.

g. In the event that this does not meet your approval, please notify the writer as to your wishes.

h. In order to obtain absolutely complete information which will be agreeable and satisfactory to you, it is the consensus of our staff's opinion that we should conduct a survey and notify you of the results.

i. Pursuant to our agreement, we herewith send you the results of our investigation conducted three years ago; unfortunately we are not in a position to transmit later data at this time.

j. On the occasion of our recent meeting, you raised several questions with reference to our personnel policy.

3. Rewrite the following letters to make them more effective:

a. Dear Mr. Welch:

It is a matter of great pleasure to me—and indeed to all the members of our organization—to be able to inform you at this time that we are now engaged in the manufacture of luminous-face electric alarm clocks to sell at retail for $5.95.

Should you feel that these clocks would merit the approval of your clientele, I shall be only too happy to receive your order on the enclosed order blank which gives the wholesale prices on various quantities. The writer is firmly convinced that these clocks will appeal not only to you yourself but also to your customers.

Along these lines, I can confidently state without fear of contradiction that our new electric alarm clock—which we have named The Titan—is the finest alarm clock in its price field. Thank you again for your consideration.

Yours truly,

b. Gentlemen:

We wish to acknowledge your check in the amount of $27.46.

As per our records, the amount of our bill, sent on the 10th was $31.01. We note that you claim you are entitled to a discount, but this is not in accordance with our records.

We shall, therefore, await the balance of your remittance.

Sincerely,

c. Dear Mr. Putnam:

With reference to yours of recent date would state that we are enclosing herewith our latest sales prospectus. Should the need arise for any of our parts, we will be very glad to fill your order for same.

Very truly yours,

d. Dear Mr. Caldwell:

Your communication of May 2 is at hand and in answer wish to assure you that the damage to your radio cabinet is not, as you claim, our fault.

The writer is certain that this damage must have occurred in shipment. The fact of the matter is that our inspection tag shows the cabinet was in A-1 condition when it left our plant. Hence we cannot accept the blame for this situation.

The matter is being referred by us to the Smoot Trucking Company and you will doubtless hear from them in due course.

Yours truly,

e. Dear Sirs:

We are in receipt of your communication dated 7/9/53 and have duly noted the contents.

Since shipping costs on such heavy items as second-hand pianos are prohibitive, would suggest that you contact a dealer in your immediate vicinity. In re the make of piano we would recommend, I am forced to state that ethics will not permit such recommendation.

Hoping you will find the type of instrument you are looking for,

Sincerely,

4. As a class project, select a member of the class to interview a correspondence supervisor suggested by your instructor on the subject "What the _____ Company Has Done to Eliminate Business Jargon from Its Letters." Report to the class on the results of the interview.

5. Select five companies which your instructor recommends as being well known for the effectiveness of their letters. Write to them for information for a report you will make to the class on "How to Write Direct and Concise Letters." Prepare a summary of their answers for an oral report to the class.

You write with ease to show your breeding,
But easy writing's curst hard reading.
                    Richard Brinsley Sheridan

CHAPTER V

Making Letters Easy to Read

Every letter writer likes to think that the message which is his brain child will completely absorb the attention of the reader. Actually, nothing could be further from the truth; most businessmen have many claims on their attention and other letters than that most important one of ours to read. Furthermore, the vast increase in the number of sales letters within recent years has made letter readers increasingly skeptical and more likely to toss letters into the wastepaper basket. As a result, certain letters may be given only a perfunctory reading or a hasty glance. This situation allows the letter writer no time for stalling with his message nor for hesitancy in coming to the point. He must start to say something from the first word and stop when the necessary message is complete. His letter must, in short, be easy to read if it is to have maximum success as a message which seeks to get the reader to take some desired action or point of view.

In the last chapter we emphasized the importance of avoiding Business Jargon because such pompous wordiness is definitely not easy to read. We also discussed the importance of thought and analysis before writing; this, too, will aid in ease of reading. Let us now examine some of the specific methods of organizing and arranging the letter to make it easy to read.

The correspondent who realizes how his letter will probably be read is better prepared to organize his thoughts effectively. He thinks of his reader as glancing through the mail—in which there are inevitably several sales letters whose products don't much interest him; the reader's technique is probably to glance at the first paragraph of each letter, to let his eye run hastily over the first sentence of each succeeding paragraph, and perhaps to read the last paragraph completely. He is like a man reading the newspaper, scanning the headlines, reading the "leads," and letting his eye glance through the topic sentences of the rest of the news story. If that sort of "skimming" arouses his interest sufficiently, he may go back and read the story from beginning to end; if it doesn't, he will pass on to other news stories that do interest him. How can such a reader's interest be caught and held?

THE FIRST PARAGRAPH

This reading technique puts a premium upon the first paragraph of the letter, for it is both the headline and the lead for the message that follows. Ideally, the first paragraph of the business letter should do four things:

1. It should get favorable attention.
2. It should indicate what the letter is about.
3. It should set a friendly and courteous tone for the whole letter.
4. It should link up with previous correspondence by a reference to date or subject.

If the opening paragraph is direct and interesting, the whole letter may be read with care; if it is not, the rest of the message may be skimmed or skipped entirely. To be effective, the first paragraph of a business letter should observe two principles:

1. It must be short.
2. It must say something.

1. It Must Be Short

Nothing more discourages the reader than a whole section of closely packed print or type. The reader's eye is repelled by it and refuses to take it all in. The novel reader who says, "I read all the conversation and skip the long descriptions," is merely giving expression to the dislike that bulky paragraphs arouse in most readers. Our eyes are attracted to short snatches of printed conversation simply because they are short. For this reason, the first paragraph of the letter should be brief to lead the reader on to the rest of the message. It should never contain more than two or three short sentences.

2. It Must Say Something

That the opening paragraph should say something seems sufficiently evident. Yet many letters in modern business tell the
reader nothing he does not already know. Two things should
appear in the first paragraph:

a. A reference to the date of the letter being answered or to
similar details which will give continuity to the correspondence
b. A statement of what this letter is about, unless it is a sales letter
in which the first paragraph is designed primarily to attract
attention

The reference to the date of earlier letters or to similar details
should always be subordinated. A surprising number of correspondents begin their letters with some such sentences as

This is to answer yours of October 14.
We have received your letter of October 14.
Referring to yours of October 14. (An incomplete thought.)

The fact that a specific letter is being answered should be taken
as sufficient evidence that it has been received; why waste the
most important part of the letter—the equivalent of a newspaper
headline—merely to tell a reader that his letter has been received
or that it was dated October 14? When it is necessary to refer to
previous correspondence, the reference should be subordinated;
it should never be featured. The important task of the first paragraph is to announce what this letter is about in order to arouse the
reader's interest; all else should be subordinate. Notice the effectiveness of the second method of writing each of the following
opening paragraphs:

Weak and ineffective be-cause the first 10 words tell the reader nothing he doesn't already know:	Replying to yours of May 10, we wish to state that our research staff has been working for a long time on the problem that you mentioned and has finally succeeded in solving it.
Direct and effective:	Our research staff has successfully solved the problem of insulating old homes about which you inquired in your letter of May 10.
Weak and full of Business Jargon:	In reply to yours of July 16, we wish to state that we regret the error made in your last order.

More effective:	Thank you for your letter of July 16 calling attention to our mistake in filling your last order.
Incomplete sentence:	Acknowledging receipt of your letter of February 15 in which you asked for a copy of "Better Homes for Small Incomes." We are glad to send you a copy of this booklet.
Better:	We gladly enclose "Better Homes for Small Incomes" which you requested on February 15. In it you will find the answers to your questions about design, construction costs, and financing of your new home.
Trite and ineffective:	Yours of January 15 received and contents duly noted. We wish to say that we are referring your question to our sales department.
More concise and direct:	Our sales department is assembling material which should prove helpful in answering your inquiry of January 15.

Good writers never begin a letter with a participial expression. Almost invariably such a beginning indicates that the writer has not thought out what he wants to say and is merely stalling for time until an idea strikes him. One can almost see him pacing up and down, while his secretary sits with pencil poised: "Referring to yours of March 21"—a long pause while he gropes for an idea—"our representative, Mr. Smith, will personally handle your problem of insulation." This is not only a waste of words and an unnecessary featuring of the date of his letter; it is ungrammatical because the participle, "Referring to yours of March 21," obviously does not modify "our representative."

If you insist on using participial constructions in your letters, you can at least insure grammatical correctness by observing the rule that the agent or doer of the action in the participle is the same as the subject of the sentence:

Wrong:	Referring to yours of March 21, our representative will personally investigate this problem.
Correct but ineffective:	Referring to your letter of March 21, I have asked our representative to investigate this problem.

Wrong:	Thanking you for this assistance, it is our hope that we may return this favor sometime.
Correct:	Thanking you for this assistance, we hope to be able to return this favor.
Better:	We appreciate your assistance and hope to be able to return this favor.

The best rule, however, is to avoid participles at the beginning of a letter.

How would you like to attend a baseball game which *featured* the players warming up? Or a symphony concert *highlighting* the babel of sounds when the orchestra tunes up? Yet letter writers frequently use their opening paragraphs—the most vital part of their message—as a kind of practice session before they get on with the main business at hand. Don't warm up with inane expressions: "Referring to your letter of January 27"; don't rehash what your reader already knows: "Your order of March 12 has been received." Avoid all unnecessary preliminaries in your first sentence and get into your message fast. Here are some good beginnings.

You need not pay a cent to examine this new book at your leisure.

Thank you for your request for information about our reproductions of antiques.

The catalogue you requested on May 27 was mailed today.

You can help me greatly by sending a copy of your article on "Executive Training."

Here is the bulletin you asked us to send.

Thank you for your helpful suggestions about our sales conference.

Congratulations on the fine progress your annual report reveals.

We are pleased to send you the material you requested.

We're sorry that we can't comply with your request of November 19.

The material on page 16 of the enclosed brochure will answer the questions in your letter of June 16.

Just as soon as we received your letter, we wired our New York office to ship your fishing tackle.

The tires which complete your order LL-138 were shipped today.

You are certainly correct in thinking that we now produce lighter, stronger utensiles.

PARAGRAPHING THE ·REST OF THE LETTER

In business correspondence, a different conception of the function of the paragraph is needed from the literary one which defines the paragraph as a group of related sentences forming a unit of thought. Indeed, if this literary definition were accepted, most letters would be messages of one paragraph, for all of the sentences in a letter usually concern one central idea. In business letters, the paragraph is used as a device for making the message easier to read. The following two letters illustrate how the paragraph can contribute to the ease of reading:

Dear Mr. Potter:·

We are glad to tell you, in answer to your letter of May 4, that our service department has found nothing seriously wrong with your Blank Camera, Model 12 A. A few comparatively inexpensive repairs and adjustments are needed, the chief of which are replacement of one part of the shutter mechanism and readjustment of the timing. The camera appears to have been dropped or seriously jarred. Our guarantee covers "any defect of workmanship or materials within one year of normal use," but, as you doubtless realize, it does not cover careless handling. If you will send us your check for $2.17, we will put your camera in first-class condition and renew our guarantee on workmanship and materials for another year. Just as soon as you sign and mail the enclosed, stamped, addressed post card, we'll return your camera as good as new—ready to catch that picture ahead that you'll treasure as a moment of happiness recaptured.

Sincerely yours,

Dear Mr. Potter:

We are glad to tell you, in answer to your letter of May 4, that our service department has found nothing seriously wrong with your Blank Camera, Model 12 A.

A few comparatively inexpensive repairs and adjustments are needed, the chief of which are replacement of one part of the shutter mechanism and readjustment of the timing. The camera appears to have been dropped or seriously jarred.

Our guarantee covers "any defect of workmanship or materials within one year of normal use," but, as you doubtless realize, it does not cover careless handling. If you will send us your check for $2.17, we will put your camera in first-class condition and renew our guarantee on workmanship and materials for another year.

Just as soon as you sign and mail the enclosed, stamped, addressed post card, we'll return your camera as good as new—ready to catch that picture ahead that you'll treasure as a moment of happiness recaptured.

Sincerely yours,

A glance shows how much more inviting to the eye the second version of this letter is than the first, which repels the eye by its lack of paragraphing. If the literary definition of the paragraph is accepted, however, the first letter is quite correct because all the sentences concern one central idea. It should be apparent from this example that the literary concept of the paragraph must be abandoned in business letters in favor of a concept that uses the paragraph as a device for breaking up a thought into more readable units. Thus, in the four-paragraph letter above, the division is made on the following basis.

Paragraph 1: A reference to the date of the letter being answered and a statement of what this letter is about

Paragraph 2: A statement of what is wrong with the camera and why

Paragraph 3: An explanation of why the guarantee does not cover this situation and a statement of the cost

Paragraph 4: An incentive to action

To present these subdivisions of the thought in the most readable fashion, the paragraphs of the business letter should be kept short. This does not mean that each paragraph should be just one brief sentence; such an extreme is to be avoided. But the general principle is sound: Keep the paragraphs of the business letter as short as is consistent with completeness because that makes the letter easy to read.

THE FINAL PARAGRAPH

Every host is all too familiar with the guest who says "Good night" and then sits down for another half-hour to tell one more story or experience. After this process has been repeated several times, the guest actually leaves and the weary host breathes a sigh of relief. Many writers of business letters use a similarly annoying technique. After they have said everything necessary, they go on repeating the same ideas in different words. One principle should be followed in the closing paragraph of the letter: Stop when the message is complete.

The function of the last paragraph of every letter is to make it as easy as possible for the reader to take an action or to accept a point of view that the writer wants him to take. If the you attitude is properly employed, the final paragraph will show the reader how easily he may do this thing that will benefit him. Hence, when a department store wants to get a customer to return some piece of merchandise which has been replaced, the last paragraph of the letter should not read,

We hope that you will return this dress for credit as soon as possible.

but it should offer some such incentive to the customer as,

Just as soon as you return this dress, we shall gladly credit your account with $11.75.

By enclosing self-addressed envelopes or post cards and referring specifically to these enclosures in their final paragraphs, many correspondents stimulate action by making it very easy. Especially effective are such closing paragraphs as the following, which make definite suggestions and offer an easy means of taking action:

Just sign and mail the enclosed post card and you will receive all the news in concise, readable form for the next 52 weeks.

Your check in the enclosed envelope will enable you to maintain that high credit reputation you have always enjoyed.

A wire—collect, of course—to our sales department will bring a trained member of our staff to give you an estimate, at no obligation to you.

A direct question constitutes a good close because it gives the reader a specific query to consider and to answer.

May I have an interview with you at your convenience? You can reach me at my home address or Fairmount 4289.

Are you willing to give Blanco Fuel a 10-day trial to let it demonstrate in your home its efficiency and economy? Your signature on the enclosed card will bring you a 10-day supply without cost. May I have 10 minutes in which to substantiate these statements?

Would you jeopardize your credit rating for so small an amount?

The most ineffective of all closes is the participial ending. It is weak, hackneyed, incomplete in its thought, and offers no incentive to action because it eliminates the possibility of taking the you attitude. "Thanking you in advance" and "Trusting we shall have your cooperation in this matter" are the products of the same type of mind as that which begins the letter with the incomplete "Referring to yours of October 15." Such closes can always be changed into direct statements, as "We shall hope to hear from you soon" or "We appreciate your cooperation in this matter." By the use of the you attitude, these closes can be transformed into direct incentives to action or builders of good will such as the following:

If we can help you in any way, please let us know.

Mail us your check today and your order will arrive on Thursday.

Just sign your name at the bottom of this letter and return it in the enclosed postage-free envelope.

Will you let us know by April 14 so that we can place our order promptly?

We think this brochure will answer your questions, but if you need more information, please let us know.

Just fill in the card and we'll gladly send a representative to help you.

Remember—when your message is complete, stop! Good letter writers, like good railroads, pride themselves on their terminal facilities—and both want their customers to get to their destination as soon as possible.

WORDINESS IN THE LETTER

Invariably, the worst fault in the letters of inexperienced writers is an excessive wordiness. The scientist, Pascal, in a postscript to a 20-page letter written in 1656, said: "I hope you will pardon me for writing such a long letter, but I did not have time to write you a shorter one." This paradox contains a real truth. A short, well-organized letter takes more time than a discursive, repetitious one, because an effective letter requires thought and a willingness to spend enough time to eliminate unnecessary words and ideas. No quality that the correspondent can possess is more valuable in improving his letters than a readiness to revise them. We learn by our own errors, and by correcting them we can improve most rapidly. The writer who spends the necessary time going over his letters in a sincere effort to better them will soon be writing more directly and with less wasted effort.

As he writes and revises, the correspondent should concentrate on applying certain fundamental principles of good, clear writing. In the last analysis, the only way to learn to write is to write and then rewrite. The correspondent who sincerely wants to learn to write well must constantly strive to achieve the highest standards of which he is capable. Many business writers alibi their mediocre performance by such statements as, "I didn't have time to revise" or "It won't make any difference to my reader" or "He won't recognize good writing from bad." Such superficial and superior attitudes ignore a fundamental fact—that readers recognize good, clear writing even though they are vague about, or even ignorant of, the principles from which it stems. Read this superb sentence which the late Edwin L. James of *The New York Times* wrote for the lead of his Armistice story at the end of World War I: "In a twinkling, four years of killing and massacre stopped as if God had swept His omnipotent finger across the scene of world carnage and had cried 'Enough.'" Does anyone doubt that this is good writing?

No one expects highfalutin literary style in business letters; but readers have every right to expect direct, forceful, and readable style, and they will recognize such writing for what it is.

Because every letter conveys a definite impression of the correspondent or the company he represents, writers in business have a special obligation to write clearly and concisely, to avoid sounding pompous and impersonal, and to do credit to themselves and their company. And since the business letter is a comparatively short form of communication, every word should do its job. As one writer said, "Words are like inflated money—the more that are used, the less each one is worth." Here, then, are a few principles that will help business writers to deflate their wordiness and to produce readable letters:

1. Use Active Voice Wherever Possible

Active voice is direct, forceful, personal; it tells *who . . . does . . . what.* Whereas passive voice says, "The game was ended when a third strike was thrown by Feller to Mantle," active voice says, "Feller ended the game with a third strike thrown to Mantle." In business letters, similar roundabout expressions can be changed as follows:

Wordy: Consideration is being given to this matter by our Sales Department.

Improved: Our Sales Department will consider this matter.

Wordy: It is desired by Mr. Swain that this be called to your attention.

Improved: Mr. Swain asked me to call this to your attention.

Wordy: Our Atlanta Office has been instructed to be prepared for a visit from your representative.

Improved: We have told our Atlanta Office to expect a visit from your representative.

Wordy: This manual of instructions was prepared to aid our dealers in being helpful to their customers.

Improved: We prepared this manual of instructions to aid our dealers in serving their customers.

Excessive use of the passive voice results in more wordiness in letters than almost any other form of expression. Its name implies just what it is—*passive*—and, therefore, indirect and impersonal. Get used to personalizing, to direct and *active* expression.

2. Make Verbs Carry the Load

Verbs are words of action; they carry readers along; they should not be watered down.

Instead of: Application of these principles is the best way for us to obtain the cooperation of our retailers.

Say: By applying these principles, we can get our retailers to cooperate.

Instead of: This sales message is something of vital concern to all our personnel.

Say: This sales message vitally concerns all our personnel.

Instead of: This contract has a requirement that it be signed by you.

Say: This contract requires your signature.

Instead of: This makes it necessary for us to refuse your request with regret.

Say: We regret that we must, therefore, refuse your request.

Instead of: This does have a direct bearing on the possibilities for future sales.

Say: This directly affects future sales.

Notice that some of this wordiness stems from the passive and that some of it comes from roundabout expressions like "is something of vital concern," where one verb will express the idea, and from abstract words like "application," which can usually be replaced by verbs. Remember the advice of John Hookham Frere, an English diplomat and writer of the nineteenth century:

> And don't confound the language of the nation
> With long-tailed words in *osity* and *ation*.

3. Use "There is," "It is," and Similar Expressions Sparingly

Instead of: It is my personal opinion that . . . .

Say: I think . . . .

Instead of: There are certain problems which confront us . . . .

Say: Certain problems confront us . . . .

Instead of: It was our understanding that . . . .

Say: We understood that . . . .

Instead of: It is the responsibility of our Production Department to see that it meets the requirements of our Sales Division. (Note that the first "it" is indefinite, the second refers to "Production Department," making a very confusing sentence.)

Say: Our Production Department must meet the requirements of our Sales Division.

Instead of: There is a need in today's business for properly qualified correspondents.

Say: Today's business needs properly qualified correspondents.

4. Keep Sentences Short and Concentrate on One Idea in Each Sentence

How short is "short"? No simple answer will suffice; Dr. Rudolph Flesch, who wrote *The Art of Plain Talk*, believes that an *average* sentence length of 17 words makes high readability. Writers of business letters should aim at variety in both the length and pattern of their sentences. They should occasionally check the average length of sentences in their letters to see that they fall somewhere between 15 and 20 words. If not, they should use a very useful device—the period—more frequently; most long sentences lend themselves logically to this chopping-up process.

I should greatly appreciate your letting me know what your decision is so that I can send the report to Mr. Jones in our Memphis office with a request for more information which we will need to make our plans for the coming year and to encourage him to make any suggestions he may want to incorporate. (One sentence, 57 words)

I should greatly appreciate your letting me know your decision. I can then send the report to Mr. Jones in our Memphis office requesting more information. We will need his suggestions for next year's plans. (Three sentences, 35 words)

The classic definition of the sentence is "a group of words to convey a single thought." Too many correspondents err on the side of putting qualifying phrases and clauses into their sentences and hence lengthen them to a point which passeth understanding. Aim at conciseness, at clean-cut sentences, and put the qualifiers in separate sentences.

Usually we find that our refrigerators give maximum efficiency when they are stored in a very dry place until they are used, but occasionally we hear of a case where such storage has resulted in a drying out of the insulation around the door in which case we recommend that it be treated by applying a damp cloth so that the moisture in the rubber may be replaced. (One sentence, 68 words)

We find that our refrigerators give maximum efficiency when they are stored in a very dry place. Occasionally, this results in drying out the insulation around the door. We then recommend applying a damp cloth to the insulation to replace the moisture in the rubber. (Three sentences, 45 words)

Business letters are written to convey information, to get action, to build good will. They accomplish these purposes best with sentences which carry the reader along step by step. Don't force your reader to go along until he is breathless from the sheer length of your sentences. And don't clutter your sentences with too many ideas at once.

5. Watch Clauses to See Whether They Can Be Expressed More Concisely

Wordy: You will be pleased with this clock which is dependable and attractive in appearance.

Improved: You will be pleased with this attractive and dependable clock.

Wordy: This service, which is offered without any charge whatsoever, is available to all of our customers.

Improved: This free service is available to all our customers.

6. Rearrange Sentences to Make Them More Direct

Wordy: Sign the enclosed card and drop it in the mailbox today.

Improved: Sign and mail the enclosed card today.

Wordy: Its point is made of metal and it will not break.

Improved: Its point is made of unbreakable metal.

7. Choose Words Carefully for Greater Simplicity and Directness

Very wordy: We must, therefore, keep each method of paying our salesmen a matter of information to be known only to those affected.

Much improved, with one word replacing the last eleven:
           We must, therefore, keep each method of paying our salesmen confidential.

8. Write in Language That Your Reader Will Understand

In Chapter II, we emphasized the importance of keeping the reader constantly in mind so that the letter may have the proper tone and the right psychological approach. This also affects the language of the letter; by trying to visualize his reader and by using words familiar to the reader, the correspondent can avoid the shoptalk, technical terms, or specialized vocabulary which often require additional letters of explanation.

Instead of: Please forward your remittance.

Say: Please send us your check (or payment).

Instead of: Unfortunately an error was made by our Collection Department in posting your account.

Say: Unfortunately, we made an error in your bill.

Instead of: We have instructed our C. & C. Department to investigate this matter.

Say: We have asked our Credit and Collection Department to find out what happened.

Instead of: Our Sales Manager is putting a bring-up on your file for the 15th.

Say: Our Sales Manager will send you a reminder on June 15.

Instead of: You can expedite the finaling of your electric service at your cottage by notifying us when we may reach you there.

Say: Please let us know when you will be at your cottage so that we can cut off the service promptly.

Samuel Johnson once described Oliver Goldsmith's writing in these words: "He makes his little fishes talk like whales."

The best way to attain directness of expression in applying these principles is through constant revision. The examples above, all taken from actual business letters, show how much may be accomplished by revision. The writer should ask himself, "Have I said this as directly and as simply as possible?" If he is willing to change his letters until they meet this standard, he need have no concern about wordiness.

SUMMARY

In the last four chapters, we have been discussing the desirable qualities of business letters in general; now we are ready to go on to some of the problems of such specific types of letters as inquiries, claims, collection, sales, application, and memorandums. But regardless of the exact type of letter to be written, the general qualities thus far discussed and the techniques mentioned should be made an integral part of it.

By way of a brief summary of these opening chapters, we might insist that the writer of any business letter—that message which attempts to influence its recipient to some action or attitude desired by the sender—do the following things:

1. Before writing, analyze what it is that the letter attempts to do. (Chapter II)
2. Use those qualities which will be most effective in influencing the reader to do what the letter writer desires. (Chapter II)
   a. Use the you attitude, which influences the reader to do a certain thing or take a definite point of view because it is to his advantage.
   b. Adapt the letter to the reader's interests and background.
   c. Give the letter a natural tone or "personality."
3. Select the appropriate form of the letter and see that the letter is correct in such details as letterhead, stationery, grammar, spelling, and punctuation. (Chapter III)
4. Avoid Business Jargon and wordy, trite, or meaningless expressions. (Chapter IV)
5. Make the letter as easy to read as possible. (Chapter V)
   a. Keep the paragraphs short.
   b. Make the first paragraph say something directly and concisely.
   c. Stop when everything necessary has been said.
   d. Avoid wordiness.
   e. Revise the letter wherever it may be improved.

The rating scale on page 86 offers a convenient way for readers to apply to their own letters the principles discussed in the preceding chapters.

A RATING SCALE FOR LETTERS

Every letter creates a definite impression on the reader. While the factors involved in such an impression cannot be reduced to a mathematical formula, the following rating scale will help correspondents to evaluate their efforts. If they can answer "Yes" to questions listed, they are on the road to successful letter writing.

Appearance Does the letter's appearance make a good first impression? Does it comply with correct usage for this letter 20% form? Is it free from erasures, strikeovers? Is it well balanced on the page? Are the paragraphs short enough to invite easy reading? Has it been checked for errors in grammar, punctuation, and spelling?

Thought Does it reveal careful thought about the fundamental purpose of the letter? Does it achieve that purpose? 20% Does it answer all the necessary questions? Is the material presented in logical order?

Attitude Does it point out to the reader how he benefits from the action you suggest? Does it build good will? Does 20% it include all the information he needs? Is it written in language your reader will understand?

Style Is it clear, concise, and readable? Does it avoid Business Jargon and trite, meaningless, or wordy expres- 20% sions? Are the sentences short and direct? Has it been revised to correct all errors in style?

Tone Does it sound as if one human being had written it to another? Is it friendly, courteous, and tactful? Does it 20% avoid exaggerated claims and overstatements? Does it sound sincere?

EXERCISES

1. What changes would make the following letters easier to read?

a. Dear Mr. Byers:

This is in reply to your letter of October 12, 1953, in which you said you were interested in the details of how to use insulation to make your house warmer in the winter months. We appreciate your interest and we hope we can be of service to you as we have to thousands of other customers who have solved the same problem by the use of Warmtex Insulation. The enclosed booklet entitled "A Warmer Winter for You" will show you how Warmtex Insulation is installed and how its cost may be estimated as well as how you may estimate your fuel savings on the basis of the savings of our thousands of other customers.

We hope you will get in touch with our representative in your territory, Mr. W. Smails, Pittsfield, Mass. You can call him at Pittsfield 4327-M. We appreciate your interest and we hope you will arrange to see Mr. Smails. Thank you again for your inquiry. We shall be glad to count you among our thousands of customers.

Sincerely yours,

b. Dear Mr. Whitney:

Referring to yours of July 10, in which you asked our opinion of Mr. J. Willoughby Murch as a credit risk.

In reply we wish to state that Mr. Murch has been a customer of ours for many years and our business relations, we believe, have been entirely satisfactory; at least, for our part, we can say so. As you undoubtedly know, Mr. Murch conducts The Feed and Grain Supply Co. at Libertyville, N. Y., and enjoys what seems to us to be a profitable business; at least, he pays his obligations to us rather promptly. About five years ago, illness forced him to turn over the management of his business to a son-in-law, and during that time, payments fell somewhat in arrears, but when Mr. Murch took active control again this situation was changed for the better.

We hope this answers all the questions you asked.

Sincerely yours,

2. The following sentences are taken from actual letters, memorandums, and reports. How would you rewrite them to make them more readable?

a. We are in receipt of your application for employment and regret

to inform you that at present there are no openings for which a
person with your qualifications and experience might qualify.

b. It is obvious that it is becoming more and more important that top
management should be furnished with timely and up-to-date reports. It is therefore necessary that the methods of getting information from our branch offices be improved.

c. Many of our dealers have advanced the thought that it was better
at present to hold accounts in the local office and try to collect
them rather than to turn them over to the main office where they
might possibly be handled by the legal department.

d. Another advantage of the use of prepunched form cards is that by
reducing the time required for the processing of a credit transaction, the next customer to be served will not be kept waiting as
long as he normally would be under the present system.

e. It may be noted from this statistical analysis which was carefully
prepared by our Operations Analysis group under the supervision
of John Light that worthwhile reductions in our sales presentation
appear to be possible.

f. This safety policy is called to your attention because our day-to-day
experience seems to indicate that a review of the facts from a
safety point of view is advisable and that our policy should be
finalized in the light of these facts.

g. In accordance with your telephone request of December 17, an
investigation was made relative to the bills rendered to you for
furnace repairs over the past three months.

h. There is a strong probability that tax-wise our present situation
renders us liable to a precarious position in the event of a diminu-
tion of sales.

i. Steps are being taken to make improvements where they are found
to be necessary, but in lieu of an absolutely complete revision of
office space, it is felt that this piecemeal maintenance policy may
prove to be more expensive in the long run.

j. A master file of vendor information is being prepared for the
mutual use of our dealers and salesmen to give them complete
information.

3. Revise the following letter to make it as concise and direct as possible:

Dear Mr. Wilson:

Thank you for inquiring about the possibility of becoming our agent
in your territory. The consensus of opinion among each and every one
of us in the New York office, to which your letter was referred, is that
this territory offers fine prospects.

We are sending under separate cover our prospectus which outlines
the opportunities, duties, and sales methods of our various agents in

all parts of the country. This prospectus, which is available without any charge of any kind to all of our dealers, is sent with the hope that you will read it carefully so as to profit from the experience of our other agents all over America.

Thank you again for your kind expression of interest in our company and its product. I am sure that you will enjoy representing us in what we believe to be a fine territory, and we sincerely hope that you will fill out, sign, and return the contract blank which is also being sent to you under separate cover.

Sincerely yours,

4. Revise the following opening and closing paragraphs to make them more effective.

 a. Acknowledging receipt of your letter of February 27, this order will be shipped within the next three days. As per your instructions, shipment will be by express collect.

 b. I have your letter of April 12 at hand and wish to advise that at the present time there are no vacancies in our accounting division although there is some possibility that a vacancy will occur within a few months. Since we keep each and every applicant's letter on file, you will undoubtedly hear from us along these lines at an early date.

 c. This is to acknowledge your favor of May 4, and in reply would beg to state that your request for credit will be considered as soon as we hear from your references.

 d. Thanking you in advance for any information you may care to send, the undersigned will await your favor eagerly and when he is in receipt of the questionnaires from all the companies will send you a comprehensive analysis which should prove useful to you.

 e. We expect you to send us your check by April 30 because we have bills of our own that must be met. Thank you again.

5. By using a short phrase to summarize the material that should be included in each paragraph of the finished letter, *outline* what you would do in each of these letters:

 a. A letter to collect $37.19 for automotive repairs which you have made on Mr. Julian Santee's car.

 b. A letter to convince a junior executive that he should enroll in your college's evening course in Business Correspondence.

 c. A request to an official in the company where you have just been employed that he rent his house to you and your wife during his two months' vacation.

 d. A request to the Dean of your college asking that you be permitted to substitute a different course for Economics III in which you have been enrolled for one week.

6. Indicate how you would break the following material into paragraphs for a business letter:

    a. We are sending in today's mail our latest catalogue of electrical appliances which you requested recently. We hope you will find it as helpful and informative as thousands of our customers already have. You will notice on page 41 a description of our latest model electric stove, the Economiser, which incorporates the newest techniques in design and construction. The Economiser carries a five-year guarantee against any defect in workmanship or materials. Since we are now in full production of this type of stove, we can make delivery within two weeks of your order. A convenient order blank is enclosed in our catalogue. With prices on electrical appliances due for a rise within the next few months, you can save money by acting now.

    b. At this time of the year, our certified public accountants are making preparations for their annual audit of our books and analysis of the condition of accounts. Since we notice that your account is overdue, we suggest that payment be made immediately so that you will not be listed among those considered in arrears. We know that you will wish to protect your credit rating. Please return this letter with your check for $120 in the enclosed convenient envelope.

7. Rewrite the following sentences to make them less wordy:

    a. I want you to know that we have missed your former visits to our store because it has been such a long time since it has been our pleasure to see you.

    b. At the present moment we must express our regret at having to inform you that we cannot now fill the order which you so kindly sent us.

    c. In response to your valued communication which was dated February 2, I can only say at this time that we shall have to take more time to make an investigation and to carry on the necessary research.

    d. This new manual was written for the man who practices accounting, for the individual who runs his own business, for the man who keeps his own accounts, and, in short, for anyone who keeps financial records for himself, his company, or anyone else.

    e. Our each and every wish is to assist our customers in every way possible, to help them with those difficult problems which they have trouble in solving themselves, and to render every possible service so that we may both prosper mutually.

    f. We made a thorough survey of all the milk consumers in a certain Middle Western city, and it was found that the average daily consumption of milk per family in that city was less than two quarts a day.

    g. As the end of the year approaches, with Christmas and the start of the new year close at hand, we want to take this opportunity to thank you for your patronage and to express our appreciation for your interest in our company and its products.

h. You will undoubtedly be interested to know that it has come to our attention through channels that we are unable to divulge because they are confidential that a rival photographic studio will soon be opened close to yours.

i. This situation to which you referred in your letter of September 16 is in my judgment, if I may express a personal opinion, not only dangerous to our hope of expansion in the next year but also renders it practically impossible for us to enlarge the scope of our organization.

j. This complete and definitive work was not written for laymen, or for the man on the street, or for the average man, but it was intended for experts in the field of statistics.

8. The following letter is an exact transcript of a communication sent to the placement director of one college. How would you rewrite it to interest your fellow students in working during the Christmas holidays?

Dear Sir:

May I take the liberty of respectfully requesting you to announce to the student body that those who are interested in modestly augmenting their personal allowances, reducing accumulated incidental expenses, replenishing and increasing their bank accounts, may secure, during the Christmas period of December 15th to January 1st, temporary employment at our Main Plant, located at 630 Blank Street.

Applications are now being accepted and honored at this unit for temporary positions at $1.10 an hour for a 40–48 hour week.

It would be of material assistance to us if applicants possessed knowledge and could advise when their services would be available.

Please accept, in advance, my deep and humble gratitude for your kind cooperation.

Respectfully,

*It is the modest, not the presumptuous, inquirer who
makes a real and safe progress. . . .*
Viscount Bolingbroke in a letter to Alexander Pope

CHAPTER VI

Inquiries, Answers to Inquiries, Orders

Among the types of letter most frequently received in business is the letter of inquiry. This letter seeks information on such varied matters as the operation of machinery, the price of certain products, the construction of various models or the uses to which each may be put, the details of financing, or any one of an infinite number of similar subjects. These letters are of two kinds:

1. *The solicited letter of inquiry,* which is usually a response to an advertisement inviting the reader to write in for further information to a certain department or division.
2. *The unsolicited letter of inquiry,* in which the writer takes the initiative in asking for information.

The Solicited Inquiry

Resulting as it does from a specific suggestion, the solicited inquiry presents no difficulties. It should be very brief, usually no longer than one or two sentences, and should state definitely what is wanted. Usually, a mention of the advertising medium in which the suggestion to write appeared is appropriate. The following examples are typical:

Zenith Radio Corporation
Chicago 39, Illinois

Gentlemen:

Please send me the name of your nearest dealer who handles the new Rivera Table Model Radio-Phonograph advertised in the *Saturday Evening Post* last week. I would also greatly appreciate your letting me know whether this or any of your other phonographs can be operated with batteries. I am interested in purchasing such a phonograph for my summer camp where we do not have electricity.

> Sincerely yours,
>
> Howard Bartlett
> 7 Pine Street
> Wells, Vermont

Burroughs Adding Machine Company
Detroit 32, Michigan

Gentlemen:

Please send me information about the features and cost of the adding machine which you advertised in *Life* for November 13, 1953.

> Yours truly,
>
> Robert Black

Polk Miller Products Corporation
Department 52-G
Richmond 11, Virginia

Gentlemen:

In accordance with your offer in *Time* for July 12, 1953, please send a free copy of your *Dog Book* to me at 2719 Park Street, Seattle 14, Washington.

> Sincerely yours,
>
> Esther A. Marshall
> (Mrs. Robert Marshall)

The inquirer should be careful to include his address if he uses paper without a letterhead. Advertisers testify unanimously to the large number of requests which can never be granted because writers forget to include addresses.

The Unsolicited Inquiry

The unsolicited inquiry letter is more complex and much more detailed. Since the writer is asking a favor, he should strive beyond all else *to make his inquiry easy to answer*. This can best be done by making the question as direct and specific as possible or, if the inquiry is lengthy, by tabulating the questions or by using an arrangement in which they may be answered by "yes" or "no" or by checking. No writer of an unsolicited letter of inquiry should expect a complete stranger to spend several hours answering questions of a general nature; instead, he must phrase his queries so carefully that answering them will require the shortest possible time. Courtesy demands that a stamp or a self-addressed, stamped envelope should be enclosed if the inquiry is addressed to an individual or to a small firm; if it is sent to a large company with its own mailing department, the stamp should not be included because it will probably interfere with the regular mailing routine.

To give the reader sufficient information to enable him to answer intelligently and easily, the well-planned unsolicited inquiry usually contains:

1. A clear statement of the information desired or of the problem involved. This should include:
   a. What is wanted
   b. Who wants it
   c. Why it is wanted
2. A tabulation of questions or a reference to an enclosed questionnaire
3. An expression of appreciation

To ensure getting the maximum amount of information from his letter, the writer of an unsolicited inquiry should:

1. Ask as few questions as possible.
2. Phrase them so that they are clear, direct, and easy to answer.
3. Where confidential information is requested, promise to keep it confidential.
4. Try to send the inquiry at those seasons when the pressure of business is least heavy.
5. If possible, stress the way in which the recipient will benefit by answering the questions.

The following examples show how unsolicited letters of inquiry may be used to obtain information:

Gentlemen:

Have you any information about the economies achieved through using dictating machines? We are trying to find out about the experience of similar companies before we finally decide to install these machines. For that reason, we will appreciate your answers to these questions:

1. How many machines have you installed?
2. Do your dictators and transcribers prefer them to your former method of transcription?
3. What savings have resulted from their use?

You can help us greatly by supplying this information. I hope that we may be able to repay your kindness sometime. In the meantime, I want you to know that we will be very grateful for any assistance you can give us in making our decision.

Sincerely yours,

Dear Mr. Bryant:

The Ohio Division of the Association of College Placement Advisers is making a survey to collect data bearing upon the best technique for college seniors to use in finding their first positions and becoming oriented in them. Our purpose is to ease the transition from college to the first job. We are, therefore, asking several hundred personnel men in this area to check their answers to the following questions:

1. Does a member of your personnel department regularly visit colleges in this area to interview seniors for positions?

Yes   No

2. Would you prefer to have seniors write to you, giving complete information about themselves, or would you prefer to have them come to talk to you first?

               application letter
I prefer
               interview

3. Does your organization have any kind of training school or course to acquaint young college graduates with the details of your business?

Yes   No

4. Do you find young college men you have recently hired to be untrained in any of the following:

Technique of interviewing?
Knowledge of business procedure?
Ability to write reports and letters?
Ability to organize work efficiently?

5. At what monthly salary do you start college men in their first jobs? (This will be kept in strict confidence; only the average of all answers to this question will be published.) Check the amount closest to your firm's salary:

   $250 $275 $300 $325 $350

6. If you have any suggestions that may help us give better training to college students or that bear upon the technique of getting oriented in their first jobs, please write them on the reverse side of this letter.

The Ohio Division of the Association of College Placement Advisers will be very grateful to you for your cooperation in answering these questions. We expect to publish the results of this survey and will send you a copy of our complete report, which we hope will be helpful to you in comparing the attitudes of your own company with those of others in this area. The enclosed envelope is stamped and addressed for your convenience in replying.

> Sincerely yours,
>
> The Association of College
> Placement Advisers, Ohio Division
>
> Charles Conrad, Secretary

Such a letter should elicit a large percentage of replies because the phrasing of the questions and the enclosed self-addressed, stamped envelope make it easy to answer. Furthermore, by the use of the you attitude in the final paragraph, the value of this survey *to the reader* is clearly indicated.

Quite aside from the value of questionnaires in obtaining information is the fact that they may also be used in impressing a sales story on readers. Whenever modern business wants to learn the reactions of its customers or whenever it aims at building good will, the effective letter of inquiry offers a high sales potential. It can be useful for testing customers' opinions of services offered, for ascertaining trends in certain areas and types of business, and for keeping accounts and mailings up-to-date.

The following letter sent by the Air Express Division of the Railway Express Agency is a remarkable example of an inquiry with sales appeal. Sent with a questionnaire to 105,000 people, it elicited a response from 21 per cent and, more important, placed the facts about air express before thousands more.

Mr. Joe Doe
100 Doe Street
Doeville, Ky.

Dear Mr. Doe:

May we ask a favor of you—one that will take only a few minutes and perhaps may ultimately benefit you? It consists simply of checking the brief points in the enclosed folder and returning it to us.

Here's our problem: Every business has certain fundamentals which must be gotten over to the public. They're facts which are mentioned consistently in promotional material—so consistently that often a firm believes that they've registered their story and they stop featuring basic points. Then a check is made—and they wake up to find they were wrong.

Undoubtedly, your firm is no exception—and Air Express, with a very factual story, certainly isn't. That's how you can help us. For we're writing to representative business people like yourself to determine what success we've had in making people aware of the basic features of the Air Express story.

The folder enclosed contains a series of brief facts about air express—each one boiled down to the utmost to save your time. If a fact is old stuff to you, simply check the little "Did Know" box to the right of the statement. If it's news to you, check the "Didn't Know" box.

You'll notice that there's no space for your signature in the folder. That's because we're only seeking answers—we're trying to gauge public opinion. The more answers we get, the more representative will be our results, and the better will we be able to check the success of past efforts and guide our future educational work.

When you've finished checking the folder, please be good enough to enclose it in the self-addressed, postage-paid reply envelope and return it to us. And thanks for your cooperation.

Sincerely yours,

The following letter demonstrates a good solution to the problem of keeping a mailing list active by an easy-to-answer inquiry:

Gentlemen:

We'd like to mail a special portfolio of manufacturing forms to the person in your organization who is most responsible for the methods you use in writing, routing, and supervising office and factory records.

This portfolio is a handy filing folder containing actual samples of forms being used by manufacturers whose problems are similar to yours—factory orders, bills of lading, receiving records, invoices, and the like.

As this is really a research project and not an "advertising stunt," we are anxious to place it in responsible hands, so that it will be filed for reference along with other material dealing with modern business methods.

By jotting down the name and title of the proper person, you can help your organization improve its methods of handling records. There's no charge or obligation, of course.

Cordially yours,

Name ....

Position ....

Our business is ....

And here's a questionnaire letter which was followed up by a post card; as a result of these two mailings, 69 per cent replies were received.

Dear Mr. Whitacre:

A manufacturer of equipment for liquefied petroleum gas has asked me to find out which magazine serving the LP-gas industry is best edited to give you help on your problems.

So I am asking *your* help. It will take only a minute to check the answers to the simple questions listed below and to drop this letter in the mail.

If you do it today, I'll be doubly appreciative. A stamped, addressed envelope is enclosed. *Thank you.*

Sincerely,

1. To which of these magazines do you subscribe?
   _____*Butane-Propane News*
   _____*LP-gas Magazine*
2. Please list as first choice the magazine you find most helpful in your work.
   First Choice_____

   Second Choice_____

ANSWERS-TO-INQUIRY LETTERS

A few years ago, businessmen generally regarded the letters of inquiry they received as a nuisance or, at best, as trivial matters requiring routine treatment. Their answers, even to solicited letters of inquiry, lacked imagination and foresight. Usually, they answered these inquiries in the following manner:

Dear Sir:

As you requested in your letter of December 5, we are sending you, under separate cover, a copy of our new spring catalogue. Inside the back cover, you will find an order blank to assist you in obtaining any items you want to order.

Sincerely yours,

This is a good example of the "thought-less" letter which we discussed in Chapter II. Its writer goes just as far as the occasion demands and no farther. He fails to comprehend the possibilities of his letter for building good will or making a sale. His attitude is simply "Here's your catalogue; take it or leave it." He may make a sale, but if he does, it will be in spite of his letter.

Such answers to inquiries are still being written, but the majority of businessmen now realize that these letters represent a real opportunity to turn requests for information into orders and good will. This attitude is well expressed in the following excerpt from a speech, "Putting Good Will in Your Mailbox," by Mr. W. G. Werner, Manager of Public Relations of the Procter and Gamble Company, a preponderance of whose mail comes from housewives:

A letter to the Company is a personal act of the writer. When we are confronted with a pile of mail, this fact is easy to forget. Business correspondence, through the years, not only in its traditional stilted phraseology, but also too often in its very physical handling, has been considered a mechanical process, like operating an adding machine—almost a nuisance—instead of a most important channel for building friendship and good will.

When a woman takes up her pen to write a letter, she is entering into quite a different and unique relationship—a personal relationship—with a company. Suddenly she has stopped being one of the mass market; she is a human being writing to some rather mysterious entity which she knows only as a "company" or a "corporation." Whether she is expressing appreciation for the way a product serves her, writing a complaint, seeking help, or offering an idea, she hopes that she is writing to another human being like herself.

The way in which her letter is handled may determine whether she is a friend for life, a disappointed and embittered antagonist, or a confirmed cynic concerning "cold-blooded corporations." It may determine, also, whether a favorable, good will–building message about the company, or the other kind, is what clicks over that supercharged grapevine of gossip over the back fence between one home and another.

In startling contrast to the point of view which Mr. Werner presents so well is the actual practice of many firms in answering inquiries. There is considerable evidence to show that after they invest substantial amounts in advertising to invite inquiries, many companies answer tardily, sloppily, or not at all. Paul Vincent reports in *Printers' Ink* on an experiment he conducted in writing to 50 concerns whose ads invited inquiries. He received only eight replies within ten days, nine others between three weeks and thirty days, four of his requests were ignored entirely, and the rest took more than thirty days to get an answer back to him. Mr. Vincent's name, which had been typed below his signature on his inquiries, was misspelled 12 times on the envelopes, six circulars came with postage due, four circulars arrived in bad condition, and two envelopes were empty.

These statistics certainly point up two principles for students and correspondents who want to handle inquiries efficiently:

1. Answer all inquiries promptly.
2. Take special care in addressing, posting, and enclosing material.

In fact, one progressive company issues the following instructions to its correspondents:

1. Answer all inquiries the same day they are received. Strike while the iron is hot! Give inquiries the right of way over all other correspondence.
2. Size up the needs of the prospect and answer his inquiry in terms of the advantage of our product *to him.*
3. Don't make him wait for information while you refer him to "local representatives" or "branch offices." Answer him first— and let your local agents follow it up.
4. Allow a reasonable amount of time for an order or a reply to come in, and then follow it up with another letter. Keep on writing at regular intervals as long as the percentage of returns from similar follow-ups makes it profitable.

To these model instructions, we might profitably add that the letter should answer all the questions raised, in language that is clear and understandable, and that it should refer specifically to any catalogue or brochure enclosed or sent separately.

Granting a Request

Answers to inquiries may be grouped in two general categories: those granting requests and those refusing requests. The very nature of the situation makes the first type easier to write; however, if the letter merely grants the request in a routine fashion, the correspondent will miss an unusual opportunity for building sales or good will. In the final analysis, he is writing to someone who has already shown enough interest in the company's products, operations, or methods to write an inquiry. Hence, the answer to an inquiry has passed the first hurdle inherent in every sales situation—arousing the reader's interest. Letters granting requests should capitalize on this fact.

Frequently, such letters contain enclosures such as catalogues, brochures, pamphlets, or reprints which have been requested. Experience shows that better results are obtained when a letter accompanies these enclosures and when the letter and the enclosure are tied together. For that reason, the letter should refer to the enclosure but should not duplicate it; the primary aim of the enclosure is to present detailed information, the primary aim of the letter is to sell. To avoid the weak "here is your catalogue" letter shown on page 99, correspondents answering requests with enclosures will do well to write at least three paragraphs organized around these functions:

1. State the action taken.
2. Refer specifically to the enclosure.
3. Motivate action or build good will.

Notice how this is done in the following examples:

Dear Mr. Slobody:

We are pleased to send you a copy of our pamphlet "Greater Efficiency in Office Layout," which you requested.

You will be interested in the diagrams of typical office layouts on pages 14–19. Surveys by our architects and engineers show that these arrangements effect savings of 50 per cent by utilizing space efficiently. And because our lightweight Acme Partitions are tailored to individual needs, more privacy and greater efficiency result, as shown in the five typical installations on pages 26 to 30.

Our agent, Mr. John J. Pratt, will call on you within the next three days to demonstrate how Acme Partitions can make your office a more efficient, comfortable, and economical place to work.

Very truly yours,

Dear Mr. Thompson:

We are sending you our booklet "Modern Insulation for Older Homes," which you requested on October 15.

As the owner of a home which was not originally insulated, you will be particularly interested in the description on pages 23 and 24 of the simple technique by which Blanktex Insulation can make older homes as snug and warm as those with original insulation. You will want to read on pages 37 to 41 the unsolicited statements by satisfied users of Blanktex Insulation proving that as much as 20 per cent of the annual heating cost can be saved by our modern methods.

After you have read this booklet, which has won us thousands of warm friends, you will undoubtedly have questions pertaining specifically to the insulation of your home. Our heating expert in your territory is Mr. Robert Vaughan, 69 Main Street, Scranton 2, Pennsylvania (Phone Diamond 3109).

As a graduate engineer, Mr. Vaughan can give you exact figures on costs, fuel savings, and similar facts regarding your home—all without obligation on your part. A card or phone call to Mr. Vaughan can make this winter the warmest you have spent in your home.

Yours truly,

The tone of these letters and their references to specific pages of the requested booklets make them effective sales emissaries. Their writers properly use an answer to a letter of inquiry as the first step in making a sale. Many companies use a definite follow-up system as the second step, as shown in this example from The Upson Company of Lockport, New York:

Dear Mr. Conroy:

Will you answer just three questions, please?

Several days ago you were kind enough to send for our new booklet, "New Interiors for Old." This booklet was mailed to you promptly. An additional booklet, "Upson Panels," was sent a day or two later to give added information regarding Upson dependable products.

We hope you received these booklets promptly and that they proved helpful in guiding and inspiring you with your home remodeling plans. Naturally, we are interested in your progress and wonder if you have had the opportunity to get started.

We would appreciate it, therefore, if you will answer the questions and mail us your reply in the following envelope provided. (No postage necessary.)

THE UPSON COMPANY   LOCKPORT, NEW YORK

WILL YOU TELL US, PLEASE?

1. Have you contacted your lumber dealer? Yes_____No_____or carpenter-contractor? Yes_____No_____

2. Has your lumber dealer contacted you? Yes_____No_____

3. Is there anything we can do to help you get started?

   (Please name)_____

   _____

   _____

   Name_____
   Address_____
   City_____

   Would you like the name of our sales representative for your area?
   Yes_____No_____

In situations where answers to inquiries do not directly involve sales, the correspondent should aim at building good will. Above all else, these letters should convey a tone of helpfulness and should contain sufficient information to answer the inquirer's questions. Here is an effective example:

Dear Mr. Fife:

Your letter asking about our program for executive development interested me greatly. I am glad to have an opportunity of telling you about our policies.

The answer to both of your questions is "yes." We do have a definite program for developing potential executives, and we feel that it has been very worth while. I am enclosing a program showing the topics which have been discussed during the past year.

We believe that the success of such a program depends largely on the method of selection by which men are admitted to it. For that reason, we developed a very elaborate personnel appraisal sheet by which candidates for the program are rated by their superiors and their coworkers. The enclosed blank will show you the personal qualities we are concerned with.

If we can help you in any way, please let us know.

Sincerely yours,

This letter avoids the two main pitfalls which characterize many answers to inquiries: giving the reader a sense that he is receiving a perfunctory treatment or a "brush-off"and conveying an impression of answering questions grudgingly or in such general terms as to be useless.

Refusing a Request

The refusal of a request is one of the more difficult types of letters. Great tact and courtesy must be used if the reader is not to be antagonized. Many of the requests or inquiries that are made of businessmen are inconsiderate or unreasonable, but the answers to these requests should never be brusque, even when the request is refused. A harsh refusal may antagonize a potential customer or develop a source of ill will toward a company. Regardless of how thoughtless the request may seem, the intelligent technique is to refuse it tactfully. By doing this, good correspondents have learned that they can say "No" and still retain the reader's good will.

The refusal of an inquiry usually follows this pattern:

1. A statement of appreciation to the inquirer for his interest.
2. A refusal of his request without hedging and without apology.
3. If it is convenient, an explanation of why the request must be refused. Wherever possible, avoid vague terms like "company policy" or similar generalities.
4. If possible, a constructive suggestion or offer in the closing paragraph to be of service in the future.

The individual circumstances of each request and the person who makes it will, of course, govern the amount of detail included in the refusal. In many instances there need be no elaborate explanation of the reason for refusal; in others, no constructive suggestion can be included. But whatever the details of the situation, the tone of the letter should be tactful and helpful. This is especially necessary when the request comes from a friend, an acquaintance, or a good customer; the refusal of a request from such a source would follow *in detail* the outline above. To illustrate the application of this outline, let us assume that Mr. Lawrence Miller, a customer of yours, is opening a new business which is similar to yours but will not compete with you in any way. Mr. Miller has written to you asking for information concerning the basis on which you pay your salesmen and you must refuse his request. What is the best way to refuse Mr. Miller? Notice the contrast in the point of view of the following letters:

Dear Sir:

I have your letter of April 12 asking about the basis on which we pay our salesmen.

I regret that I cannot let you have this information because confidential reports have a way of getting out. I might say that our system of remuneration has been very successful and our salesmen are completely satisfied with it.

It is my hope that you will not consider this refusal an uncooperative act on our part and that our pleasant business relationship may continue in the future.

Very truly yours,

Dear Mr. Miller:

Thank you for the interest expressed in your letter of April 12 concerning the way in which we pay our salesmen. We are flattered that so successful a businessman should ask our advice.

We regret that we cannot divulge this information. Since each of our salesmen works under an individual contract, we would be violating the confidence of our employees if the terms of these contracts were given out. Because our employees themselves have requested this secrecy, you will understand why we cannot comply with your request.

You undoubtedly are already familiar with E. J. Smith's booklet entitled "Setting Up a Sales Organization"; we have found it invaluable in its practical suggestions for dealing with specific problems. It might prove very useful to you at the present time.

If we may be of assistance to you in some other way, please feel free to write us. We want to offer our best wishes for success in your new venture, along with the hope that our pleasant business relationship with you may continue.

Sincerely yours,

The first letter is completely negative with its wrong emphasis, such as hoping "you will not consider this refusal an unco-operative act"; it is almost insulting in its thoughtless suggestion that the reader cannot be trusted—"confidential reports have a way of getting out"; it is aggravating in its teasing tone of "our system of remuneration has been very successful—*but* we can't divulge it." The second letter, by contrast, is tactful, sincere, and as constructive as possible. Its reader cannot help feeling that the explanation is honest.

ANSWERS TO ORDERS

That there is room for originality and humor even in the prosaic business of acknowledging orders is illustrated by the following exchange between a customer and one of America's largest mail-order companies. The former wrote:

Gents:

Please send me one of them gasoline engines you show on page 785 and if it's any good I'll send you a check for it.

To which the company replied:

Dear Sir:

Please send us the check, and if it's any good, we'll send you the engine.

Under more normal circumstances, however, most companies follow a definite procedure in acknowledging orders.

Since almost every firm has its own order blank, there is little necessity for dwelling upon the form of the order itself. Letters acknowledging orders are usually of a routine nature, except when the order is the first one from a new customer or an unusually large order from an old customer. At such a time, a letter of acknowledgment may appropriately be written. Although the sequence of parts in such a letter can be varied, it will usually contain:

1. A reference to the order and a statement of how it is being shipped
2. A statement of appreciation
3. A brief sales message on the quality of service you expect to render or an expression of interest in the customer's needs

The following letter illustrates how this outline may be applied:

Dear Mr. Havens:

We were delighted to learn from your order of May 15 that you are planning to feature our line of Spring Weave men's suits in your store.

You will be pleased, we know, with the way these suits sell. Spring Weave is a name that men know because of our ten-year national advertising campaign.

Your order is being shipped by express today. With it, we are sending you a set of displays, keyed to our advertising campaign, which you will want to use in your shop windows.

Thank you very much for your order. We are looking forward to a mutually profitable relationship, and if there is anything we can do to help you with the promotion of Spring Weave suits, please let us know.

                    Sincerely yours,

When a new purchasing agent is appointed in a cor pany with which a Chicago firm does business, the following excellent letter is sent to acknowledge an order and to build good will with the new man:

Dear Mr. Jenks:

Thank you for the fine order that came in this morning. Naturally, we always appreciate orders, but this one makes us especially happy because it represents our first dealing with you.

We've done business with your firm for a number of years and have always enjoyed a friendly relationship. You may be sure that we will do our best to keep it that way.

Congratulations on your new position. If we can make your job easier or help you in any way where our products are concerned, we want to do so. Please call on us—any time.

Sincerely yours,

Using Inquiries and Orders for Business-promotion Letters

Most businessmen spend more time and money welcoming new accounts than they devote to their old customers, who are the backbone of their business. This is natural, perhaps, since growth is measured largely in terms of new business. Progressive companies realize, however, that the steady customer is the bedrock upon which business success is built, and they write letters expressing their appreciation for his patronage. This type of letter is usually called a business-promotion letter. While it is often closely associated with the acknowledgment of an order, it can be effectively used on anniversaries, at year's end, on holidays, or on any other appropriate occasion.

The essence of the business-promotion letter is a statement of appreciation to the customer for his business, his cooperation, his interest, or his promptness. Highly relevant to the spirit of this type of letter is a story about Rudyard Kipling when he was at the height of his career. A group of Oxford undergraduates, upon reading that Kipling was to be paid 10 shillings a word for an article, wired him 10 shillings with the request, "Please send us one of your best words." Back came Kipling's answer, "Thanks." Correspondents who learn to use "thanks" as one of their best words will find its value beyond price. The writers of such letters certainly reap a harvest of good will from a very small investment by letting old customers know that their orders and patronage merit thanks. Here are some excellent examples of the way in which correspondents use letters, which are basically acknowledgments of orders or inquiries, as a method of promoting sales and good will.

Dear Mr. Whiteside:

Merci beaucoup, Danke schoen, Grazie infinite, Muchas grácias, Tackar sa mycke, Go Rhabh maith Agath—

I don't know how you'd say it, but I've been groping for a new way to say
THANK YOU

. . . for the confidence you've shown in us
. . . for your increased orders
. . . for your prompt payments

Because we want you to know how grateful we are, we think the best way is simply saying

THANK YOU FOR EVERYTHING.

Cordially yours,

Dear Mr. Byers:

BEFORE a man marries—
He'll send the girl flowers and take her to the theater in a taxi.

AFTER—the only "flour" she gets is Gold Medal. And she has to lug it home from the Cash and Carry in a 24-pound sack.

Business is a lot like that.

Firms spend much to make a man a customer. And then the best he gets is an invoice.

We believe a firm should tell a customer that his trade is appreciated. And that's why we are writing you this letter to tell you how much we appreciate the steady flow of orders you've sent us during the past year.

Not to sell you—but to tell you—it's always a real pleasure to serve you.

Cordially yours,

The following inquiry letter with a penny attached has been highly successful in reactivating accounts:

Dear Mr. Jones:

A PENNY FOR YOUR THOUGHTS—

. . . and here's cash in advance . . .

We are still trying to find out why you have not used your charge account at Rosenfield's recently, and yet we do not wish to annoy an old friend by being too persistent. But we do want to know if anything has happened to displease you in the slightest.

It will take just a minute for you to tell us the reason, in the space below, and to let us know if you would like us to continue sending you your current credit card each month.

We have thousands of customers who find their charge account a great convenience in getting the things they want at Rosenfield's and we sincerely hope you will use your account again. This letter is just to find out your wishes, so that we may serve you as you want to be served.

There's a postage-paid envelope enclosed which will bring your reply to my desk. And thank you very much.

Sincerely yours,

Dear Mr. Selig:

I plan to use my charge account again, so continue to send my credit card each month. (Please check.)   (   )

I prefer to pay cash so please close my account. (Check)   (   )

I have not used my account recently because of the following unsatisfactory service I received at Rosenfield's. (If we have failed to please you, tell us frankly.)..
....
....

A large lumber company sends out an actual bill, keyed to an inquiry, as a business-promotion device. The bill shows a balance due of $0.00; on the bill are typed these words:

We're sad about "nothing"!

Your account is paid in full, and you haven't bought anything from us lately. On the reverse side of this bill, you'll find three questions about the service we've tried to render. Will you help us by checking the answers and returning the questionnaire in the enclosed postage-paid envelope?

Or better still . . . send us an order so we can stop worrying about "nothing." Then we can really concentrate on "something"—how to give you the kind of service an old customer like you deserves!

Sincerely,

A more general kind of inquiry, keyed to building good will, is the following:

Dear Mr. Gardner:

We of the Barclay Family hope you enjoyed your stay with us.

That is what I say to the guests whom I have had the pleasure of meeting personally—and that is what we mean sincerely.

Maybe you would like to say something about our accommodations, our food, or our operations in general. We will certainly appreciate your suggestions.

Do come back soon—and thank you.

Sincerely yours,

A large appliance manufacturer uses this inquiry to stimulate dealers:

Mr. Jones, our sales manager, was around today asking questions.

He says he hasn't seen any orders from you for some time.

You know the answer to that better than I do. But if it's any of these reasons, just check, and I'll take care of your needs immediately:

Need order blanks?_____

Need our new spring catalog?_____

Need display items?_____

Anything else?_____

With the spring construction period just one month off, your customers are going to need many electrical appliances. The enclosed order blank will help you to meet their needs and to build increased sales and profits for your store.

Cordially yours,

Finally, an effective acknowledgment of an order from an old customer expresses gratitude and builds a sound relationship for future sales:

Dear Mr. Goodwin:

When a friend helps us on with a coat, we smile and say "Thank you." If we drop something and someone picks it up for us, we practically burst with gratitude.

Strange? Not at all.

But it is strange that when we get into business, we take so many things for granted that we forget to say "Thank you." Take old customers like you, for instance.

You did something pretty important for us—important because we think so much of your business that it gives us a great deal of pleasure to see it grow.

I just wanted to write you personally, telling you how much we appreciate your order, and saying "Thank you" for your confidence in us.

Very truly yours,

Many a sermon has been preached on the text, "If a man ask you to go with him a mile, go with him twain." The text is applicable to the whole subject of letter writing. The letter which goes beyond routine, which goes "the second mile" where others stop with the routine "first mile," is the really effective message. For that reason, these letters succeed; they reflect a policy which is designed not only to win new friends but to keep old ones.

EXERCISES

Chapters II–V of this book present the general principles pertaining to all types of effective letters. In the exercises in this chapter and those following, the student should learn to apply these principles to the specialized problems described. Before attempting to write the letters dealing with these specialized situations, *the student should prepare a brief outline or notation of the points he wishes to make in each letter;* this will insure a careful analysis of what he wants his letter to do before he actually starts to write.

1. Write to the Big Indian Mountain Club, 25 West 45th Street, New York, New York, requesting the booklet on summer homes advertised in *The New Yorker* of May 27, 1953.

2. Write a letter to a personnel manager with whom you have a slight acquaintance asking for advice on the best training you may take in order to get into personnel work.

3. The Better Business Service, 3700 Michigan Avenue, Chicago, Illinois, has requested permission to publish your series of collection letters in its monthly report to subscribers. Write refusing the request because you believe that publishing the letters would destroy their originality.

4. Your salesman in the New England area has finally persuaded the White Company, 217 Commonwealth Avenue, Boston, Massachusetts, to place an order with you, despite the fact that they have been buying from a competitor for years. Write an appropriate letter to acknowledge this first order for automotive parts amounting to $371.19.

5. As secretary for your local chamber of commerce, you are compiling material for a bulletin designed to attract new industries to your locality. Among other things, you want information about the products manufactured by the companies already located in your city, the number of employees, the weekly pay rolls, the labor conditions, and the reasons why

each of the industries chose your locality. Compile an appropriate letter of inquiry.

6. In the same capacity at your chamber of commerce, you have received the following inquiry:

Gentlemen:

I have read with a great deal of interest your advertising that (your city or locality) is "a good place for industry to locate."

Our company, which manufactures speedometers for one of the largest automobile manufacturers, is considering expanding its facilities and is thinking of your area as a possible site for this expansion.

We should like to know, therefore, about the advantages your city might have for an enterprise such as ours. Our proposed expansion would involve a plant employing approximately 1,000 workers, many of whom would have to be recruited in the place where we decide to locate.

Will you please reply as soon as possible?

Sincerely yours,

Henry G. Smith
Vice-President

7. Write a letter to accompany your booklet "Cruises on the Great Lakes" which has been requested by Mr. Harry Wilson, 431 East 25th Street, Cuyahoga Falls, Ohio. Tours from three days to two weeks range in price from $42.50 to $200.

8. A business-school student has written you requesting specific information concerning the courses he might take in his last year in order to obtain a position in your advertising department. Refuse the request because you don't want to commit your firm to hiring anyone until your personnel representative has visited the business school.

9. The university in your city is offering a number of extension courses open to the general public. Write to the proper officer of the university inquiring about the fees, hours, credits, and contents of a specific course you are interested in taking.

10. Your first assignment as junior member of the new-accounts department of an advertising agency is to compile a questionnaire to go out over your superior's signature. The questionnaire will be sent to the presidents of large companies located in small towns within a 50-mile radius of your city. Your superior has told you that the questionnaire must be organized to find out what medium of advertising—newspaper, magazine, radio, or direct mail—the various companies prefer, but it must also give some sales material on the services offered by your agency.

11. Write an appropriate acknowledgment to The Wm. Peabody Co.,

379 East Main Street, Perth Amboy, N.J., for a $400 order. In his letter accompanying the order, Mr. Peabody remarked, "Incidentally, this is the twenty-fifth year our company has purchased its garden supplies and seeds from you; we want you to know that our customers have expressed complete satisfaction with your products over that long period."

12. As student chairman of your state's Interfraternity Conference, you must report on the degree of control exercised by college administrative officers over fraternity social functions. Write a letter which might appropriately be sent to the administrative officers of the colleges in your state to obtain this information.

13. Write an appropriate letter to the E. C. Dartmore Company's president, Mr. William E. Goodman, on the occasion of his company's opening a new plant which will double its production of television antennas. For five years this company has been buying metal parts from your firm.

14. Mr. E. C. Hartmann, Director of Training for your company, has been asked to make a speech on "Improving the Reading Speed of Business Executives." He has supplied you with a list of ten companies whose executives have taken formal courses in accelerated reading. For his speech, he wants information on the average number of hours executives spend daily in reading, the best methods for developing greater efficiency in reading, and the results these executives achieved from their formal instruction. Write an appropriate letter to get this information from these ten companies.

15. The proprietor of a very exclusive millinery establishment, whose advertising is handled by your agency, has complained that the advertisements in the metropolitan daily newspapers are not bringing adequate returns to justify their expense. She has furnished you with a list of 350 of her customers; write a letter to them attempting to find out what advertising medium would be most effective.

16. Criticize the following answer to a letter of inquiry:

Dear Mr. Parker:

In compliance with your request of November 1, we send herewith our brochure entitled "Selecting a Piano for the Home" with the hope that it may prove useful to you.

In the event that you are interested in purchasing a Belltone Piano, we would suggest that you consult Mr. J. C. Wiggers, 232 West Street, in your city. It is entirely possible that he may be of assistance to you.

Hoping that you will see fit to discuss this matter with Mr. Wiggers, we are,

Very truly yours,

17. As correspondent for your wholesale company which sells photographic supplies, write an acknowledgment of the first order from The Acme Photo Shop, 3174 West Oak Street, Lexington, Kentucky. The order

consists of seven items of which four are in stock, two are expected within three weeks, and one is an item on which you cannot guarantee delivery in less than six months.

18. Mrs. James S. Knox, 76 State Street, Worthington, Pennsylvania, has sent you $12.95 for a pressure cooker which your company advertised in a national magazine. Since your company sells only through dealers, write Mrs. Knox that you are forwarding her order to The Home Appliance Shop, 1970 Broadway, Worthington, and suggest that she go there to select the exact style of pressure cooker she desires.

19. You are interested in a career as a newspaper reporter. Write to the city editor of the daily newspaper that you read and ask his advice on the best preparation for such a career and on the type of education that would prove most beneficial.

20. As the student manager of your school's speakers bureau, write a letter of inquiry, with tabulated questions, to be sent to 150 clubs, church groups, and other organizations. Your speakers bureau supplies student speakers for various occasions and is intended to give the students actual experience in talking before groups. There is no charge for this service; last year, members of the speakers bureau presented programs before 42 groups. You are now planning your program for the next school year, and your letter is intended to ascertain how many groups might be interested, what topics they wish discussed, how large an audience might be expected, and whether such facilities as projectors and amplifiers would be available.

Who said that "fine words butter no parsnips"? Half the parsnips of
society are served and rendered palatable with no other sauce.
William Thackeray, *Vanity Fair*

CHAPTER VII

Claim and Adjustment Letters

"To err is human" according to Alexander Pope, and the number of errors committed in the routine transactions of business attest the truth of Pope's words. Orders may be filled improperly or incompletely; goods may be damaged or unsatisfactory; misunderstandings may arise over discounts, bills, credit terms, and exchanges. The letters written to bring these errors to the attention of those who must take the responsibility for them are known as *claim letters;* those written to take action on such claims are called *adjustment letters.*

To anyone acquainted with the complexities of modern business, the important fact is not that errors do occur but that the percentage of error is actually very small. The surest indication of the amateur in business is a willingness, at the one extreme, to promise that mistakes will *never* occur or, at the other, to become angry and threatening as soon as such errors are made. The experienced businessman develops a rather tolerant attitude toward the errors made by his own associates and by others; this is not to say that he is complacent about mistakes made by his own organization nor ready to continue doing business indefinitely with those whose blunders are too numerous. But from experience, he has learned that there is an irreducible minimum of mistakes made in business, and this knowledge prevents him from losing his temper over the mistakes of others or from promising that he will never again let such an error occur in his own company.

THE CLAIM LETTER

The tolerant attitude just described is the correct viewpoint from which the claim letter should be written. Claim letters lack-

ing this tone usually originate with those unfamiliar with business. A letter like the following is all too typical:

Dear Sir:

That television set your store sold me last week is a disgrace. The picture is distorted and flops around so that we can't look at it. You've sent your repairman out twice and each time the set is worse after he tinkers with it. I think you knew it was no good when you sold it to me and hoped I wouldn't have sense enough to complain. This is the last time I'll ever buy anything from your store.

Yours truly,

The first and natural reaction to stupid mistakes and unreasonable blunders is anger, but, on second thought, we realize that *we* make mistakes too. Good manners alone should prevent such explosive reactions. To write such an angry and accusing letter is simply to let one's emotions run away with his reason. In fact, the worst attitude for the claim writer is nicely summed up in an old ditty:

> In controversial moments
> My perception's very fine;
> I always see both points of view,
> The one that's wrong—and mine!

A little thought before writing a claim letter will show that *it is to the writer's own advantage to be tolerant and even-tempered in his claim letter.* Is it likely that the dealer who receives the vindictive letter about the television set will try to be as scrupulously fair as he might otherwise be if this situation had been called to his attention without malice? Obviously not. If for no other reason than that one stands a greater chance of getting a reasonable adjustment by being fair, the claim letter should avoid anger, sarcasm, and accusations. In its phrasing, the claimant should shun such accusing terms as *complaint, disgusted, dishonest, false, unfair, untrue, worthless,* and *no good.*

An analysis of the claim letter shows that four elements are usually present:

1. An explanation of what is wrong. This explanation should give exact dates, amounts, model numbers, sizes, colors, or any other

specific information that will make a recheck easier for the reader.

2. A statement of the inconvenience or loss that has resulted from this error.

3. An attempt to motivate action by appealing to the reader's sense of fair play, his honesty, or his pride. Don't threaten him with loss of business at the first error.

4. A statement of what adjustment is considered fair; if the writer doesn't know what adjustment is equitable, he should try to stimulate prompt investigation and action.

This analysis puts a premium upon specific facts rather than emotions in the claim letter. It is predicated on the assumption that the overwhelming majority of businessmen want to do the fair thing, if only because it is good business to do so; hence, an appeal to fairness or honesty is the best possible motivation. With regard to the actual adjustment, the claimant may not know exactly what he wants or what would constitute a fair settlement of the claim. In that event, *it is generally best to let the adjuster suggest a satisfactory settlement.* Several surveys of department stores and retail establishments have shown that when the customer has a reasonable claim and has left its settlement completely up to the store, the adjuster will usually grant more than the customer would ask. This technique will not appeal to those who believe that all business is conducted on the plane of "beat the customer before he beats you." But for those with a realistic background of experience in business such a technique is the best method of writing claims, because it stems from a belief on which modern American business is founded—that honesty in business is the best policy.

Contrast the tone of the following letters with the first one presented in this chapter.

Gentlemen:

On your bill for February, I was charged $22.75 for a fishing rod and reel which I purchased in your sporting goods department on December 18.

This bill was paid on January 14 by my check on the Guaranty National Bank. This canceled check was returned with the bank statement which I received on February 2. The next day I received your bill showing this amount still unpaid.

Will you please see that my payment is credited to my account so that I am not billed again?

Sincerely yours,

John H. Middleton

Gentlemen:

The 6.50 — 15 Rubbertex Tire which I purchased on July 23 from The Standard Supply Company, 237 Broadway, Colton, New York, has proved defective after 8,000 miles of use.

Since I bought this tire while I was on a business trip in the East, I am unable to take it to the dealer from whom I purchased it. I have, therefore, asked your local representative, Mr. John Ostrander, 5 Park Street, Galesburg, Illinois, to replace it. He has suggested that I write to you about the matter.

As a user of your tires for the past ten years, I have learned at first hand about their long mileage and safety. This past experience makes me curious to know just why this Rubbertex Tire should wear out so rapidly.

In view of the fact that I have come to expect 24,000 miles from Rubbertex Tires and that I have been caused considerable inconvenience, I feel certain that you will give me a new tire at a 66 per cent discount as figured on the mileage basis.

Very truly yours,

Alvin C. Harding

Gentlemen:

On September 15 we ordered 50 maple kneehole desks to be shipped on September 28 for delivery here on September 30 in time for the opening of our new dormitory.

When this shipment arrived on September 28, we found that it contained 25 desks, which we had ordered, and 25 maple tables. I attempted to get the cartage company, which delivered the furniture from the freight station, to leave the desks and return the tables to the station. They insisted they had no authority to do this and that we would have to accept the whole shipment or return all of it.

When I attempted to call you long distance, I could locate no one who knew anything about this situation. This has caused us considerable inconvenience since we were forced to open our dormitory for inspection before it was completely furnished.

We are, therefore, asking you to send the 25 desks immediately and to arrange to have the tables removed from our dormitory locker room as soon as possible because we urgently need this space for trunks and luggage.

Sincerely yours,

Henry Green
Business Manager

THE ADJUSTMENT LETTER

Typical of the attitude of modern business toward handling complaints are the following comments:

It has been our invariable policy to let people know we appreciate hearing from them if they are dissatisfied in any way. We have always recognized the customer's right to expect our products to fulfill any claim we made for them in our advertising. (H. F. Jones, Vice-President, Campbell Soup Company)

I make it a rule to answer every letter of complaint that I can personally handle. If a busy schedule prevents me from doing this, an associate takes care of the letter for me; but the point is—every letter is answered. (John C. Whitaker, President, R. J. Reynolds Tobacco Company)

I think that to fail to answer an intelligent letter about one's product, flattering or the other kind, is to lose an opportunity . . . (G. H. Coppers, President, National Biscuit Company)

I certainly do welcome flattering letters . . . but I also welcome the other kind because they give me a check on what's happening from indignant sources. It's a standing rule here that each letter addressed to me, in which the writer has a gripe, comes to me personally . . . and is acknowledged at once by me. (L. A. Van Bomel, President, National Dairy Products Corporation)

These and similar comments by business and industrial leaders show that alert businessmen welcome comments from their customers. Actually, claim and adjustment letters offer an excellent check on the quality of service or merchandise, and many companies keep a continuous record of these letters as a control mechanism for their products and service. Furthermore, progressive businessmen realize that there is nothing more detrimental to good public relations than the discontented or dissatisfied customer who goes around telling all his friends and acquaintances that "the Blank Company is a poor place to do business." If he can be persuaded to write directly to the company and thus get his troubles "off his chest," the company has an opportunity to convert a potential liability into a booster who tells his friends, "The Blank Company is reliable; if they make an error, they'll make good every time." Of such small elements is that intangible but invaluable quality called "good will" composed. In building it, the adjustment letter can play a vital role if correspondents keep these principles in mind:

1. Every complaint or claim, no matter how trivial it seems, is important to the person who makes it.
2. It, therefore, requires a prompt answer or acknowledgment.
3. The answer should be factual, courteous, and fair.
4. Above all else, it should not argue or take a critical attitude. Remember, instead, an old Italian proverb: "One good word quenches more heat than a bucket of water."

Naturally, the adjustment letter will reflect the company's attitude toward claims. In general, there are three policies in effect concerning the granting of claims:

1. "The customer is always right"; therefore, all claims are granted. This policy is used by only a few firms at present who deal in expensive merchandise for an extremely reputable clientele.
2. "Grant adjustments wherever the claim seems fair." This is by far the most widely used policy toward claims. It offers the advantage of letting each case be decided on its merits, and it avoids committing the company to a single policy regarding adjustments.
3. *"Caveat emptor."* "Let the buyer beware!" He bought the goods and he can assume the reponsibility; therefore, no claims are granted. No reputable firm can afford to adopt such an unfair policy.

Unless there are peculiar problems connected with the particular business, the second policy outlined above is the most effective one.

But regardless of what the policy is, correspondents have a special obligation in handling adjustments to make the policy clear, to apply it to the situation at hand, and to emphasize its fairness and consistency. For that reason, vague statements like "company policy prevents our doing this" should be replaced by specific explanations against the broad background of a company policy which is applied impartially. A company which operates from principle rather than expediency, from policy rather than partiality, has gone a long way toward winning customer acceptance of its fairness.

Notice how effectively policy is explained in the following letter written by Kermit Rolland of the Public Relations Department of the New York Life Insurance Company, which owns and operates Fresh Meadows, a residential community on Long Island. When the problem of bicycles, roller skates, and tricycles became acute, the management sent this form letter to handle a difficult situation:

Dear Mr. Bailey:

Recently one of our special patrolmen picked up a wheeled vehicle belonging to you—it had been left out in a public area apparently through an oversight by some member of your family.

We recognize that wheeled equipment is an important part of family life. That is why, when our community was planned, the architects included special rooms for the convenience of residents, so that they might store these vehicles when not in use. It has been estimated that Fresh Meadows families own a total of 5,500 baby carriages, velocipedes, bicycles, and other wheel toys. When any of these are left in public halls, passage ways, outside of buildings on paths, sidewalks or roads they not only are a nuisance to other residents who must walk around them, but more important, they create a real hazard, for people have been known to trip over them. Such accidents could result in serious injuries.

In a community like Fresh Meadows it is necessary that all residents cooperate in the care of vehicles belonging to their families. Our leases contain a provision concerning the use and care of such equipment. As you may know, should one of these vehicles cause an accident, the responsibility would be the owner's.

Last year it was necessary for us to remove nearly 2,000 baby carriages and assorted wheel toys which were left out. Because of this demand on our staff, we have found it necessary to make a service charge of $2 each time equipment is removed from a public area. No charge, however, is being made to you for the pick-up this time. But we want you to know that we will have to make a charge in the future if it is necessary to perform this service again.

Out of consideration to your neighbors, will you help us with this problem?

Sincerely yours,

The writer of the adjustment letter should always realize that he is handling a delicate situation. The customer is disgruntled and probably believes sincerely that he has a very real grievance, whether he has or not. The aim of the adjuster should be to make the reader see that he is trying to be fair; yet he must steer a straight course between the two extremes of sympathizing too much with the claimant and thus making him believe that his grievance is indeed greater than he originally thought and, on the other hand, of seeming to argue or to accuse the customer of making an unjust claim. He ought especially to avoid such phraseology as "you state" or "you claim" or "we cannot understand," because such phrases antagonize the reader; nor should he use such words as "failure," "breakdown," or "poor results," because they imply that the product has indeed failed. Instead of saying, "You claim that our heater is no good," the trained adjuster will write, "Thank you for telling us of your experience with our heater."

Test your own reaction to the following negative letter:

Dear Mr. Sinclair:

We cannot comply with your claim for an adjustment on the radio you purchased from us.

In rejecting your request, we want to emphasize that we never make adjustments on merchandise after the customer has kept it three days. You state that the radio was marred when it reached you, but our final inspection showed it was in good condition when we sent it. Unfortunately our policy prohibits our making any adjustment in this case.

Sincerely yours,

Instead of this negative approach, this letter should explain in a matter-of-fact way the facts of the situation. In short, it should be expository rather than argumentative in tone.

Granting the Adjustment

The letter granting an adjustment is usually easy to write. It should make the adjustment *cheerfully* and should admit the error frankly. Its ultimate purpose, if the writer thinks about it carefully, is not just to grant the adjustment but to retain the good will and the business of a disgruntled customer. The following four points are usually included:

1. An expression of regret over the inconvenience suffered
2. An explanation of the cause of the error
3. A statement of what adjustment is to be made
4. An attempt to build good will

These points may be arranged in various ways, but it is important that they should be adapted to the reader and that the letter should sound sincere, as in the following:

Dear Mr. Middlefield:

We regret very much that the radio you purchased from us was unsatisfactory. You have every right to expect merchandise from this store to be in perfect condition, and we appreciate your telling us of this experience.

Our shipping department makes every effort to see that every piece of merchandise is thoroughly inspected before it is sent out. Unfortunately, your radio was not inspected because of the negligence of one of our temporary employees.

We expect to receive another shipment of Finetone Radios tomorrow, and on Thursday we shall send you a new radio to replace the one you have.

Your patronage of our store during the past six years has been greatly appreciated. We want you to know that we value your friendship highly, and, for that reason, we wish to make each transaction satisfactory to you. If it is not, we hope you will inform us, as you did this time, so that we may make an equitable adjustment.

Yours very truly,

By frankly admitting that a mistake has been made, the next letter carries an air of sincerity which renders it effective:

Dear Mr. Gaston:

I certainly appreciate your writing me about the fact that your last two bank statements have been sent to you in envelopes which were unsealed.

If there is one thing the Continental Bank insists on, it is having our employees take every precaution to see that the financial affairs of our depositors are kept absolutely confidential. I am, therefore, grateful to you for calling this matter to our attention and for your fairness concerning a situation which must have annoyed you greatly.

We have taken every precaution to see that this mistake does not occur again. And we want you to know that we are especially sorry that this happened to one of our oldest depositors.

Sincerely yours,

The friendly tone of the next letter, together with its recognition of the fact that errors will occur in the best managed business, goes far toward promoting a friendly relationship:

Dear Mr. Woodside:

I am sorry we blundered on your order. Maybe if I could handle every order myself, we wouldn't make so many mistakes, but, of course, I have been in this business for forty-seven years and might be expected to know more than a clerk who has been with us only thirty-five days.

Some of our people have been with us for twenty-five and thirty years, but even they slip up once in a while. I suppose the penalty of bigness is that mistakes are bound to be made. If we made only one mistake out of a thousand orders, we would make several hundred mistakes. This may seem like a lot, but the percentage would be very, very small. Naturally, the one person in the thousand on whose order we did make a mistake thinks we made a mistake on the other 999 too, which is not the case.

I am sure you could send us 999 more orders and every one of them would go through without the slightest hitch. The law of averages is now all in your favor! Won't you put the law—and us—to the test?

Sincerely yours,

When a major error was made by a printing company, the following letter saved the situation by its frank admission of error and its willingness to grant whatever adjustment the customer desired:

Dear Mr. Carlson:

I wish this were a letter I didn't have to write you. . . Not for fear of the outcome, as I propose to do whatever you suggest, but because a friend of mine feels that he is let down.

I'm terribly sorry that you feel as you do about the print job, although I admit we "pulled a boner." They say that ignorance of the law is no excuse. And, after the crime is committed, it is too late to feel sorry about it. So here I am the "criminal." You are the judge.

Our foreman feels very bad about the mistake and admits his error. Realizing nothing can be done about it now, I'll be glad to give you whatever allowance you feel is necessary, even to the point of rerunning the job. I want to be fair.

From here on, the case rests in your hands.

Sincerely,

Refusal of Adjustment

Much more difficult is the refusal of an adjustment, which may be defined as any letter that does not grant the original claim. A partial adjustment may be made, but if it does not comply with the request, from the customer's viewpoint it is still a refusal of adjustment. The correspondent who is frequently called upon to refuse claims might well take as his text the Biblical injunction that "a soft answer turneth away wrath"; there is no better advice for the refusal of adjustment. If a "soft answer" is the tone to be given such a letter, its contents will usually be as follows:

1. An attempt to get on common ground with the reader by agreeing with him in some way
2. A clear explanation of the situation from the adjuster's point of view
3. A complete refusal of adjustment or a statement of a partial adjustment
4. An attempt to get the reader to accept the adjuster's analysis of the situation

For example, the claim letter on page 119 requesting a new tire might be answered as follows:

Dear Mr. Harding:

We agree that you should expect more than 8,000 miles of service from the 6.50 — 15 Rubbertex Tire that you wrote us about on September 3. As you know from previous experience, Rubbertex Tires are built to give 25,000 miles of trouble-free service under normal conditions.

Our service department has carefully examined your tire, which was sent on to us by your local dealer, Mr. John Ostrander. They find that your tire was driven when seriously underinflated; this caused the side walls to crack. To make this as clear as possible, we enclose a booklet which, you will notice from the illustration, shows a tire injured in the same way yours was. By following the suggestions given in the part we have marked with red pencil, you will have no further difficulty of this kind, and you will be greatly pleased with the increased mileage you will receive.

Looking at this situation from your point of view, we can appreciate how you feel. Our guarantee of "at least 20,000 miles for Rubbertex Tires under normal conditions" still holds. But your tire, probably without your even knowing it, was subjected to abnormal strain, which no tire could stand; it, therefore, does not fall within the scope of this guarantee.

Because we want you to know the miles of carefree service that Rubbertex Tires can give, we are willing to bear a portion of your loss by offering you a new 6.50 — 15 Rubbertex Tire at a 20 per cent discount. Just take this letter to your local dealer, and he will mount your new Rubbertex on your rim—ready to protect you from dangerous skids and blowouts.

Sincerely yours,

The Rubbertex Tire Company

C. J. Cowan, Adjuster

Notice how tactfully the following letter fixes the responsibility for the breakdown of a washing machine without accusing the customer:

Dear Mrs. Kelley:

We certainly agree with you that it's inconvenient to run a home without a Supreme Washer. For that reason, we have lost no time in investigating the source of the trouble in your machine.

The report from our repair department indicates that your washing machine has a burned-out bearing which was caused by the fact that it has not been oiled. Although we guarantee the Supreme for three years against all defects in workmanship or materials, we cannot assume responsibility for repairs necessitated by improper care. You will understand, therefore, that we cannot grant your request to repair your machine without charge.

We shall, however, be glad to put your Supreme in brand-new condition at the actual cost of the parts, $3.67. When your machine is returned to you, it will be completely oiled and ready to operate. Then, if you will follow the directions for oiling, which are given on page 3 of your instruction book, you will get years of trouble-free service from your washer.

Just mail the enclosed post card today, authorizing us to proceed with the repairs, and we'll return your Supreme on Saturday in plenty of time to banish those washerless Monday blues.

Sincerely,

Let us assume that you are the adjustment correspondent for a department store to which a mother has returned a pair of shoes purchased for her ten-year-old son. After six weeks' use, the shoes are very stiff and badly cracked. Your investigation shows that the shoes have been worn constantly in snow or rain and then dried too near a stove or radiator. The real fault is, therefore, the customer's, and you must refuse any adjustment. This problem, which was used in a letter-writing contest for students in six American colleges and universities, requires considerable tact and careful handling. Here is the best solution as reported in the May, 1952, issue of the excellent *Bulletin* (published at Urbana, Illinois) of the American Business Writing Association.

Dear Mrs. Sherman:

That old saying, "Boys will be boys," is never more true than when it is associated with boys and shoes. I think everyone agrees that no one gives a shoe harder wear than a young boy.

Our product is fortified against such wear, and it has been tested for effectiveness against such things as scuffing, water, and snow.

When your boy's shoes reached my desk I was curious about the reason for their breakdown, so I sent them to our San Francisco laboratory. There they found that the shoes had been subjected to moisture and then to heat. This is the one thing leather cannot stand, for it cooks the life and flexibility out of it. It is for this reason that we cannot allow an adjustment on your purchase.

We do have a possible solution for you, however. During the last war our soldiers needed something to apply to their shoes to keep their feet dry and still retain flexibility in their shoes. The A. A. Bailey Company came to their rescue with "Stopwet," which is applied just like a wax polish. Not only does it do all that it was required to do, but it does not rub off on clothes or soak through on socks.

If you care to purchase another pair of our Strongbilt shoes, we will gladly prepare them with this compound for you, and you will never have to worry about your boy's shoes being wet.

We want to please you, so call on us whenever you have any shoe problems.

Sincerely,

These letters show that one of the chief functions of the adjustment letter is to educate the customer to the proper care of the product. If he can be shown that the adjuster is completely fair, he will accept the refusal of adjustment without any loss of good will.

One of the most difficult situations requiring a refusal of adjustment occurs when customers take unjustified discounts on their bills. Suppose, for example, that your firm has a policy of granting a 2 per cent discount for bills paid within ten days. One of your customers has paid a $600 bill three weeks later but has taken a $12 discount and has protested angrily when you billed him for the $12. Obviously, in this situation it is not the amount, but the principle, which should count. Here is the way one correspondent handled this delicate situation:

Dear Mr. Leavengood:

Thank you for your letter of November 12. I appreciate your giving us an opportunity to explain a situation which might lead to a misunderstanding if you had not written.

As you know, we have had a long-standing policy of permitting a 2 per cent discount to customers who pay their bills within ten days of the date of their bills. We maintain this policy because it enables us to effect similar savings by paying our own bills promptly. Actually, then, we pass these savings on to our own customers as a reward for their promptness.

Since we make no savings when our customers do not pay within the pre- scribed time, we must adhere rigidly to our principle. Actually, the amount of $12 is in itself a trivial matter; but in fairness to all our customers, we maintain a consistent policy. I think you would rightly object if we granted certain terms to other customers and different ones to you.

Now that you have the facts in this situation, I am sure that you will see the fairness of our bill for $12. We want you and all our other customers to take advantage of our discount policy, but we want to treat everybody fairly and consistently. To do so, we have to follow our principle, and I am sure you will agree that this is the only just and equitable method of operating.

I am grateful to you for writing to me because I realize that only by frank discussion can our companies work together for their mutual benefit.

Sincerely yours,

No exact formula will solve the problem of writing effective ad- justments. Whether the claim is granted entirely, partially, or not at all, the correspondent must seek to:

1. Convince the reader that he is being treated fairly
2. Gain his confidence in the products, services, or policies of the company
3. Regain his good will

Although much of the procedure in claims and adjustments is rather routine, it would be a mistake to conclude that the treatment of any adjustment situation must necessarily be stereotyped. Originality and a sense of humor can be most helpful in solving situations which might otherwise become rather tense. As a classic example of these qualities, consider the following exchange between Mr. L. E. Kaffer of the staff of the Palmer House in Chicago and Mr. Harry Bannister of radio station WWJ, Detroit. Several days after Mr. Bannister had stayed overnight at the Palmer House, he received a letter from Mr. Kaffer telling him that "two woolen blankets, replacement value of $8 each, were missing from the room you occupied" and asking Mr. Bannister to look through his luggage when unpacking since "guests frequently, we find, in their haste inadvertently place such items in their effects and, of course, return same when discovered." Instead of losing his temper, Mr. Bannister used his sense of humor as the basis for the following rather devastating reply:

Mr. L. E. Kaffer
Assistant General Manager
Palmer House
Chicago, Illinois

My dear Mr. Kaffer:

I am desolated to learn, after reading your very tactful letter of September 1, that you actually have guests at your hostelry who are so absent-minded as to check out and include such slight tokens of your esteem as wool blankets (replacement value of $8.00 each) when repacking the other necktie and the soiled shirt.

By the same token, I suppose that passengers on some of our leading railroads are apt to carry off a locomotive or a few hundred feet of rails when disembarking from the choo-choo on reaching their destinations. Or, a visitor to a big city zoo might conceivably take away an elephant or a rhinoceros, concealing same in a sack of peanuts—after removing the nuts (replacement value of $.05).

In this particular case I may be of slight assistance to you in running down the recalcitrant blankets. As I had a lot of baggage with me, I needed all the drawer space you so thoughtfully provide in each room. The blankets in question occupied the bottom drawer of the dresser, and I wanted to place some white shirts (replacement value of $3.50 each) in that drawer, so I lifted said blankets and placed them on a chair. Later, the maid came in and I handed the blankets (same blankets and same replacement value) to her, telling her in nice, gentlemanly language to get them the hell out of there.

If you'll count all the blankets in your esteemed establishment, you'll find that all are present or accounted for—unless other absent-minded guests have been accommodated at your emporium in the meanwhile. That's the best I can do.

Very truly yours,

Harry Bannister

P.S. Have you counted your elevators lately?

To this, Mr. Kaffer replied as follows:

Dear Mr. Bannister:

I wish to thank you for one of the most delightful letters it has been my pleasure to read in my entire business career. It would take a radio executive to compose a letter that would cause Damon Runyon, Mark Hellinger, and a lot of other writers radio might hire, to blush with futile envy. My sincere congratulations to you.

Yes, Mr. Bannister, we do a lot of counting around here. I've counted the elevators—and they're right where they should be, and operating, every one of them. What I want to count now is more important to me. I want to continue counting you as a friend of the Palmer House.

You, in your executive capacity, must of necessity supervise countless counts of so-called "listening audiences," "program polls," and all the bothersome promotions that annoy countless people in the middle of their dinner, or get them out of bed on cold nights to answer telephone queries. I shall assume, therefore, that you have naturally realized that you were most unfortunately a victim of a machine-like routine made necessary by the very vastness of an organization so well managed as the Palmer House.

There are a lot of folk in this merry world that would, as you so naïvely put it, "carry off locomotives, hundreds of feet of rails, and pack away an elephant or a rhinoceros." Just put a few ash trays, towels, blankets, pillows, glassware, and silverware in your public studios and reception rooms and see what happens.

Twenty-five thousand dollars' worth of silverware (actual auditors' "replacement value") is carried away annually by our "absent-minded" guests. A similar total (in "replacement value") is cherished annually by sentimental guests who like our linens as a memento of their visit to the Palmer House. They even go religious on us and take along the Gideon Bibles to the number of several thousand yearly. Nothing is sacred it would seem.

And so it goes. We are sorry, Mr. Bannister, that you were bothered as a result of a maid's mistake. Her lapse of memory started a giant wheel of routine. I am, in a way, happy the incident happened, because it gave me a chance to read your letter. It was a swell missive.

As the song says, and WWJ has no doubt played it "countless" times, "Let's Call the Whole Thing Off." And there's another song you also use, "Can't We Be Friends?"

Very sincerely yours,

L. E. Kaffer

So long as letters such as these can be written within the province of claims and adjustments, there is no need for further refutation of the charge that business letters must necessarily be dull and routine. Originality, humor, and cleverness can play an important role in any letter. In closing, we might well adopt Mr. Kaffer's idea of the theme song; for claims and adjustments, our theme should certainly be, "A soft answer turneth away wrath."

EXERCISES

1. How would you improve the phraseology and general tone of the following adjustment letter? Rewrite the letter on the assumption that one of your new employees has made an error and included 500 old shades in the order.

Mr. Harry White, Purchasing Agent
The Johnson Manufacturing Company
Peoria, Illinois

Dear Sir:

We were greatly surprised to learn from your letter of October 12 that the 3,000 silk lamp shades ordered on October 1 were unsatisfactory.

You claim that many of the shades were discolored and streaked. If this is true, we are at a loss to understand how such damage could have occurred because all of our merchandise is carefully inspected before it is shipped.

You also state that several hundred of the shades give evidence of having been in our stock room for a long period of time because they are dusty and faded. We cannot understand this because the lamp shades sent to you were manufactured only one month ago.

Since you have been a good customer of ours, however, we are willing to take back the shades which you claim are discolored and to replace them. We hope this will be satisfactory.

Sincerely yours,

2. The carpeting for your living and dining rooms, which you ordered from samples submitted by Mr. John Hawkins, salesman for The Elite Home Furnishing Company, does not match the sample which Mr. Hawkins showed you at the time you purchased your carpeting from him. Since your drapes and furniture were ordered to blend with the sample of carpeting, your whole decorative scheme is ruined. Write a claim letter to The Elite Home Furnishing Company, 27 East 55th Street, Chardon, Ohio.

3. As adjuster for The Elite Home Furnishing Company, you have received the claim letter mentioned in Exercise 2. Your salesman has apparently neglected to tell the customer that no two dyes of carpeting are exactly the same and that samples and the delivered carpet do not match exactly. Since the carpeting is already cut to the dimensions of the customer's rooms, you face a considerable loss if the customer does not accept it. Write, offering her a discount of 20 per cent and endeavoring to get her to accept this adjustment.

4. Mr. Will Carmen, 14 Amherst Street, Poughkeepsie, New York, has returned a $49.50 wrist watch, claiming that it stopped running three weeks after he purchased it. An investigation by your service department shows that the watch has been dropped or seriously jarred. The actual cost of repairs will be $4.27; write explaining why your one-year guarantee against defective materials or workmanship does not cover this sort of damage and attempt to get Mr. Carmen's authorization for the necessary repairs.

5. On August 1, just before starting on a long trip, you took your Buick coupé to the Economy Service Station to have it greased and the oil changed. Because of a mechanic's negligence, the plug in the crankcase was not tightened and the oil drained out, resulting in a burned-out bearing, a repair bill of $67.38, and great inconvenience. Write an appropriate claim letter to the Economy Service Station.

6. Write an adjustment letter granting the claim for $67.38 made in Exercise 5.

7. How could the following claim letter be improved?

Dear Sir:

My order did not arrive on time, and as a result I did not have the goods for my spring sale. It seems to me you ought to be more careful to fill your orders on time. If this happens again, I will stop doing business with you.

Sincerely yours,

8. As adjuster for the Bleakowen Department Store, you have received the following letter:

Gentlemen:

On March 26, I purchased a size 14 tweed coat for my daughter in your Junior Miss Department. For this coat, which my daughter wanted for Easter, I paid $42.75.

One week after Easter, you advertised this same coat on sale in the *Morning Chronicle* for $29.95. It seems to me that it is outrageous for you to charge almost thirteen dollars more for a coat just because it is purchased ten days before your sale, which I couldn't have known anything about. And anyway, we needed the coat for Easter.

I expect you to send me a credit slip for the difference in price; otherwise I'll never do business with your store again.

> Sincerely yours,
>
> Amanda E. Lewis
> (Mrs. J. E. Lewis)

Your store policy is to grant such adjustments when they occur within a week. But this is almost two weeks, and, furthermore, the store has always been very careful to avoid adjustments on merchandise for such holidays as Christmas and Easter, which have always been followed by sales. Write to Mrs. Lewis, refusing the adjustment.

9. The Square Deal Furnishing Company, 1213 Atlantic Avenue, Miami, Florida, has written that a mahogany dining-room table shipped by you on October 27 arrived with its top badly scratched. Apparently your shipping department was negligent in inspecting this merchandise before shipment. Rather than pay charges for shipping a new table and for returning the scratched one—which is the adjustment the customer asks for—offer a discount of 20 per cent on the table and suggest that this saving be used to repair the damage.

10. Mr. William Pulver, 361 Greenwood Avenue, Troy, New York, has written to you indignantly protesting that twice within the last year he has received bills for merchandise for which he had paid cash. Write Mr. Pulver explaining that the errors were made by a bookkeeper who has since been dismissed for negligence.

11. Your spring hardware catalogue was printed by the General Printing Company, 797 Easton Blvd., Walla Walla, Washington. Because of a printers' strike, publication was delayed three weeks and, therefore, you had no chance to see proofs because it was essential that the catalogue be in the hands of your customers by March 1. When the 10,000 copies of the catalogue arrived on February 26, you found errors in the prices listed for eleven of your major items. Write to the General Printing Company asking for an adjustment.

12. Rewrite the following adjustment letter:

Dear Mr. Chatfield:

Although we regret the fact that you are dissatisfied with the Model A Excello Hot Water Heater which we installed in your home last month, we feel that we have no responsibility for this situation.

We cannot understand why we have received complaints from none of the other people in your community, despite the fact that we have made over 900 such installations there. Mr. Charles Evans, who installed your heater, informed us that he strongly advised your getting our larger Model B Excello which is designed to furnish 50 per cent more hot water and that you were not interested.

You can hardly expect any better performance from your Model A since our tests show that it is performing with maximum efficiency. We, therefore, feel no responsibility in this matter; the error was made by you when you chose too small a heater for your needs. The only way to obtain the performance you desire is to install our Model B Excello at an additional cost of $96.

Sincerely yours,

13. Revise the following claim letter:

Gentlemen:

Every time I get an electric light bill from you it is higher than the one for the month before. My December bill was $6.71, which is the highest I have ever had, and I am getting sick and tired of paying such exorbitant bills. You big utility companies take advantage of small customers like me, and it's no wonder you make the huge profits that I see reported in the papers. I want someone to come out and examine my meter because I know I'm being overcharged.

Sincerely yours,

John J. Fallon

14. Write an answer to Mr. Fallon's letter based on your investigation showing his meter is accurate. Make use of such other information as the fact that while the price of other commodities has increased greatly, the cost of electricity has gone down; that the bill was for the month of December when the Fallons probably had a lighted Christmas tree and additional lighting; that Mrs. Fallon informed your investigator that the family had received a new radio, an electric toaster, and an iron for Christmas.

15. Your fur coat, which was sent for summer storage to the Reliable Fur Company, cannot be located. You have made repeated phone calls but have been informed that under the terms of the storage contract, your coat must be declared missing for three months before any adjustment can be made. Since it is now November and you would have to wait until January under the terms of this agreement, write to the general manager of the Reliable Fur Company asking for an immediate adjustment.

16. Rewrite the following claim letter:

Dear Sirs:

You certainly did a fine job of doing everything wrong on my order for a day bed. Personally, I don't see how an outfit like yours can stay in business.

I probably shouldn't expect you to remember anything I told you, but I gave you specific instructions to send that bed to my summer camp. Instead of that, you tried to deliver it to my home—so the neighbors told me—while I was on my vacation. I wanted it particularly because we were entertaining extra guests during my vacation and your careless disregard of my instructions spoiled everything—but you don't care about that.

I'd like to know what you intend to do about this. After this experience I'm through doing business with your store.

Yours truly,

Joseph Witherspoon

17. As correspondent for your store, write an adjustment letter in answer to the previous claim. Investigation shows that your shipping department was in error. You may make any adjustment you consider proper. Mr. Witherspoon has had a charge account with your store for twelve years.

18. Your company has received a complaint from an irate customer who insists that your paints are defective. Six months after his house was painted, the paint began peeling off in spots. A chemical analysis shows that the paint was properly mixed by the contractor, and your local dealer believes that the condition was caused by excessive moisture in the walls from ice backing up under the slate roof in the winter months. Write refusing his claim that your company pay the cost of repainting.

19. Which of the following three letters dealing with the same adjustment problem do you regard as most effective? Give reasons. Select the letter which in your judgment is least effective and point out how it violates fundamental principles of adjustment letters.

a. Dear Mr. Cartwright:

The Cinemotion Movie Projector, mentioned in your letter of December 27, arrived this morning. We were indeed sorry to learn that you ran into difficulties so soon after Christmas.

A careful examination of the projector discloses that the oscillating arm is broken. We have minutely examined this part for any defect which might have caused the break but are forced to the conclusion that the projector must have been dropped or possibly knocked unintentionally. We most sincerely regret that our guarantee will not take care of this repair, as it includes "defects in materials and workmanship" only.

However, the cost of repairs is slight, only $2.78, which includes postage. If you will write us immediately, enclosing your check for the above amount, we shall see that the projector is returned to you in tiptop shape within ten days.

Very truly yours,

b. Dear Mr. Cartwright:

We are glad to tell you, in answer to your letter of December 27, that, after careful examination of the Cinemotion Movie Projector No. 483, we find nothing seriously wrong with it. A few inexpensive repairs are needed. The machine appears to have been dropped or otherwise damaged, for the oscillating arm is broken.

As you will recall, our guarantee covers only defects in material and workmanship, but, if you will send us $2.78 for repairs and postage, we will be glad to repair the projector and return it within a few days.

May we put your machine in first-class working condition at once?

Very truly yours,

c. Dear Mr. Cartwright:

Thank you for your letter of December 27. We have carefully examined the Cinemotion Movie Projector No. 483, which you returned to us, and we find that the merchandise is not defective as stated in your letter. The projector has been dropped or damaged by careless handling and the oscillating arm is broken. This is, of course, not covered by our guarantee, which expressly states that it covers only "defects in materials and workmanship."

If you want this projector repaired, please send us a check or money order for $2.78 to cover the cost of repairs and postage. These repairs will take at least ten days.

We regret that our guarantee does not cover this work, and we thank you for past favors.

Very truly yours,

Business? It's quite simple.
It's other people's money.
                Alexander Dumas

CHAPTER VIII

Credit Letters

Although Dumas' oversimplified definition of business was written strictly for humor, it contains a basic element of truth. For estimates show that between 85 and 90 per cent of American business is transacted annually on a credit basis; other surveys show that less than one per cent of the credit granted is actually written off as a loss. These statistics indicate both the magnitude and the efficiency of the American credit system. Credit (from the Latin *credo* "I believe") is based on faith—faith in people and in their willingness and ability to fulfill their obligations. Economists, businessmen, and textbook writers have their own definitions of credit. For instance, businessmen often speak of the three C's of credit—character, capacity, and capital. J. P. Morgan is said to have remarked that "credit is 99 per cent character."

Such observations are interesting, but if we are to get a useful idea of what credit means, as applied specifically to the letters concerned with its ultimate granting or refusal, we must think of it in simpler terms. To the individual who seeks it, credit is simply a device by which he may have something now and pay for it later. To the businessman who must decide whether or not to grant it, credit is an estimate of the individual's ability and willingness to pay later; whether that ability rests on his character, his capacity, or on a wealthy uncle need not concern us.

The statistics mentioned in the first paragraph show that the granting of credit is no haphazard technique but an efficient process which has emerged from the combined experiences of American businessmen. The pooling of credit information in the cooperative credit bureaus of various American cities has greatly diminished the number of letters that must be written concerning a given credit situation. The scope and efficiency of the largest of these bureaus are described humorously in the following excerpt from *The New Yorker:*

WHERE CREDIT IS DUE[1]

You undoubtedly ought to know more about the Credit Bureau of Greater New York, considering that it undoubtedly knows so much about you. Of the many places where, for good or ill, your name is entered in a card index, it is certainly among the most important. It's a cooperative organization, like the Associated Press, the biggest of over a hundred of its kind in the nation, with some twelve hundred members, big hotels, department stores, professional people, bookshops, silversmiths, liquor dealers, and most businesses you could think of. Its headquarters occupy a whole floor of the building at 350 West Fourth Street, and there it has the names of four million people on file, with their retail purchasing and paying history.

By telephoning or, in the case of the biggest stores, querying by telautograph, a store can get a Trade Clearance Report on a prospective customer in just a few minutes—useful when an impetuous buyer wants to open an account, charge something then and there, and carry it off with him. This report tells what New York accounts the customer has had in the past, how big the accounts were, and the length of time he took to pay. (The Bureau considers payment within two months prompt. Three months is fair. Four months is slow and if you take longer than that you're called delinquent.) The Bureau assesses its members thirty-five cents for this report.

Then there's the special report, which costs a dollar, but is well worth it, for it details not only your paying record, but your income, what rent you pay, your employment record, the size of your family, and a general estimate of your character. Some credit investigators, like the gumshoe men for the insurance companies, go about putting shrewd questions to landlords and doormen, but the Credit Bureau doesn't care about your habits especially, except in the matter of paying your bills.

The Bureau circulates a weekly bulletin listing men who will not be responsible for their wives' debts, and passers of bad checks. It operates a Collection Department which the members may make use of if they want to. And there's a Clipping Department, which searches the newspapers for news of things that might affect a person's financial standing (lawsuits, marital difficulties, and what not); and there's a Locate Department, which locates people.

The whole system functions so well that the stores expect their annual loss from bad accounts to be down around one-half of one per cent.

A more serious description of the Credit Bureau of Greater New York, by Mr. Rudolph M. Severa, its Executive Manager, in *The*

---

[1] "Where Credit Is Due" originally appeared in *The New Yorker.*

Credit World, points out the magnitude of this efficient agency. It maintains a staff of 264 people to answer approximately 5,500 inquiries daily on an annual budget of almost a million dollars. One of its major activities is its liaison with other credit bureaus throughout the nation; in 1951, according to Mr. Severa, the New York bureau ordered 94,805 reports from associated credit bureaus.

Naturally, the information supplied by such organizations and by other sources obviates much of the delay previously considered inevitable in the granting or the refusal of credit. But since the coverage of these agencies is necessarily incomplete, the whole technique of obtaining credit information by mail should be understood. If a person or firm not listed in any of these sources applies for credit, the following types of credit letters might be written:

1. A letter acknowledging the customer's order or his application for credit and requesting that he send credit references
2. Letters to the references furnished requesting credit information
3. Letters from these references giving the credit information
4. The final letter to the customer
   a. Granting him credit
   b. Refusing him credit

A general understanding of the problems and principles of each of these types is invaluable to any correspondent. Since the credit letter is closely connected with the sales letter on the one hand and the collection letter on the other, a familiarity with the technique of making final judgment of the individual's credit aids in comprehending the problems of sales and collection.

The only realistic attitude toward credit letters is to regard them as part of a three-legged stool on which business is built—credit, collection, and sales. And their net effect should always be to build good will. This fact is underscored by Mr. Joseph L. Wood, Assistant Treasurer of the Johns-Manville Corporation, when he writes:

Today's credit executive is one who is imbued with the obvious fact that his company is in business for only one reason—to earn profits. He knows, too, that in order to earn profits, his company must obtain maximum sales, and that maximum sales cannot be obtained without preservation and enhancement of good will.

One of the most delicate phases of credit management is registering the company's payment terms with a new customer. This is especially true in retail business where many customers, not conditioned to fiscal require ments, are inclined to resent being told when they are expected to pay. If the situation is handled bluntly, defense mechanisms go into action and the seller starts off with two strikes against him in the good-will zone.

1. ACKNOWLEDGING APPLICATIONS FOR CREDIT

Salesmen habitually encourage new customers to place orders and are inclined to dismiss the whole matter of the granting of credit as incidental. Thus, the customer is led to expect his order promptly and is impatient of any delay caused by the credit routine; yet to protect itself the firm must make a thorough investigation. The purpose of the letter acknowledging the order or the application for credit is, therefore, to stress the fact that its request is routine and to encourage action by telling the customer that the sooner the information arrives, the sooner his order can be sent. The letter usually follows this pattern:

1. A statement welcoming the new customer or expressing appreciation for his first order.
2. An explanation of the firm's policy with regard to credit and payment of bills.
3. A request that credit references be sent or that the enclosed credit blank be filled out. (Usually three references are requested: a bank, a mercantile establishment, and a personal reference on the applicant's standing in his community.)
4. An incentive to action by emphasizing the fact that as soon as this routine is finished, the cutomer may receive his order.

Since the situation and the specific company policy dictate whether the order can be shipped before or after credit information is received, the following letters indicate how this pattern may be applied in both cases:

Dear Mr. Weldon:

We certainly appreciate the opportunity you have given us in your first order to do business with your firm. Your expression of confidence in us is most gratifying, and we will do everything in our power to live up to it.

Since we are anxious to serve you, your first order is being shipped to you by express tomorrow. So that we can handle your future needs without delay, we'd appreciate your sending us your financial statement. Or if you prefer, just fill out and return the enclosed credit form.

This credit information will, of course, be kept absolutely confidential. We are looking forward to having you as a regular customer. May we have your credit information soon?

Sincerely yours,

Dear Mr. Barrett:

We greatly appreciate the order for $237.21 worth of canned goods which you placed with Mr. White, our representative in your territory.

Since this is our first transaction with you, we must ask you to fill out and return the enclosed blank from our credit department. This is part of our regular routine in handling all new accounts; the information you send us will, of course, be held in the strictest confidence.

Your account will be opened and your order will be shipped as soon as this information reaches us. It is our hope that this is the beginning of a long business relationship. We shall do our best to make it a pleasant and profitable one for you.

Sincerely yours,

Dear Mr. Reichert:

Your first order pleased us greatly, and we are eager to add your name to our list of customers who have established credit with us.

To do this, you will realize that we need financial information about your firm. Since this information is not available in the usual sources, will you please send us your most recent financial statement. Or if it is more convenient, you may fill in the enclosed form. This information will, of course, be kept in the strictest confidence.

Your cooperation will enable us to ship your order promptly. May we have the information as soon as possible?

Yours very truly,

Acknowledgments of credit applications offer no serious problems. In dealing with the general public rather than with businessmen, the credit department will lay even greater stress upon the usualness of its request for information, lest the inexperienced customer be antagonized by what his ignorance of business technique may lead him to think is prying into his affairs.

2. REQUESTING CREDIT INFORMATION

Basically, a request for credit information is a letter of inquiry, which has been discussed in Chapter VI. Above all else, it should be easy to answer. The questions asked should be specific rather than general; the customary procedure is to enclose a credit blank to be filled out. Where less detailed information is required, such a form as the following, with the credit applicant's name typed in, is used:

Gentlemen:

We should like to have your opinion of

> Mr. John Dickson
> 316 Fernway Road
> Los Angeles 26, California

Your estimate of his financial responsibility, his credit reputation, and his previous methods of borrowing will be very helpful to us. We shall be grateful for this information, which will, of course, be kept confidential. We enclosed a stamped, addressed envelope for your convenience.

> Sincerely yours,

Gentlemen:

The _____ Company of (_____ address _____)
has given us your name as a credit reference.

We will appreciate your giving us the benefit of your experience with this company. If you will answer the questions listed on the form below and return this letter in the enclosed stamped envelope, we shall be very grateful.

Your reply will, of course, be kept in strict confidence.

> Sincerely yours,

How long has this company dealt with you?...
The terms were...
Amount now owing is $...................
Highest credit you will extend is $..................
Date of the last transaction...
Remarks ....
....
....
                 (Signed) ....
                 (Date) ....

3. LETTERS GIVING CREDIT INFORMATION

The letter giving credit information varies considerably, depending upon whether the correspondent speaks favorably or unfavorably of the credit applicant. Where a favorable reply can be given, the letter is frank in answering any necessary questions, as in the following instance:

Gentlemen:

Mr. Allen Eaton, 27 Broadway, Hurley, Indiana, about whom you asked us on July 26, has always had a good credit rating with us. He has been a customer of ours for seven and a half years, and he has usually paid his bills on the first of the month following purchase. His credit limit with us has been $500.

Sincerely yours,

The Taft Brothers

Where the information is unfavorable to the applicant, the letter should be much more guarded and careful in its language because of the legal implications involved in expressing an unfavorable opinion of someone's credit reputation. It is customary to avoid using any names in letters reporting unfavorably on the applicant's credit reputation, as in the following example:

Gentlemen:

The individual about whom you inquired on July 3 has a poor credit record with us. He has been a customer of ours for less than a year, and we are already having great difficulty in collecting from him. His credit limit with us was $250, but at present we are making shipments to him only on a strictly cash basis.

Sincerely yours,

4. THE FINAL LETTER, GRANTING OR REFUSING CREDIT

Thus far, the letters in the credit series have been of a rather routine nature, offering no very serious problems. But in his final letter, the credit man must express, however indirectly, his estimate of the customer's willingness and capacity to pay later. If the opinion is favorable, the letter is comparatively easy to compose; but if the opinion is unfavorable and credit is refused, the most difficult of all business letters must be written. Because of the resulting difference in technique, each of these types is discussed separately.

A. The Letter Granting Credit

The letter granting credit is not merely a statement of terms and conditions; it is also a sales letter which tells the customer of the quality of the merchandise and of the excellence of the service the firm tries to give. It may be compared in its general tone to a note of welcome to a friend who has just arrived in the writer's city; it should welcome him and express the hope that his "visit" will be enjoyable and that he will take advantage of the many facilities "the city" offers. The general tone of welcome, of interest in the customer's welfare, and of willingness to serve him is invaluable at the beginning of what the credit man hopes will be a long and pleasant business relationship. Consider the difference in the cordiality of the following letters:

Dear Mr. Jones:

In accordance with your request of May 11, we are granting you credit with a top limit of $500. Our bills are sent on the 28th of each month and are payable by the 10th of the next month. We hope you will enjoy shopping in our store.

Sincerely yours,

Dear Mr. Jones:

We are happy, indeed, to grant your request of May 11 for a credit account with us. Bills, payable by the 10th of each month, are mailed on the 28th of the month and include all charges up to the 25th.

Formerly, it was possible for the Blank Company to welcome each of its new customers personally. The size of our company and the number of our customers now prevent that, but our growth has come, and will continue to come, from our interest in serving all of our customers in the friendly manner that has become a tradition at Portland's most modern store.

As part of our service to charge customers, you will be given opportunity in advance to shop at all our sales before advertisements reach the general public. You will want to take advantage of our shopping service, which enables you to shop by phone to avoid the tiresome trip downtown. A call to Miss Parker will give you this efficient service and, of course, at no extra charge. All you need say now is, "Just charge it to my account."

The enclosed booklet will tell you of the hundreds of services offered for your convenience. We want you to use them because they will save you time and money. For our part, we hope that we may express our appreciation by serving you efficiently for many years to come.

Sincerely yours,

Dear Mr. Conover:

Thank you very much for sending us your financial statement so promptly. You are to be congratulated on the fine credit record your company has established.

We have shipped your order of March 21 by express today, and you should receive this merchandise by the first of next week. As you know, we will bill you on the 10th of each month for goods purchased the previous month. Payments within ten days of the date of our invoice entitle you to a two per cent discount.

We hope that you will like doing business with us. For our part, we want to do everything we can to deserve the confidence you have placed in us. We regard every order as an opportunity for prompt and efficient service.

Yours sincerely,

The second and third letters are far more deft than the first in expressing the hope that this new business relationship will be mutually profitable. By indicating a determination to make it so, they go far toward building good will at the very start of a business relationship. Usually the letter granting credit contains:

1. A granting of credit
2. A statement of terms
3. A sales talk on the type of service the company hopes to render
4. An expression of appreciation

Although the order of these parts may vary, all of them are generally present. The personality of the letter is as important as its contents; if the granting of the credit is friendly, cordial, and helpful in tone, it will be adequate.

B. The Letter Refusing Credit

Correspondents customarily believe that the letter they are engaged in writing at any given time is the most difficult of all types of letters. The immediate problem before us always seems the most perplexing, but if we objectively consider what is the most difficult of all the usual types of business letters, there is little doubt that we would select the letter refusing credit. The mere refusal of the credit is not so difficult, although the implication that the applicant represents a poor risk is hardly a pleasant one. The problem in refusing credit arises from the intelligent writer's desire to make his letter something more than just a refusal. Far too many businessmen are content with a routine form letter starting with the unimaginative words, "This is to inform you that we are unable at this time to extend credit," and ending with a pious hope that things may be different at some indefinite time in the future.

What else should the writer try to do? The applicant has been judged so poor a risk that no credit can be granted. Why not let the whole matter end with a vague or indefinite refusal? That is obviously the easiest way out for the credit man, but it is not the intelligent way. If the writer has thought out what he is trying to do in this letter (as described in Chapter II), he is not refusing credit so much as *he is trying to get the applicant's business on a cash basis.*

There are perfectly sound arguments which can be used to convince the customer that cash buying is to his own advantage. The credit man can advance such incentives as a discount for cash, or the advantages of buying in small quantities for cash and thus keeping up-to-date merchandise in stock, or the pleasures of end-of-the-month freedom from bills, or the fact that cash buying over a period of time will establish his reputation so that credit may be granted in the future. Perhaps the applicant won't accept these suggestions; perhaps he can get credit from another source. But the alternatives for the writer of this type of letter are to refuse him and stop there or to try to do something constructive. The intelligent correspondent will not be content to be negative; he will try to prevail upon the customer to buy for cash.

In its structure, the refusal-of-credit letter, then, should accomplish two tasks: it should tactfully refuse credit and it should attempt to get a cash order. The anomalous character of the refusal-of-credit letter comes from the fact that although it constitutes an unflattering comment on the applicant's financial standing, its language must not reflect this at all. Notice how tactless and inept the following letter is:

Dear Mr. Haley:

Thank you for your order of February 16. We regret to state that our investigation of your credit standing shows that your firm is not a good credit risk.

We hope that you will understand our position in this matter as we want your business, but we operate on so small a margin of profit that we dare not risk any credit losses.

You stated that 2,100 of our No. 14 cardboard containers would fill your needs for the next three months. In that case, we think we would be placing no hardship on you if we ask you to order C.O.D.

If you still want to place an order with us, we shall be glad to take care of it. As you know, our workmanship is better and our prices are lower than any of our competitors'.

Yours truly,

Prices and workmanship should indeed be incomparable to make up for the ineptitude of this letter. Such antagonizing phrases as "not a good credit risk" and "you stated" and such negative approaches as "we would be placing no hardship on you," "we dare not risk any credit losses," and "if you still want to place an order with us" certainly tend to drive customers into the arms of competitors. However true they may be, the correspondent must not use such statements as "you are a poor credit risk" or "your credit references were unsatisfactory" or "the report on your financial standing was not satisfactory." These facts must be glossed over, and the language must be selected to express the situation in less harsh terms.

With all these aspects of the problem clearly in mind, the writer of the refusal-of-credit letter will probably attempt to attain his two major objectives as follows:

1. Refuse credit by
   a. Acknowledging receipt of the credit references or credit information
   b. Analyzing the situation by beginning with its more favorable aspects but ending with a clear statement of refusal of credit
2. Attempt to get an order on a cash basis by
   a. Making some practical offer to cooperate (such as, for ex-

ample, cutting down the size of the order and paying part cash and the balance on specified terms)

or by

b. Advancing arguments to show that the customer himself benefits by cash buying, such as

(1) An offer of cash discount, usually 2 per cent

(2) A suggestion that cash buying in smaller quantities will give a wider selection and more up-to-date stock

(3) An inducement to establish credit within a short period by buying for six months or a year on a cash basis

Notice how effectively one credit man handles a difficult refusal, making no mention of what is probably the fact that Mr. Travis is a very poor credit risk:

Dear Mr. Travis:

Thank you for your promptness in sending us the credit information we requested. We are glad to report that all of your credit references spoke favorably of you as a businessman.

The new store which you are opening in Bellport should eventually prosper, since yours is a thriving community. But its location within 20 miles of New York City forces you to compete with the larger stocks and lower prices of the metropolitan department stores, so readily accessible to commuters from Bellport and similar communities. Because your resources do not indicate that you can meet such competition by starting with a large indebtedness, we must refuse your credit application.

We would suggest, therefore, that you cut your order in half and pay cash for it. This will entitle you to our 2 per cent cash discount, a saving which you may pass on to your customers. By ordering frequently in small quantities, you can best meet the competition of the New York stores through keeping up-to-date merchandise on your shelves. Thus, through cash buying you will establish your business on a sound basis that will entitle you to an excellent credit reputation.

The enclosed duplicate of your order will assist you in making your selection. Just check the items you wish and sign the order. Your merchandise will arrive C.O.D. within two days after our receipt of the order—in plenty of time for your opening sale.

Sincerely yours,

This credit man takes the very realistic point of view that half an order is better than none. To get it, he uses all the arguments he can muster. A comparison of the tone of this letter with that on page 148 will show how ineptly or how deftly credit can be refused, depending entirely on the technique used.

The following letters also reveal a tactful technique of refusing credit in such a way that the prospect will not take offense:

Dear Mr. Doe:

Thank you for your order for 50,000 tags. We are glad to have it.

Unfortunately, however, we now find that the credit information we have in our files is not complete enough to enable us to accept your order on open account. We realize that a thorough credit investigation would probably show that your organization is in good shape financially, but elaborate investigations cost quite a bit and usually require several weeks to complete.

Since you probably need the tags as soon as possible, I thought you might like to send us your check for $79 to avoid the delay that would be caused by our making a credit investigation. Or, if more convenient, send $40 and we will ship them "balance due C.O.D."

We will enter your order as soon as we receive your check—or, if you prefer, send us a list of two or three credit references and your latest financial statement.

Sincerely yours,

Gentlemen:

Thank you for your order given to Mr. Burton on June 11 for Safeway heaters.

As is the usual custom before a new account is opened, we have tried to obtain information that would serve as a basis for extending credit. Such information as we have thus far obtained does not permit us to form a definite conclusion, and for the present, therefore, we are not warranted in opening the account.

We realize that misunderstandings sometimes occur through trifling matters, which, if particulars were known, would have little or no bearing on the consideration of one's credit standing. If you feel that our action is not justified, we shall be glad to have you call at our office or write us so that we can arrive at a better understanding.

Please feel sure that we are anxious to serve you; and, after all, credit is a convenience and not a necessity.

Possibly in the future, conditions may change so as to allow us to open an account for you. Meanwhile, we hope you will instruct us to send this merchandise to you collect. We assure you that we will furnish you with the best of merchandise and give you the best prices and the friendly services offered by the Magnolia Heater Company.

Yours very truly,

USING CREDIT SITUATIONS FOR BUSINESS-PROMOTION LETTERS

As we have seen in inquiries and acknowledgments of orders, modern business uses any opportunity from birthdays to New Year's greetings as the occasion for letters designed to stimulate business or good will. Although these letters are fundamentally sales messages, certain types of business-promotion letters are also closely associated with credit. One of these is an offer of credit to those who are known to be good risks. The following letters sent by two department stores are typical of the whole class of such promotion letters:

Dear Mrs. Blake:

Miss Rita Conway, the head of our book department, has told me of your interest in our spring book sale and has suggested that you might be interested in opening a charge account with us.

You will find such an account of the greatest convenience, for it will enable you to call Miss Conway at any time and order the books you want without the inconvenience of making long trips downtown. In this way you will be able to keep up with the latest books and still have the benefit of Miss Conway's expert advice.

With a charge account, these same privileges are available in all the 51 departments of our store. Just call any one of the departments listed in the enclosed folder, order what you wish, and say, "Charge it"; or if you are undecided about gifts for friends, our Personal Shopping Service is available without cost to charge customers. Furthermore, you will receive advance notice of our many sales in the various departments of the store.

Just sign and mail the enclosed card which offers you carefree and convenient shopping.

Sincerely yours,

Dear Mr. Lowman:

Have you ever forgotten your wife's birthday? Need we say more? It takes years to live it down in most families.

It's a funny thing how the average wife, after a certain age, likes to have everyone, except her husband, forget her birthdays. If you should forget the date—it won't be funny—it'll be tragic.

So here we are taking the liberty of reminding you that your wife's birthday is

Friday, February 14

a red letter day for you—a blue day for her if you don't remember it!

At our uptown store, 1515 Second Avenue, between Pike and Pine, you will find two very helpful women, Mrs. Reeser and Miss Ball. They are eagerly awaiting a personal visit or telephone call from you. From their knowledge and wide experience in what women like, they can and will save you lots of valuable time in selecting that gift which will be most appreciated. They'll help you choose an appropriate birthday card and wrap your gift so beautifully that you'll be proud to present it to your "best girl."

Just call Elliott 8870 and ask for either Mrs. Reeser or Miss Ball of the K.H.O.O.D.* Department; if you can't shop in person, they will do it for you. Just tell them to "charge it to my account."

Happy days—if you don't forget!

Sincerely yours,

* Keeping Husbands Out of Doghouse.

The general pattern of the business promotion letter is comparatively simple:

1. The use of some special occasion such as a holiday, an anniversary, or a sale as the reason for offering credit or for acknowledging a good credit record
2. A detailed explanation of the advantages to the customer of having a credit account
3. A convenient method by which the customer may take advantage of the offer

Another method of business promotion used increasingly by credit correspondents is an expression of thanks for prompt payment:

Dear Mr. Franklin:

With a new year just around the corner, we want you to know how much we have appreciated your cooperation during the past year.

Your account has been paid promptly, and we hope that you have enjoyed doing business with us as much as we have with you.

That's why we want to say THANK YOU and to wish you a happy and prosperous NEW YEAR.

Cordially yours,

Dear Mr. Emerson:

It's your Anniversary!

Maybe you don't keep records of such things, but it was on March 21, 1953, that you sent your first order to us.

On that same date a year later, we want you to know how much we've appreciated a year of doing business together. You've met all your obligations promptly, and we feel privileged to have you as a customer.

And so, as we start our second year, we want to express our desire to give you the best possible service and to say THANK YOU.

Cordially yours,

Dear Mr. Kenyon:

We feel that there is something wrong with the general business practice of giving attention to the man who is "out of step."

In fact, we think the people who stay "in step" are the ones who really deserve recognition. And with this letter we want to recognize a man who has kept in step—*you*.

Month after month you have paid your installments on your loan with promptness and regularity. We want you to know, therefore, that we not only appreciate your business but also the manner in which you have met your payments.

Thank you for your fine cooperation. We have considered it a privilege to serve you.

Sincerely yours,

Dear Mr. Kilroy:

A credit manager is usually up to his neck in misery and frowns, but it's companies like yours that give us a chance to smile once in a while.

In checking over our accounts, I was impressed with the prompt record of payment you have established with us over the years. It is really appropriate for me to say that you build up a credit man's morale!

So before I get back to my dunning and frowning, I wanted you to know how much I appreciate your account. And my thanks, of course, go for our entire staff.

Sincerely,

Another important use of business-promotion letters, closely allied to the credit function, is the message designed to revive inactive accounts. Ostensibly this is an inquiry to find out why the customer is not using his credit account; actually, it is an important sales medium to express an interest in the customer and to point out how he benefits from using his account. Since customers stop using their accounts for many reasons, the number of letters sent varies considerably with the type of business and the buying habits of its customers. Increasingly, however, letters to revive inactive accounts are sent in series over a period of months. One Chicago department store, for instance, sent a series of five letters to 500 inactive accounts and found that the fifth letter produced more results than any of the first four. The first letter revived 50 accounts; the second, 24; the third, 48; the fourth, 48; and the fifth, 76.

Since most businesses have a considerable investment in putting customers on their books, common sense dictates that they do what they can to protect their investment and that they make it produce dividends in the form of steady orders. To do this, their letters should make the customer feel that he is important, that his past business was appreciated, and that future business is wanted and will benefit him. The following examples show how these aims can be achieved:

Dear Mr. Alexander:

Old friends are the best friends . . . .

That's the way we feel about the old friends we've made in our 22 years of business. And when you don't see an old friend for a long time, you're naturally concerned.

That's why we're writing you. Because we're concerned that we have unintentionally done something you didn't like. If so, we want to know about it and remedy the matter.

We have valued the confidence you've placed in us for many years now. A lot of new customers have been entered on our accounts during that time, but the old friends are those we treasure most. Because we've missed you, may we hear from you soon?

Cordially yours,

Dear Mr. Hightower:

We've missed you . . . .

And we're wondering if we haven't somehow slipped up without realizing it.

Your account and your friendship are important to us, because we like to think that we continue to deserve the confidence and the good will of customers like you. For that reason, if we have not rendered the kind of service you should receive, we'd appreciate your telling us so that we can do whatever we can to correct the situation.

We realize, of course, that you may not have needed any of our products in the past few months. But with the holidays approaching, we have many novelties and children's toys which will be attractive to your customers and profitable to you.

Because we've counted it a privilege to serve you in the past, we are looking forward to hearing from you soon.

Sincerely,

Dear Mrs. Kern:

When we sent you your Charga-Plate last year, we wrote you about the convenience and speed with which you could make purchases at our store.

Since you have not used your account during the past three months, we are wondering if somehow, we have not given you the kind of service to which you are entitled. If so, won't you let us know? We'll do everything we can to correct the situation.

Your Charga-Plate still offers the easiest and simplest way to shop. With it, you can take advantage of the savings at our advance sale of house furnishings and children's wear starting on February 10. In fact, we are putting hundreds of items on sale at values which you've been waiting for a long time.

We want you to feel that Millet's is *your* store and that our first interest is serving our customers. Won't you visit us soon?

Sincerely yours,

These letters demonstrate how well credit situations can be integrated into a general plan of public relations. In writing such letters, credit correspondents must particularly guard against the danger of sounding "gushy" or insincere. When it is properly handled, however, the business-promotion letter offers countless opportunities for creating favorable impressions, cementing established relationships, and maintaining customers' good will.

EXERCISES

1. Criticize the following letter refusing credit. Rewrite the letter.

Mr. James Glick
The Complete Haberdashery
Beacon, New York

Dear Sir:

We appreciated your promptness in sending us all the necessary credit information, but we regret to advise you that your references spoke rather unfavorably of you.

You will, therefore, understand why we cannot send you the merchandise which you ordered on August 15 on a credit basis. As a businessman, you yourself know how difficult it is to collect money these days, especially from those with poor credit rating.

We think that you should order about half the amount of your original order and pay cash for this merchandise. For our part, we shall be glad to extend you our 2 per cent discount for cash.

We know you will prefer to stock Wearwell Men's Suits in your new store because of their finer quality and lower price of $27.50. We shall hope to receive your order in a few days.

Sincerely yours,

Wearwell Clothing Company

James Bryant
Credit Manager

2. Write a letter requesting credit information from Mr. Harry Whitacre, 9 Main Street, Somervillle, Massachusetts, who has sent in his first order for $225 worth of electrical appliances on a credit basis.

3. Write an appropriate letter to one of the references furnished by Mr. Whitacre inquiring about him as a credit risk.

4. The Standard Hardware Company, 379 Broadway, Seattle, Washington, has written to you for credit information regarding Mr. John Jones, 31 Warren Street, Smithport, Washington. Mr. Jones has been very slow in his payments; at present he owes your firm $371.19; altogether, you regard him as a very poor credit risk. Write an appropriate answer to the inquiry of The Standard Hardware Company.

5. Mr. Joel Markey, 791 Pond Street, Westfield, Massachusetts, has ordered $431.67 worth of merchandise from your company. Investigation shows that Mr. Markey has an excellent credit rating. Write granting him the credit with a top limit of $500.

6. Your company is celebrating its twenty-fifth anniversary in the sporting-goods business. It started as a partnership when the two founders opened a shop producing carved gunstocks and special trout flies. It has since expanded as The Sporting Goods Corporation, which now supplies a complete line of sports equipment. Your credit manager has compiled a list of 156 dealers who have purchased supplies from you for more than twenty years. All of them originally paid cash for small orders, but they, too, have grown in size and now order substantial quantities for which they pay promptly. Write an appropriate letter to these dealers.

7. Mr. John Winthrop, 3621 Canal Street, Ellenville, New York, has ordered $279.47 worth of kitchen utensils, garden implements, and paint from your wholesale house. Investigation reveals that Mr. Winthrop is a very poor credit risk. Write, refusing him the credit for which he has asked.

8. Mr. C. I. Lee has ordered $450 worth of men's suits from your wholesale clothing firm and has asked for credit. Mr. Lee has had no previous business experience and is opening a new clothing store with the financial backing of his father. Write, suggesting that he pay $150 down, and $100 on the first of each succeeding month until the account is paid.

9. Write a letter offering credit privileges to Charles C. Lamb, 301 Spring Street, Auburndale, Pennsylvania. Mr. Lamb has made a number of cash purchases in the garden department of your store. Use the fact that you are having a sale of gardening equipment as the occasion for the letter.

10. What changes would you make in the following letter answering a request for credit information:

Gentlemen:

The Exclusive Men's Store, 765 Main Street, Peoria, Illinois, about which you inquired on March 18, has a poor credit rating with us. During the past year and a half, we have had a great deal of difficulty in collecting the amounts owed us, and three months ago, we were forced to insist that all their purchases be on a cash basis.

Sincerely yours,

11. Rewrite the following letter granting credit:

Gentlemen:

We are glad to grant you the credit which you recently asked for. We want
you to understand clearly that your account with us will carry a top limit
of $400 and that our bills sent on the last day of each month are payable
by the 20th of the following month. We hope you will enjoy the privileges of your credit with us.

Sincerely yours,

12. Write a letter that will go to 175 customers who made substantial
cash purchases during your January sale of men's furnishings. Offer them
the opportunity to open a charge account with your store and use as the
occasion for your letter the fact that your men's department is having
another sale during the last week of March.

13. Harold T. Sterling, R.F.D. #1, Hillside, New York, requested credit
for bedding, furniture, and kitchen equipment amounting to $900 about a
year ago. At that time you refused the credit to Mr. Sterling and persuaded
him to reduce his order and pay cash for it. In the meantime, Mr. Sterling
has prospered moderately in his roadside restaurant and tourist camp,
which he now wishes to enlarge. Write, granting his request for credit on
an order amounting to $600.

14. As the president of your fraternity, which is moving into a new
house, you must obtain credit for the purchase of new furniture amounting
to approximately one thousand dollars. Write a letter asking such credit,
which you might appropriately send to three wholesale furniture companies in your area.

15. Criticize the following letter:

Dear Mrs. Hoag:

We have noticed that you have purchased various items from us on a cash
basis during the past year.

We wondered if perhaps you did not find this inconvenient and if, like
many of our other customers, you would not prefer to have a charge
account, which offers many advantages. That way you can simply call us
up, order whatever you want, and just say, "Charge it."

If you do prefer to open a charge account with us, simply fill in the
enclosed card. We want to take this opportunity to express our deep
appreciation for your past patronage and to hope that we may continue to
merit your approval.

Yours truly,

16. Rewrite the following refusal of credit:

Gentlemen:

In answer to your request of February 2, we must say that we cannot grant the credit which you asked for.

You probably realize that new enterprises such as yours have very heavy risks, and if things do not go well with you, we would incur a big loss. We have had so much experience with new businesses that we just do not dare take a chance, much as we would like to.

In the meantime, we hope you will see your way clear to buy from us on a cash basis because we are really interested in expanding our new accounts.

Sincerely yours,

17. As credit manager for your paint manufacturing company, write an appropriate year-end letter to Mr. Charles E. Higgins, President, The Higgins Hardware Company, 3917 East Avondale Road, Charlotte 4, North Carolina, who has been a customer for five years. During the year, purchases from The Higgins Hardware Company have more than doubled and bills have been paid promptly to merit your 2 per cent discount.

18. Write an appropriate letter to the First National Bank of Blankville, Tennessee, asking specific information about John Doeson of Blankville, who has sent you an initial order for a substantial amount and has given the bank as a reference.

19. You have received an order for 500 sets of skates from Mr. Joseph C. Lunderberry, 397 Main Avenue, Westville, New York. Mr. Lunderberry is opening an indoor skating rink in two weeks and wants immediate delivery of the skates. The Credit Association has reported that Mr. Lunderberry's record is unsatisfactory. Write, refusing his request for credit.

20. An alert salesman in the men's department of your department store has reported that a Mr. C. J. Evers purchased $36 worth of ties, shirts, and accessories. During the conversation, Mr. Evers told your salesman he was a newcomer to your city since he had just been appointed chief engineer for a large manufacturing company. The salesman also learned that he was greatly interested in your camera shop and your music department. Write an appropriate letter offering him credit.

Annual income twenty pounds, annual expenditure nineteen and six,
result happiness. Annual income twenty pounds, annual expenditure
twenty pounds and six, result misery.

Charles Dickens, *David Copperfield*

CHAPTER IX

Collection Letters

The relationship between the granting of credit and the collecting of debts is a close one; when credit has been expertly managed, the work of the collection department becomes much simpler. Equally important is the relationship between the collection and sales departments. The customer who has owed money for a period of time ceases to be a customer, for if he needs additional merchandise, he may turn to competitors of the firm that has carried him on its books.

Many collection men discuss this situation quite frankly in their collection letters. One firm has had good results with the following brief note which states the problem in forthright terms:

Dear Mr. McMaster:

We send you this not just to collect the $47.52 you owe us but also *because we want you to buy from us again.*

Sincerely yours,

The following letter links sales and collection appeals:

Dear Mr. Warner:

One of the reasons we dislike seeing your account go unpaid for so long is that it may cause you to hesitate in ordering material you may need from us.

When you have been owing us for several months, you are apt to be a bit timid in reordering even though you are dangerously low on some of our merchandise.

In that case, we both lose. You lose the sales and profit that you should have, and we, in turn, lose the business you might give us.

That's the reason why we'll both benefit by your sending your check for $89.74 to pay our invoice of April 15. Why not check over your stock now, make up an order, and mail it with your check in the envelope we are enclosing?

Yours truly,

Another firm sends out this letter showing the amount due in very large figures in a drawing of a magnifying glass:

Dear Mr. Locke:

Little things sometimes get magnified out of all proportion.

Maybe your outstanding balance doesn't seem a "little thing" to you—but we don't want it magnified so that it affects our relations. We appreciate all the business you ·have given us in the past and we want it to continue.

Won't you send us your check—in full, if you can—or a substantial payment? After all this time, you must need a number of our products . . . and we, of course, want you to have them.

Sincerely yours,

Unfortunately, the letters of many companies sound as if their collection correspondents and their sales correspondents were not speaking to one another. While the salesmen have been dealing with the customer under the theme of "how to win friends and influence people," the collection department all too often takes over with a rough, offensive tone more than likely to nullify all the sales effort. This situation—a little like the contrast between the sweetness and light of fraternity rushing and the grim reality of the pledge period—can be corrected only through the closest co-operation between sales and collection policies. To do this, correspondents must remember the twofold object in collecting a past-due account—to get the money and to retain the customer's good will and patronage. The language and the tone of the collection letter should be carefully scrutinized on the principle that a collection letter which retains the customer's good will stands a better chance of collecting the amount due than one which irritates or antagonizes him. Try your own reaction to the following letter sent out by a company that spends a considerable amount for advertising and sales-promotion efforts:

Dear Mr. White:

We cannot understand your failure to reply to our previous reminders about your delinquent account amounting to $47.43.

By ignoring our letters, you leave us little choice but to decide we were wrong in extending your credit. After all, you must realize that the expense of sending repeated reminders makes this a very unsatisfactory experience for us.

You can prove we were not wrong in our judgment by sending us your check, now.

Yours truly,

The needless negative emphasis of such words as *cannot understand, your failure, delinquent, ignore, wrong, unsatisfactory* certainly cancels a lot of sales-promotion effort; and without appearing "soft," the correspondent can collect and still keep good will by being persuasive and constructive. Notice the difference in point of view and general tone of the following letter dealing with the same situation:

Dear Mr. White:

We have sent you several reminders about your past due account for $47.43, without a response from you.

In fairness to yourself, we hope you'll consider how important an asset your credit standing is. Certainly, you would place a far higher value on it than the amount you owe us.

To protect this asset, you can write us frankly as to when you will make payment—or better still, send us your check now. By doing so, you'll get this off your mind. Use the envelope we are enclosing for your convenience —and mail it today, please.

Yours truly,

In recent years, the collection letter has taken on new and varied hues. Formerly the product of a bookkeeper, it wore the drab garb of routine and impersonality. Typical of such uninspired letters is the following:

Dear Sir:

Our books indicate that your account with us shows a balance of $116.17 due for goods shipped on November 13. Please remit at once.

Sincerely yours,

By contrast, the debtor of today gets a lot more thought, originality, and humor expended on him than did the debtor of a few years ago. This change has occurred because collection men have come to realize the value of *selling the debtor the idea that it is to his own advantage to pay.* Instead of the dull, routine notice of payment due, the collection letter has assumed all the sales arguments, the attention-arousing devices, the humorous stories, and the colorful stunts previously associated only with the sales letter. While this "trick stuff" should not be overemphasized, many a collection man has nevertheless discovered that if he can entertain or amuse his debtor, the chances of payment increase.

Naturally, the technique of collection varies greatly with the individual debtor, who will probably be classified in one of the three general groups of good, fair, or poor credit risks, or "prompt pay," "slow pay," and "poor or uncertain pay," as they are sometimes called. If a utopian situation prevailed, all the customers would belong to the good or fair categories where they could be easily entertained, amused, or cajoled into payment, but since the poor are always with us, the collection man must deal with this group of customers on the theory that they will pay if they are made to pay—and with this group his letters take on a sterner tone. Without completely disregarding all the different situations and debtors involved, can we determine the basic structure of collection letters? When properly considered as sales messages, collection letters usually contain the following elements:

1. The opening paragraph states the business at hand—*i.e.,* the amount due, dates of letters or orders, and mention of specific merchandise where necessary—unless the first paragraph is an attention-arousing device.
2. The next two paragraphs present the argument for payment.
3. The closing paragraph motivates action.

This analysis ought to be regarded merely as the framework of the letter; the actual details may modify or change it greatly. It is a guide to what the letter should try to accomplish rather than a formula to be followed exactly.

Within this framework, most collection letters carry a strong appeal to the reader's self-interest or to his sense of fair play. In tone, they should sound confident that the debtor will pay; especially to be avoided are any statements which indicate exasperation or an abused feeling on the part of the collector. In general, effective correspondents operate on the theory that most people want to pay their debts, that persuasion and perseverance are the best means to get bills collected, and that curtness, sarcasm, or righteous indignation merely antagonize the debtor.

Actually, there is no such thing as *the* collection letter; like troubles, collection letters "come not singly but in battalions," known as *the collection series.* This series of letters is a practical expression of the fundamental belief behind all collection procedure—*that the customer will pay if he is reminded regularly and with increasing insistence that payment is due.* The frequency of the reminders and the degree of insistence will depend entirely upon the type of credit risk the customer is. But whether he deals with a good, fair, or poor risk, the efficient collection man knows that the debtor must be handled according to a plan, which starts with a gentle reminder that payment is due and, if payment is not made promptly, goes through to its most insistent point of threatening to take drastic action to collect.

Each of the letters in such a series contains some basic assumption which colors the whole letter. To show the logical relationship between the individual letters of the series, we must now examine the fundamental assumption on which each of the letters is based and the manner in which each assumption contributes to the increasing insistence of the series as a whole.

1. The Assumption That the Customer Wishes to Be Reminded That Payment Is Due

This reminder may be a very brief letter or simply a statement. Its assumption that the customer really wants to be reminded of the debt is perhaps artificial, but the collection man certainly feels that the debtor ought to be reminded. Many firms save time in the early stages by sending out form letters in which the amount and the date may be inserted. As the opening step in his campaign, the collection man sends a statement or a very brief note, such as the following:

Dear Mr. Davis:

Just a friendly reminder of our terms, which are full payment monthly. Our account will be off your mind if you send us your check for $13.48 in the enclosed envelope.

Very truly yours,

Gentlemen:

Your account today shows an unpaid balance of $. . . . .

Not enough to worry about, of course, but many unpaid balances like this add up to a substantial sum.

Won't you remit today?

Very truly yours,

Dear Mr. Brady:

We thought you'd appreciate a reminder that your account is past-due.

If you have sent us your check, please accept our thanks and disregard this notice.

Sincerely yours,

Gentlemen:

Balance past due: $312.41

Will you accept this letter as a friendly reminder to send us your check for the amount shown above, which is now past due?

If your check has already been mailed, accept our thanks.

Yours very truly,

2. The Assumption That the Customer Has Forgotten to Pay

This second letter is brief and suggests that because of the rush of business or through an oversight, the customer has simply forgotten to pay. Actually, it is very similar to the first letter of the series and is sometimes called "the follow-up reminder." Many companies do not use these intermediate or follow-up reminders on the theory that one reminder is sufficient. On the other hand, there are undoubtedly good reasons why the customer does not respond to the first reminder, and, particularly if he has dealt with the firm for some time, the follow-up has an important place in a well-balanced collection series.

Dear Sir:

Your account has a birthday today. It's ..... days old.

As birthdays go, this is one type that ages fast, and the older it gets the harder it is to handle.

You've probably forgotten this birthday, so let's take care of it while it's still young. Won't you please send us your check for $19.75 today?

Sincerely yours,

Dear Mr. Black:

This little flag is designed to call your attention to the amount of your past-due balance.

Undoubtedly you have overlooked this. If your check is already in the mail, please disregard this notice. If not, will you please send your check today?

Sincerely yours,

Dear Mr. Graham:

We previously reminded you that your account, as shown on this statement, is past-due. Since we have not yet received your payment, may we again ask that you send us your check as soon as possible?

Sincerely yours,

Dear Mr. Snow:

An expert recently selected these seven words as the most expressive in the English language:

1. Most beautiful—"love"
2. Most tragic—"death"
3. Most revered—"mother"
4. Warmest—"friendship"
5. Coldest—"no"
6. Most bitter—"alone"

And the 7th and saddest is "forgotten."

And that's the word that bothers us—because you have apparently forgotten us. Won't you please remember to send us your check for $17.31?

Sincerely,

Dear Mr. Franklin:

Perhaps you overlooked it—

Possibly you forgot—

At any rate, we haven't received the monthly payment of $...... requested in our recent statement. We want to explain that Club Plan Accounts are opened with the understanding that the installments shown on the contract are to be paid each month when due.

A stamped, addressed envelope is enclosed for your convenience in remitting.

Yours truly,

3. The Assumption That Something Is Wrong with the Goods, the Service, or the Records of the Transaction

At first thought, this may seem to the uninitiated a curious letter to include in the collection series because it is actually an offer of adjustment. But this letter, suggesting that perhaps the customer is dissatisfied or that the firm's records of the transaction are wrong, performs two important tasks in the collection series.

First, it gives the customer a chance at an early stage to express any dissatisfaction he may feel; if he doesn't respond to this offer, he can't in good faith tell the collection man later in the series, "I haven't paid your bill because I didn't like the service you gave me." The effective collection series forestalls that alibi; the customer is given an early opportunity to make any complaints—if he doesn't make them then, he can't very logically do so later.

Second, the contents of this letter are designed to crack the armor of the most difficult of all debtors, the "silent customer." Collection men work on the principle that any response is better than none; they feel that if debtors can be persuaded to make some sort of reply, even an unsatisfactory one, a solution to the problem may be worked out. Their most vexatious problem is the silent customer who gets all their letters, probably reads them, and then makes no reply. If any letter will dent this silent defense, the offer of adjustment will. For these two reasons, it plays an important role in the well-planned collection series and, in addition, it offers an excellent and logical opportunity for a sales message couched in terms of the kind of service the firm wants to render. If this individual has not received that kind of service, he is not being fair to himself by keeping silent. The following are good examples of this type of letter:

Dear Mr. Colby:

HELP!

Yes, we've had our share of troubles with help during the past year . . . and maybe we've slipped somewhere on your account, which is now $249.40 past due.

Since we've sent you two reminders without an answer, we thought you might like to let us know if anything is wrong. If there is, we'll do our best to correct it.

If not, will you please send your check today?

Sincerely yours,

Dear Mr. Robertson:

This is not a dunning letter. We want the $219.17 you owe us—but we also want to keep your friendship.

You have always paid your bills with us promptly in the past. Therefore, we know there must be some special reason for nonpayment in this instance.

We try our best to render the most efficient service possible, but we are aware that errors occur occasionally. If there has been any tardiness in delivery or any mistake in our records, we want you to tell us about it.

Or, if you will write us frankly, we can perhaps work out some plan whereby you can take care of the past-due balance without imposing too heavy a burden on yourself while, at the same time, we can continue to make shipment to meet your immediate needs. The enclosed self-addressed envelope is for your convenience in replying.

Yours very truly,

Dear Mr. King:

Since we have not received your check for $13.26, we are wondering if you have some reason for not paying us.

Naturally, we try to the best of our ability to avoid errors, but you will realize that mistakes do happen, and, being human, we do occasionally make them.

If you have found an error, please tell us so that we can make the necessary adjustment. If there are no corrections to be made, we shall expect you to send us your check today.

Yours truly,

Gentlemen:

DID WE OVERLOOK SOMETHING?

Is it because of some omission on our part that we have not received your check? If so, may we please have an explanation? We'll do our part toward making any necessary adjustment.

On the other hand—if we've performed our part of the sales contract, won't you now complete yours? Your check will do the trick. And, by the way, if you need any more cups, include your order.

Cordially yours,

Universal Paper Products Co.

4. The Assumption That the Ideas of All the Previous Letters Were Erroneous

Since there has been no reply to his letters assuming that failure to pay was caused by oversight or dissatisfaction, the collection man now frankly admits that he is puzzled. Actually, if he has had much experience, he isn't as baffled as he may sound in his letter; by this time he is well aware that he must increase the tempo and the insistence of his series. Like the previous letter, this is primarily intended to get the debtor to break his silence. By summing up what has been done thus far, the letter appeals to the customer's sense of fairness. Its theme is, "We have delivered the goods you ordered and given you service which you accepted as satisfactory, since you made no reply to our last letter—and still you remain silent. Is this fair?"

In the collection series, this fourth letter constitutes the transition between the first phase of the collection campaign to a second and much more urgent phase. If there is no response to this letter, the collection department properly feels that it must follow through, quickly and with great insistence.

Dear Mr. Drake:

Let's take a look at the record!

> . . . We delivered $279.10 worth of our products in February.
> . . . We mailed your first bill on March 1.
> . . . We've sent you three reminders and a letter asking you to tell us if anything was wrong with the goods, the service, or our records.
> . . . And still we have no reply from you.

Maybe you'd like to put something else on the record. Frankly, we hope that "something else" will be your check for $279.10; but at the very least, we hope you'll let us know if we can work out some satisfactory method of settling this account.

We're asking you to go on record by sending us your check or an explanation of why we have had no response to our previous letters.

Sincerely yours,

Dear Mr. Whitcomb:

In our letters of June 16, July 2, and July 20, we tried unsuccessfully to obtain payment of your past-due account of $84.02 or to gain some explanation from you.

We are sorry that you have made no reply because we want to help our customers whenever possible. We filled your order promptly and in a manner that must have been satisfactory to you since you have made no reply to our offer of an adjustment.

As you know, our credit terms call for payment within 30 days. You have not complied with these terms nor given us the facts by which we might arrive at a solution.

Won't you use the enclosed envelope to send us your check or an explanation of why your payment is so long overdue?

Very truly yours,

Dear Mr. Henry:

Ever hear of a Well Witcher?

No, that's not a misprint for "well-wisher." A well witcher is a fellow who, with the aid of a forked stick, finds water below ground. Farmers employ him to find locations for wells.

That forked stick business sounds like the magic wand of fairy tales but, somehow, we can't help wishing that we had such a friendly persuader to solve our problems.

Right now, the problem with us is to obtain payment of your past-due account for .... amounting to ...., and we are wondering what kind of friendly persuasion it is going to take to bring us that check. This is the fourth request, as you know. Will you cooperate by making it the last? Please mail your check today, or tell us the reason why.

Very truly yours,

5. The Assumption That the Customer Is Not Taking His Proper Responsibility

This letter places the burden of responsibility squarely on the shoulders of the debtor. There is no longer any talk of reminders, adjustment, or similar reasons for the delinquency. This letter points out that the customer is not fulfilling his responsibility. It appeals to his sense of pride, or his honor, or best of all, his self-interest. No time is wasted on sales talk about merchandise or service at this stage; the sales message of this letter concerns the value of a sound credit reputation. It points out that credit is the very lifeblood of business; that no businessman can long survive without a sound credit reputation; that by paying this bill he preserves his most valuable asset—thus, it is *to his own interest* to see that the delinquent account is settled. Otherwise, there will be unpleasant action.

Dear Mr. Meyer:

From school days on, we learn the importance of "good marks."

In business, for example, we all know the value of silver marked "sterling," of jewelry by Tiffany, of cars by Cadillac.

Your "mark" is your credit standing. To keep it high requires constant vigilance. We're sure that you don't want your past-due account for $113.43 marked "Delinquent."

For your own sake, don't neglect this account another day. We expect your check by return mail.

Yours very truly,

Dear Mr. Martin:

As a businessman you certainly realize the value of a good credit reputation. You know that it is probably your most valuable asset.

Yet you are jeopardizing your credit rating for $89.26, the balance of your account with us. Surely you are being unfair to yourself to place so low an estimate on your most valuable asset.

Prompt attention to your obligations is the one way to maintain your credit reputation. Otherwise, we shall have to report your account as delinquent to the local credit bureau. Your check will make it unnecessary for us to make such a report.

Sincerely yours,

Dear Mr. Miller:

Up along the west coast of Canada lies one of the greatest aids to ships and commerce—the world-famous Inside Passage. Its reef of rocks several miles out from the mainland acts as a barrier against the wild north Pacific and the Bering Sea.

Outside that reef, the storms lash the ocean into a fury, while ships move safely and easily in the Inside Passage. Without that channel, commerce between America and Alaska would be seriously curtailed.

A sound credit rating is like that Inside Passage, Mr. Miller, and because of it, your "ship" of business can move smoothly and easily. The barrier which protects that rating is the promptness with which you meet your obligations.

You can form a protective reef for yourself by sending in your check for $31.19. Why not take care of it today?

Sincerely yours,

Dear Mr. Jones:

A business transaction that is not to the advantage of both parties concerned is to the advantage of neither.

When you originally asked for credit in March of 1952, furnishing our company with a signed financial statement, we made the customary credit investigation. The information we have in our possession indicates that you have been established in business for a good many years, have the reputation of retiring your obligations in a satisfactory manner, and are well and favorably known in your community.

Our credit manager had every confidence in your ability and willingness to pay and extended to you a liberal line of credit on the time-payment plan. Now your account is delinquent the February and March installments of $50 each, totaling $100, and our many requests to you for payment have received no attention whatsoever.

We, as the manufacturers of the equipment, are naturally interested in your welfare. We are anxious to see you protect the sizable equity established in the equipment, and we have no doubt but that you are vitally interested in continuing to maintain a good credit standing.

With this thought in mind, we urge that you attach your check to the carbon copy of this letter, which we are also enclosing, and mail it to us in the business reply envelope enclosed.

Remember, one of your most valuable assets is a good paying record. Protect it.

Sincerely yours,

6. The Assumption That the Customer Will Pay Only if He Is Made to Pay

The final letter of the collection series uses fear as its motivating force. It consists of a brief statement that unless payment is received by a certain date—usually within five or ten days—the delinquent account will be turned over to a lawyer or reported to a local credit bureau. This final letter may express great reluctance to resort to this action, and it may well point out that there is a far more pleasant solution if the customer desires, but its tone leaves no doubt that the creditor intends to go through with the necessary action. The following are rather typical examples of the final letters of the collection series:

Dear Mr. Jones:

Our records show that we have received no payments on your $233.11 past-due account for merchandise we shipped to you on August 7.

Since we have not had any reply to our previous correspondence, there seems to be no alternative for us except to place this matter in the hands of our attorneys.

For you, there is still one alternative—send us your payment in full within five days. Otherwise we shall be forced to take an action which, frankly, we dislike.

Yours truly,

Dear Mr. Bender:

Frankly, we are reluctant to turn your account over to our attorney for collection. After all, though lawyers do have a way of getting money, legal action is expensive and unpleasant.

We are, therefore, going to give you every opportunity to avoid outside collection of your account.

But it will be necessary for you to do your part. Your check for $50 within the next five days and satisfactory assurances about paying the balance of the account are what we consider your part. It's your move next.

Sincerely yours,

Dear Mr. Conrad:

We have tried to handle your overdue account in the most courteous way possible.

You have had a number of letters from us, telling you that you owe us a balance of $91.44. To none of these have we had a reply.

Only one measure is left . . .

Unless we receive your check within the next five days, we shall take the necessary legal action to enforce payment.

Yours very truly,

Dear Mr. Pearson:

Occasionally we judge a person wrong. Perhaps we are too optimistic and put too much faith in our fellow men.

We have begun to believe our judgment of you was overoptimistic because you have not even replied to our notices or the letters we wrote you regarding payment of your account.

If misfortune or ill health had prevented your paying us, you would certainly have informed us in order to protect your credit. You have left just one course open to us—to turn the account over to our attorneys. That will be expensive for both of us.

Your check for $27.96, received within five days, will settle the matter. It is now up to you.

Yours truly,

To impress debtors with the urgency of the situation, many firms use telephone calls or registered letters in the final stage of the collection procedure. Another device is to send a letter over the signature of the president or a high official when letters signed by subordinates have not received a response.

The telegram is also being used increasingly during the latter stages of the collection series. It is particularly good in the demand stage of collection because it attracts attention, motivates action, and its message is brief. The reader can test its effectiveness by thinking what his own reaction would be on receiving such a collection message as the following:

We have been very patient. Please remit. Urgent.

Very important your check reach us by March 15. Send today.

Unwilling to wait longer. Your account must be paid within five days.

Will take action unless check or money order is mailed today.

Your last chance to make good. Wire remittance today.

Will take immediate action unless remittance is received at once.

TIMING THE COLLECTION SERIES

The success of the collection series depends largely on the frequency with which the individual letters are sent. The timing of the letters, in turn, depends on many factors such as whether the customer is regarded as a good, fair, or poor risk, whether he is engaged in a seasonal occupation like farming, and whether the collection series represents a retail or wholesale business.

These details pertaining to the frequency of the letters are not of primary importance; what *is* important is that there must be a definite plan as to the contents and timing of the individual letters in the collection series. The collector should know from the very beginning just what he is going to do and when he will do it. Obviously, the good risk or the old customer is going to be given a longer time and gentler treatment than the poor risk, but the collection series should be planned *in advance* to deal with both extremes. To show the timing of one such series in relationship to the type of risk involved, the analysis below gives the procedure of a retail firm in dealing with collections.

Assuming that the purchase has been made in December and the invoice was received then, the following letters would be sent on approximately these dates:

Poor Risk

January 1—	A statement
January 15—	An offer to make any necessary adjustment
February 1—	A letter explaining that the collection department is puzzled by the debtor's silence and appealing to his sense of fairness
February 15—	An expression of the collector's feeling that the debtor is not assuming proper responsibility, and a sales talk on sound credit
March 1—	A demand that payment be made by March 10 or the account will be turned over to an attorney for action

Fair Risk

January 1—	A statement
February 1—	A statement
March 1—	A note assuming that the customer wishes to be reminded that payment is due
March 15—	A brief letter assuming that failure to pay is the result of an oversight
April 1—	An offer of any necessary adjustment
April 15—	All previous assumptions were wrong; the collection man is puzzled. Appeal to the customer's sense of fairness
May 1—	An urgent expression of the collector's feeling that the customer is not taking the proper responsibility, together with a sales talk on sound credit
May 15—	A demand that payment be made by May 25 or the account will be turned over to an attorney for action

Good Risk

January 1—	A statement
February 1—	A statement
March 1—	A statement
April 1—	A note assuming that the customer wishes to be reminded that payment is due
April 15—	A brief letter assuming that failure to pay is the result of an oversight
May 1—	An offer of any necessary adjustment
May 15—	All previous assumptions were wrong; the collection man is puzzled. Appeal to the customer's sense of fairness
June 1—	An urgent expression of the collector's feeling that the customer is not taking the proper responsibility together with a sales talk on sound credit
June 15—	A demand that payment be made by July 1 or the account will be turned over to an attorney for action

Such a schedule should not be rigid. There are, of course, many different kinds of poor risks, fair risks, and good risks. The experienced collection man attempts to treat his accounts as individuals; he remembers that financial emergencies and personal crises fall on all of us at one time or another. When the honest debtor writes in to tell of heavy expenses caused by illness or similar troubles, the collector is willing to temper the wind to the shorn lamb. His letters are designed to get an honest explanation of why payment has not been made; but when he is met by evasions or stony silence, he has a definite plan of action and he follows it.

"LAUGHTER MAKES THE CHECK COME FASTER"

At the beginning of this chapter we spoke of the transformation in the collection letter from a routine announcement of payment due to clever and humorous "stunt" letters designed to entertain or amuse the reader into paying his bill. Such letters are strong on attention-arousing qualities and can be used effectively in collecting small payments like magazine subscriptions, membership dues, and similar accounts. They are usually substituted for the bills and reminders which make up the early stages of the collection series.

An almost infinite variety of devices, gadgets, and novelties is used by credit and collection correspondents to implement the basic message "please pay." While such stunt letters can be carried too far, their basic idea is sound—that attracting the debtor's attention is the first step to successful collection. Typical of the gadgets and stunts used effectively in recent years are the following:

A pin attached to the letter—"This is no ordinary pin. If used to attach your check to this letter, it will work magic for your credit standing."

Letters typed in red—"It will be a red-letter day for you when you complete this payment," or "Help us get your account out of the red."

String attached—"Put this string around your finger to remind you, etc."

Letter typed on left-hand side leaving right side blank for customer—"Won't you meet us halfway?"

A miniature letter and bill—"The enclosed bill is so small we don't
want to take up too much space calling it to your attention."

Blank check or stamp attached—"We want to make it easy for you
to pay your account."

Cartoon of a man examining contents of his waste paper basket—
"We've been looking all over for your check."

Fishhook attached—"Frankly we're fishing for your check."

Several bars of music printed across the page—"We've got the
blues about your account because we haven't had a note from
you."

Since the debtor on the receiving end of a series of collection
letters is all too likely to glance at them, recognize them for what
they are, and throw them away unread, such stunts overcome a
major obstacle. In the final analysis, however, reader reaction and
collection results are the ultimate criteria. And reader reaction can
sometimes be very unexpected, as the collection agent for a furniture store found out when he sent the following letter:

Dear Mr. Smith:

What will your neighbors think if we have to send our truck out to your
house to repossess that furniture on which you have not met your last
three payments?

Sincerely yours,

A week later Mr. Smith sent this answer:

Dear Sirs:

I have discussed the matter you wrote about with all of my neighbors and
every one of them thinks it would be a mean, low-down trick.

Yours truly,

Another collection man, after months of letters, turned an
account over to his young assistant, who brought him a check for
full payment ten days later along with his unusual letter: "Doggone it, why don't you send us a check?" On it, the debtor had

penciled a note, "Doggone it, here's your check!" The following letters show how originality, cleverness, and humor can be used in the collection letter to get results in the form of "here's your check:"

Dear Mr. Engel:

An effective collection letter should be:

1. Short
2. Courteous
3. Successful

This letter is short; we hope you think it's courteous. The rest is up to you.

Sincerely,

Dear Mr. Dowling:

Said Mark Twain: "Always do right. This will gratify some people—and astonish the rest."

We won't be astonished, but we'll certainly be gratified if you'll do right by your account for $87.12.

Yours truly,

Dear Mr. Eaton:

We've done our best to follow an old Chinese saying

"Man who wants pretty nurse must be patient."

Now . . . we've been pretty patient nursing your account along . . . and we'd like to see our patience rewarded.

Sincerely yours,

The City Club of Cleveland uses this to dust off delinquencies:

Dear Member:

Man is made of dust.

Dust settles.

Be a man!

Your Treasurer

Equally brief and effective are the following:

Dear Mr. Richardson:

> How do you do?
>
> Some pay when due.
>
> Some pay when overdue.
>
> Some never do.
>
> How do you do?
>
> Your balance is $. . . . . .
>
> > Very truly yours,

Say, Mr. Smith!

> Are you still running around with my check in your pocket?
>
> > Sincerely yours,

Anecdotes, such as the next letters employ, are useful when they are made relevant to the collection message:

Dear Mr. Baker:

We've just heard about a Vassar girl who had had several dates with a Yale senior and then heard nothing from him for four weeks.

"DEAD, DELAYED, OR DISINTERESTED?" she wired.

"HUNTING, FISHING, OR TRAPPING?" was his reply.

We hope that nothing like this has happened to you, but we do want you to know that we've been hunting and fishing for your past-due check for $37.19. And while we aren't setting any traps, we are making a date for April 22 when we'll expect your check or an explanation.

> Sincerely yours,

Dear Mr. Ellsworth:

We know of a dentist who couldn't collect from a model until he sent her this message:

"Unless the denture I made for you is paid for by November 1, I shall be forced to insert the following ad in the local paper:

'For sale—beautiful set of false teeth. Can be seen any time at the residence of Miss Joan Blank, 5 Park Street.' "

As you know, there are ways of putting teeth in a collection policy, but we'd prefer less drastic methods. May we have your check for $119.91?

Yours sincerely,

Dear Mr. Millet:

A shy secretary didn't want to tell her boss the reason for her resignation, so she asked her husband to explain. He sent the following note:

"My wife's reason for leaving will soon be apparent—and so will I."

It's just as apparent to us that there must be an explanation why we haven't heard from you. Won't you write and explain—or better still, send us your check for $23.49?

Sincerely,

Gentlemen:

I have a hobby—it is looking up word sources. One day I checked on the word "dun."

It comes originally from the Old English word *dunnen,* which means making a loud noise. Now some folks would call this a dunnen letter—but I assure you there's nothing explosive about it.

It's just as apparent to us that there must be an explanation why we ask is a fair effort on your part to meet this indebtedness, or a word of explanation.

Yours truly,

Widely used, but still getting results, is this brief letter concluding the collection series:

Gentlemen:

Will you please send us the name of a good lawyer in your community? We may have to sue you.

Sincerely,

One small-town merchant got quick results from this brief message to a delinquent account:

Dear Mr. Albrecht:

If you don't pay me the $61.37 you owe, I'll tell all your other creditors that you did.

                              Very truly yours,

   That such letters as these are effective is due to their originality and sense of humor. Nevertheless, the writer of collection letters should not lose sight of the fact that his job is not entertainment but the collection of money. Where amusement gets results, it should be used. But in the general work of collection, there is no substitute for the basic principle which lies behind all collection series—that *the best way to collect money is constantly to keep after delinquent accounts with a gradually increasing insistence culminating in action.* Perhaps this insistence may result in a reply such as the following received by a Georgia firm in answer to a long series of collection letters:

Dear Sir:

Here is your money and you won't be one bit gladder to git it than I am to send it. Please don't send me no receipt for I don't want to hear from you no more.

                              Yours truly,

But at least the debt *was* collected.

                         E X E R C I S E S

   1. Revise the following collection letters:

   a. Dear Sir:

      Your account shows a balance due of $87.27 for oil purchased during February and March.

      We wish you would pay this promptly because this is the time of year when we must settle our accounts with the oil distributors and we need every cent we can lay our hands on.

      We should therefore appreciate your prompt payment.

                              Sincerely yours,

   b. Dear Mr. Jones:

      We are getting very tired of sending you bills and collection letters for the $42.37 you have owed us for three months.

Our expenses in running a garage are heavy, and we cannot afford to spend a couple of dollars on stamps and stationery to collect small accounts like yours. Why don't you send us a check and save us additional expense?

Awaiting your remittance, we remain,

Yours truly,

c. Gentlemen:

We cannot understand the attitude of your company regarding your past-due account of $312.26 for radio supplies.

How would you like it if we had taken three months to deliver these supplies? Well, you have made us wait three months for our money, and we don't have it yet.

If you think that you can remain in business long without paying your bills, you have an unpleasant surprise coming to you.

Very truly yours,

d. Gentlemen:

We should appreciate very much your sending us your check for $61.25 to cover your past-due account.

We confess that we have done everything possible to collect this amount during the past three and a half months and that we are puzzled as to just what we should do next. Perhaps we should turn your account over to our attorney for collection, but we dislike taking such drastic action.

Won't you help us solve this dilemma by sending in your remittance as soon as possible?

Sincerely yours,

2. Draw up suitable form letters for the first two stages of a collection series based upon the assumptions that the customer wishes to be reminded that payment is due and that he has simply forgotten to pay.

3. Mr. James Sorrell, 619 College Avenue, Durham, North Carolina, owes you $319.27 for furniture purchased on March 1. You have sent him statements on April 1 and May 1, a reminder on June 1, and a suggestion on June 15 that his failure to pay is an oversight. Assuming that Mr. Sorrell is a fair risk, write the letter which you might appropriately send on July 1.

4. Write the final letter of your collection series to be sent when none of the earlier letters has elicited a response from delinquent accounts.

5. Write the last three letters of a collection series which might be used by a department store engaged entirely in retail trade.

6. All of your statements, reminders, offers of adjustment and similar

letters have brought no response from Mr. Ezekiel Deyo, 312 South Park Street, Pittsfield, Massachusetts, who owes you a balance of $210 for an oil-burning furnace. Write Mr. Deyo the next to the last of your series of collection letters for this account which is now five months overdue.

7. Write a collection letter using one of the following as the opening paragraph:

    a. The Chinese certainly deserve credit! Every year, just before New Year's Day, they pay a visit to all their creditors to square up their bills so as to start the new year with a clean slate.

    b. We heard of the president of a tiny railroad who sent a pass to the president of one of our largest railroads with the request that the favor be returned. When his request was refused, he wrote, "My railroad may not be as long as yours, but it's just as broad." Our credit arrangements with you are as broad as they are long.

    c. A credit manager's job is no bed of roses. From the time he accepts an order until the time payment is due, he keeps wondering what percentage of his accounts will be paid on time.

    d. "Give him credit for what he's done"—those are the words in which we pay tribute to past performance. And when we gave *you* credit, we were doing exactly that.

    e. What would *you* think if we had been four months late in delivering those suits you needed so badly in April?

8. Write an appropriate collection letter to an alumnus who borrowed $600 from the school's loan fund while he was in school. Up until the time of his graduation, there was no interest charge on this amount. After graduation, the interest is computed at five per cent a year; in this instance, the total amount now due is $630.

9. As class chairman for the fund drive for the new Alumni Memorial Building, it is necessary for you to write to 30 of your classmates who have not paid their pledges made during the campaign. Write an appropriate letter, using the fact that the fund drive ends in one month as the occasion for writing. If these 30 make their contributions, your class will have 100 per cent of its membership contributing and, in all probability, will top the record for all classes.

10. As business manager for a correspondence school, write a letter to a student who signed up for a course in Electronics and made his first payment of 25 per cent of the cost. When he did not make his second payment of $15, you cut off the instruction. Write to collect the amount due and attempt to induce him to complete the course.

11. Which of the following collection letters is more effective? Give reasons.

    a. Dear Mr. Barton:

        I know that it has long been the custom for collection men to pretend that bills aren't paid because they have been "overlooked" or that the customer needs to be "reminded."

In this instance, I'm going to come right out and say that I think the reason you ignored our last letter and the previous statements is that you didn't have the money at that time. Am I wrong in this assumption?

If the situation were reversed and we owed you money, I know that you would certainly expect at least a reply from us. I am, therefore, appealing to your sense of fair play in asking you to send us a check for $69.76 to settle your account. Were the situation reversed, you would expect the same consideration from us.

We are awaiting your remittance in the envelope enclosed for your convenience.

Very truly yours,

b. Dear Sir:

Surely you knew when you ordered automotive parts from us that you must some day pay for them.

That day is here. We have given you every consideration in this matter, and in return, we have not even had a reply from you. You seem willing to ignore the fact that your credit reputation is at stake. By doing so, you jeopardize your whole future.

Won't you, therefore, relieve us of the unpleasantness of taking necessary action by sending us your check for $117.69 without delay?

Yours very truly,

12. As a class project, interview several businessmen to find out their policy of collection. Write to three or more concerns for a complete series of collection letters which they use. Analyze these letters in class to show the basic techniques, the varying degrees of insistence, and the methods by which they attempt to get a reply from the debtor.

Anything that can be sold, can be sold by mail.
John Howie Wright,
a pioneer in direct-mail advertising

CHAPTER X

Sales Letters

The discussion of the merits of the letter as a sales medium
compared with magazine, newspaper, or radio advertising has
been going on for many years. Advocates of the sales letter insist
that anything can be sold by mail. On the other hand, advertising
managers for magazines present evidence that their rates are as
low as a fraction of a cent per reader, whereas a sales letter that
costs less than ten cents must be cheaply produced and dis-
tributed in huge numbers.

Though the controversy over the advantages of various forms
of advertising scarcely comes within the province of this book,
the significant fact to those interested in business correspondence
is that American firms annually send out billions of sales letters
which justify the expense of their production. An excellent analysis of direct mail in the February, 1953, issue of *Fortune,* titled
"The Postman Rings for Sales," points out that direct mail is one
of the fastest growing advertising media and that the 1.2 billion
dollars spent on it in 1952 paid for enough mail to supply every
family in the United States with more than 300 letters a year.
Anyone within reach of the United States Post Office can name
several concerns whose business has been built up entirely
through mail advertising. Of course, ample evidence is also available to show the efficacy of the magazine, newspaper, television,
or radio in building sales. But since we are concerned only with
correspondence, the questions that should interest us are: why
is the sales letter so widely used? and when is it most effective?

The chief reason for the extensive use of the sales letter is that
it is the most selective of all advertising media. It can reach any
age group, financial class, profession, geographical area, or occu-

pation that may be interested in a given product or service. The sales letter may, therefore, be regarded as the least expensive form of advertising *per potential customer,* for if the list of prospects is carefully selected, little or no money need be spent on uninterested readers. A second advantage is that the reader of the sales letter has no other items competing for his immediate attention as does the magazine reader, for instance, who has before him on two pages several advertisements, or pictures, or a story. In addition, by its very nature the letter is a more personal kind of message than any other form of advertising. Finally, sales correspondence will carry a larger percentage of advertising than any other form; it can concentrate on material bearing directly on the product or service being sold without wasting time or space on irrelevant entertainment or pictures.

All these advantages must, however, be thought of in terms of specific products or merchandise. For example, it is abundantly evident that manufacturers of toothpastes, groceries, tires, spark plugs, cameras and films, drugs, and tobaccos use magazine, newspaper, television, or radio advertising in preference to sales letters. Why? Because these and similar products are used or needed by almost everybody, and hence, the media which reach the greatest numbers are employed. This fact answers our question as to when the sales letter may be used most effectively. Generally speaking, it is best adapted to selling products or services of specialized appeal, of a rather expensive type, or those belonging within the class of "novelties." For such products or services, the sales letter may be compared to the rifle which picks out one potential buyer from many uninterested ones, instead of to the shotgun which scatters its fire indiscriminately. The question before the advertiser is not whether "the rifle" or "the shotgun" is more efficient in any abstract sense; rather, he must determine which "weapon" he can use best in a specific situation.

In the last analysis, three fundamental factors affect the degree of success in selling by mail:

1. The product or service which is being sold
2. The prospect or list of prospects to which the material is sent
3. The sales letter itself

When the product or service is attractive, the list of prospects is carefully selected, and the sales letter is effectively written, direct-mail selling is a highly profitable medium. Progressive business-men, recognizing its flexibility and selectivity, use the sales letter for the following purposes:

1. To make direct sales
2. To obtain inquiries about services and products and to locate leads for salesmen
3. To announce and test the reaction to new services and products
4. To reach out-of-the-way prospects and to build up weak ter-ritories
5. To reinforce dealers' sales efforts and to secure new dealers
6. To build good will

THE STRUCTURE OF THE SALES LETTER

So basic is the structure of the sales letter that it can be used for almost any letter in which an attempt is made to gain agree-ment or favorable action by the reader. To make anyone act or think as we want him to, we must first gain his attention, next create a desire for the product we sell, then convince him of the truth of what we are saying, and finally make it easy for him to act. The structure of the sales letter is designed to arouse these reactions in the reader. Its parts are arranged to:

1. Attract the reader's attention
2. Create a desire for the product or service
3. Convince the reader that the product or service is the best of its kind
4. Motivate action

Frequently, the individual sales letter devotes a paragraph to each of these functions, which for brevity we shall call attention, desire, conviction, and action; in a series of sales letters, one or more of the letters may be devoted to each of them. But whether a single letter or a long series is used, the basic structure remains the same.

One of the best methods by which the novice can learn the fundamentals of sales-letter structure is through an analysis of printed advertising to see in detail how advertising experts ac-complish these four tasks. A careful reading of the advertisements in any magazine will show that the underlying structure is always the same although the details may vary considerably. For example, attention is attracted by pictures, catch phrases in large type, questions, commands, or humorous illustrations; desire is aroused by describing the pleasure, profit, or economy of the product or service offered; conviction is attained by use of statistics, testimonials, samples, tests, guarantees, and similar devices; action is made easy by suggestions such as "Send for this interesting booklet" or "Fill in the coupon below for added savings in your fuel costs" or "Go to your neighborhood druggist's today." The next few pages of this text are designed to suggest various methods of attaining the four objectives of the sales letter.

1. Attracting Attention in the Sales Letter

Because of the vast number of sales letters mailed annually, Americans are developing a rather heavy armor of sales resistance to the honeyed words and unique offers of the letter writers. To exaggerate this resistance would be pointless; yet there is little doubt that this attitude on the part of the public results in a great many sales messages being tossed aside unread. Most human beings are, however, interested in their mail and will certainly glance at a letter to see what it is about. Thus, the sales letter usually goes to a reader who has a general attitude of skepticism toward sales letters but a slight interest in the one immediately before him. The writer of the sales letter can count on this initial interest; to capitalize on it, he must make his opening paragraph attract sufficient attention to carry the reader through the rest of the letter. If the opening paragraph fails to arouse interest, the whole sales letter fails. What devices may be used to attract the reader's attention?

One method employed successfully in numerous sales letters is *a pertinent question* which has the virtue of being direct and of arousing the reader's curiosity to read further in order to discover the answer. Notice how the following questions develop a desire to read on:

Do you pick your financing plan as carefully as you pick your car?

Could you ask your boss for a raise today and get it?

Were you born in July?

Did you sleep well the last time you were in New York?

Are you satisfied with the amount of money you save?

You know about "twiggers," don't you?

Do you have to pump a clutch in your present car?

How many times have you wished that you could find time to read the best sellers that all your friends are discussing?

How about a different vacation this year? Could you enjoy two weeks of riding through sun-dappled forests, splashing through cool gurgling streams, or just sitting among blue mountains?

A courteous command is another technique used frequently to open sales correspondence.

Don't waste your time and energy in a sweltering office when you can enjoy the cool comfort of air conditioning!

To invite Romance, be yourself! So say Hollywood beauty experts.

For your family's sake, don't drive on tires that are worn smooth!

Don't read this if you have all your labor troubles solved!

A "split" beginning arranged in such a way as to attract maximum attention is widely used. The chief drawback to such an opening is that it gives the reader a feeling of being tricked or let down as in the famous sales letter that begins "Would you like to save a million dollars? Then you'd better open a mint. But we can save you $3.27!" The following illustrate the "split" beginning:

ARREST—
declining income! Our financial service is designed to do just that.

Millions of people enjoy gum—
but not in their carburetors.
(Letter with stick of gum attached to sell a carburetor cleaner.)

We can't make all the roofing in the world—
so we just make the best of it!

They canceled their order . . .
and we liked it.
(The letter goes on to explain that the original order was canceled and replaced by an order for twice as much.)

Don't spend a nickel on flourescent lighting—
unless you can answer "Yes" to these four questions.

A statement of a significant fact or *a quotation from an eminent authority or prominent individual* will arouse interest if the fact is significant or the authority is known to the reader:

You can judge a company by the customers it keeps. Forty-nine per cent of our customers have "kept company" with us for more than fifteen years.

Again, as in 16 previous years, Champion Spark Plugs equipped the winning car in this year's Indianapolis 500-mile race.

One out of three has it!

Did you know that one out of every three electric water coolers sold is a G.E.?

Napoleon's $2,500 began a million-dollar business.

In 1795, hard pressed to feed his armies far from home, Napoleon offered 12,000 francs (about $2,500) to anyone who could invent a process for preserving foods. Years later, this sum was awarded to Nicolas Appert, who developed a method of sterilizing foods and sealing them hermetically. (Sales message for Dextrose as a preservative in the canning industry.)

Surveys show that the average executive increased his work capacity an hour a day by dictating his data, correspondence, and details to an Edison Voicewriter.

Acousti-Celotex sound-conditioning can increase employee efficiency as much as 10 per cent.

Anecdotes are used almost too frequently as attention-arousing devices in sales letters. To tell a story simply for the sake of the story is one way to entertain the reader, but it does not help sales if it diverts attention from the main object of the sales letter. To be effective, the story should not only entertain but have some connection with the sales message. Your reader may be an ardent golfer, and an anecdote about golf may well arouse his attention. But if the rest of your letter is intended to sell electric fans or bolts and nuts, it is better to avoid such an unrelated opening.

No other phase of letter writing offers more room for originality than the *devices and stunts* used in sales letters to attract attention. Common is the technique of enclosing checks for the reader's time, stamps, keys, pencils, cigarettes, samples of products, and strange contraptions designed to arouse his curiosity. Sales letters are printed on all shades and all shapes of stationery from "the red-hot offer" on bright red stationery to "the circular letter" on a round sheet of paper. These enclosures and unusual-looking letters are expensive to produce; whether they pay for themselves in terms of added business should be the criterion in deciding whether to use them. The sales letter must, as we have said, attract attention, but if the reader is merely interested in a tricky device or clever opening which does not carry him along into the remainder of the sales message, the correspondent has failed as badly as if his opening aroused no interest at all. To the sales correspondent, the attention-arousing device is a means to an end rather than an end in itself.

2. Creating Desire for the Product or Service

People can be made to desire things by two basic appeals—the appeal to emotions and the appeal to reason. Perhaps it is an unflattering commentary on mankind's rational power, but a glance through the advertising in most magazines will show how much more widely the emotional appeal is used than any other form. Refrigerators, oils, automobiles, spark plugs, and similar workaday products are sold through advertisements that depict pretty girls, humorous situations, or play on our desire to "keep up with the Joneses" or the Hollywood stars. These are frequently attention-arousing techniques, but often we are made to want some product not on its merits alone but through such emotional appeals as, "Mrs. van Astorbilt of Newport, New York, and Palm Beach uses our product exclusively," or through the threat of fear as, "Your best friends won't tell you when you offend," or by descriptions heavy-laden with adjectives to appeal to our aesthetic sense.

Although the sales correspondent usually cannot use the lavish illustrations or slick copy of the printed advertisement, he has the same alternatives: whether to appeal to the reader's logic by expository and by argumentative methods or to his emotions by descriptive technique. For instance, if he is sales correspondent for an air-conditioning company, his choice might be between a description of "the cool, clean air like a mountain breeze, free of pollen and dust" or an exposition of the way the apparatus works. The deciding factor in this instance would be the type of reader; if the letter is sent to dealers, it will use a logical appeal with emphasis on profits, construction of the equipment, and exposition of its mechanism; if it is written to the general public, it will probably concentrate on the joys of air-conditioned homes or offices. The choice of the appeal is often governed by the type of product to be sold. Although there are numerous exceptions, it is generally true that the logical appeal is best for necessities, the emotional best for luxuries or novelties.

Certain human desires are rather universal, and appeals directed to these fundamental interests will reach the greatest number of readers. The Direct Mail Advertising Association lists the following 25 reasons why people spend money:

To make money	To gratify curiosity
To save money	To protect family
To save time	To be in style
To avoid effort	For beautiful possessions
For comfort	To satisfy appetite
For cleanliness˙	To emulate others
For health	For safety in buying
To escape physical pain	To avoid criticism
For praise	To be individual
To be popular	To protect reputation
To attract the opposite sex	To take advantage of
To conserve possessions	opportunities
For enjoyment	To avoid trouble

By slanting his appeal to one or more of these motives, the sales correspondent can effectively use the you attitude to produce sales. The following excerpts from sales letters show how this is done:

You want to keep intelligently informed about the rapidly changing world in which we live. You want to be able to talk confidently about national affairs and foreign affairs, about what is being invented, voted, written, painted, about what is being discovered in medicine and science. You want the news fully, concisely.

In the winter months ahead, with Chamberlin Insulation, every room in your house will be comfortable. This comfort can be achieved regardless of outside temperature or wind direction, and can save you, at a conservative estimate, 20 to 25 per cent in fuel.

We have a book that you will want; your secretary will want it; your mailing department will wonder why they couldn't have had it long ago. It is a concise encyclopedia of authoritative postal knowledge compiled with the cooperation of the Postmaster General.

Wouldn't you like to have the most successful collection men in the country explain their methods to you, show you the actual letters they use, and tell you how economically they have solved their collection problems?

Install a cooler for Coca-Cola and it will make money and friends for you. For wherever people gather, they drink Coca-Cola—and we have coolers to fit every location.

At sunset, the haze over the Catskills is a soft purple. You remember, of course, how much you enjoyed vacationing here in Rip Van Winkle Land last year—and it's just as peaceful and lovely this year.

3. Convincing the Reader of the Merits of the Product or Service

Thus far, our analysis has revealed the technique of the sales letter to be chiefly descriptive, expository, or narrative. The function of the third section is to marshal support to show that the claims made for the product are true. This is the technique of argument, which may be defined as *the art of influencing others to accept our beliefs by an appeal to their reason.* Previous claims and statements must here be supported by fact or logic; otherwise, the reader will correctly assume that the claims are grandiose and the statements untrue. In general, three types of logical support may be used in sales; they are:

a. Expert Testimony. This consists of statements by qualified experts concerning the product sold. Through the widespread use of testimonials from people in no way qualified to speak about various products, the average reader has become rather skeptical of this sort of support. But if the person quoted is really qualified by education or experience to speak about the product, his endorsement constitutes a very sound sales argument.

b. Facts. Since the statements in the first part of the sales letter belong in the category of opinion (*i.e.,* "The Colderator is the most economical refrigerator on the market today"), their truth is best shown in the third section by a solid basis of fact. Tests made by independent experts, statements made on the number of sales made within a specified period, actual cost of operation of the product, mention of the number of satisfied customers, and specific data about the product under actual working conditions —all these give an objective, factual support to the claims made for the product.

c. The Use of Logic. Since our logical faculty uses both facts and expert testimony on which to base its conclusions, this final division is somewhat arbitrary. In the sales letter, however, logic may be used to appeal favorably to the reader's reasoning or to get him to draw his own conclusions. A trial offer of the product may be made with the purpose of getting the reader to conclude, "If they are willing to let me try it out, it must be pretty good." Samples and guarantees are similarly effective. A correspondence school may use analogy to show that a student has taken a given course and has gone on to great success. The conclusion, "What he has done, you can do!" is inaccurate logic, but it seems to create sales. Widely used are causal relationships, such as "Because Pan-American coffee is packed in air-tight tins, it reaches you as fresh as the day it was roasted."

Whichever of these three types of logical support he employs, the sales correspondent should make sure that his statements do rest on a solid foundation and that his conclusions are logical. The following examples show specific applications of how these methods may be used to win conviction:

Sixty years is a long time isn't it? And that's how long we've been serving companies like yours with the technical skill that comes only from experience.

Just to substantiate these statements, I am enclosing a circular which contains the names of over a thousand graduates of our secretarial course who have voluntarily reported salary increases within the past year. Perhaps you may know, or know of, some of these people. Their record shows in dollars and cents the value of the Blank Secretarial Course.

Over 6,000 installations are proving daily that Produc-Trol opens the door to a quick, easy, accurate, efficient, and economical system of complete control.

Our company has paid off its insurance claims through four wars and a half-dozen depressions. Our eighty years' experience is your guarantee that your policy is secure in spite of unsettled conditions.

Tests conducted by the Independent Testing Laboratory of Providence show that this new fabric will wear longer and retain its color and shape after more washings than any other fabric this famous research organization has ever tested.

Our money-back guarantee is your assurance that this fan will meet your expectations in every respect. If you are not completely satisfied, you may return it and get your money back.

4. Motivating Action

The final paragraph of the sales letter should do two things: offer a specific suggestion concerning the action the reader should take, and point out how he will benefit by taking this action. The easier it is for the reader to take this action, the more effective the sales message will be; hence, stamped and addressed envelopes or the more economical business-reply permit envelopes, which do not require the payment of postage unless used, are frequently enclosed, or the reader is told to call by telephone or to wire collect. Whether these devices are economically feasible depends largely upon the product being sold. But the most inexpensive sales letter must perform these functions; otherwise, the sales correspondent has failed in what is the acid test for his letter —how many of his readers do take the suggested course of action? The following closing paragraphs show various methods to motivate action:

You have nothing to lose—and perhaps much to gain—by using the enclosed card.

Which models would you like to see on approval? Just check them on our order blank.

Won't you use the enclosed card to tell us when our representative may call at your convenience and with absolutely no obligation to you?

The enclosed card requires only your signature to bring you 52 issues full of entertainment, information, and enjoyment.

Wouldn't you like to see the way this new machine might aid you to reduce overhead? Just sign and mail this post card for a demonstration.

The coupon below will bring you a copy—without obligation. Won't you sign and mail it *today?*

Take a moment *right now* to check the items that interest you. We'll gladly send you a sample of each.

Your subscription expires with the next issue. Act now! Sign the enclosed blank and you won't miss a single issue.

Send for this booklet today. Just use the coupon we are enclosing.

You'll find our new savings plan intensely interesting. JUST FILL IN THE ENCLOSED CARD for our interesting booklet. No salesman will call.

THE SALES SERIES

Like collection letters, sales messages frequently come in series, which are known as "the wear-out" series, designed by constant repetition to wear out the reader's sales resistance. Such series are usually employed to sell costly products, since inexpensive items cannot bear the cost of a whole series of sales letters. The general technique used in such series is the same as that of the individual sales letter, but its effect is intensified because the sales series can go into greater detail. The number of letters to be included in the series cannot be dogmatically stated; often three or four follow-up letters after the original message will suffice. Other series, such as those to dealers, are never-ending. The value of the sales series lies in constantly keeping after the prospective customer.

The individual letters forming the sales series should be kept as brief as possible without sacrificing completeness. One of the most effective sales series sent out within recent years is the following group of one-sentence letters dispatched at intervals of a few days by the Schonberg Printing Company, Cleveland.

Dear Mr. Brown:

I do good printing.

> Sincerely yours,
>
> *Dave Schonberg*
>
> Dave Schonberg

Dear Mr. Brown:

I deliver good printing on time.

> Sincerely yours,
>
> *Dave Schonberg*
>
> Dave Schonberg

Dear Mr. Brown:

I don't charge much.

> Sincerely yours,
>
> *Dave Schonberg*
>
> Dave Schonberg

Dear Mr. Brown:

I said I don't charge much for good printing delivered on time.

Sincerely yours,

Dave Schonberg

Dave Schonberg

EXAMPLES OF GOOD SALES LETTERS

The following sales letters show the various ways in which devices to stimulate attention, desire, conviction, and action can be incorporated into a unified and coherent message. Try to decide which human desire they are intended to appeal to and judge their effectiveness in terms of how well they motivate action by the reader:

Dear Mr. and Mrs. Gray:

When you read the enclosed folder, you will find why I am sending it to you. As parents, you are deeply interested in the education of your children.

Therefore, I wanted to get some definite figures for you on the *value* of education. Statistics show that, on the average, college graduates may expect to earn about 40 per cent more than high-school graduates and about three times as much as those who quit school in the grades.

And, of course, there are a great many more benefits from a college education than the direct money value. That's why you will want to read the enclosed folder, "A College Education for *Your* Children." It will tell you how one of our insurance policies may play a part in your education program as a parent.

Then, if you have any question, the enclosed card will bring one of our representatives to show you how to plan now to give your children the benefits of a college education.

Sincerely yours,

Dear Mr. Cole:

Someone has said that "brevity is the art of speaking volumes without writing them" . . . and so we'll be brief.

We've been in business for 23 years . . .
    . . . supplying commercial photographs
    . . . to more than 30,000 customers

. . . for catalogues, house organs, sales brochures,
and presentations of all kinds.

May we discuss your photo problems with you? There's no obligation.
Just mail the enclosed card and I'll call at your convenience.

Sincerely yours,

Dear Mr. White:

Suppose that you had $5,000 in $100 bills in an old envelope.

Before you went to bed you tossed the envelope into the top drawer of
your dresser. This morning when you went to work you forgot it.

When you finally thought of it, you were unable to return home and re-
cover it—and no one at home answered your frantic phone calls! All day
long the $5,000 must stay in the envelope in the top drawer of your dresser.

How you would worry! The house might burn down. Someone might throw
the old envelope into the trash barrel. A thief might break in. The children
might get at it. You would have no peace of mind until that envelope was
in your safety deposit box.

Do you realize that you have a fortune of many times $5,000—not in an
old envelope—but wrapped up in you? It is your earning power! It is ex-
posed to far greater hazards and risks of daily loss than that money at
home. That fortune—your life itself—is the most precious thing in the
world to yourself and your family. It should be well guarded!

There are only two ways to realize fully your potential life value. One is to
be sure of living your allotted threescore-and-ten. I would like to discuss
the other way with you within the next few days.

May I have a brief interview when I call?

Yours truly,

Dear Mr. Ellender:

Sincerely yours,

P.S. We have an idea that's too good for words. May we stop in and tell
you about it at your convenience?

Dear Mr. and Mrs. Jones:

What's the word you associate with "kitchen?" If you're like most Americans, it's "work."

Now you can eliminate most of the work and make your kitchen the most attractive room in your home by installing modern equipment in a kitchen tailored to your individual needs—and at a surprisingly low cost to you.

My job as a contractor specializing in kitchen installations is to help you select the equipment you need, design it for the greatest efficiency, and follow your wishes in color and location.

You can have your choice of cabinets by Youngstown, Geneva, or Wood-metal, dishwashers by Hotpoint or Hobart, disposers by Waste King—and my experience with dozens of installations in the Heights area will be at your service in choosing what best suits your needs. Since I personally supervise all the work of my staff, I can guarantee that your modern kitchen will be efficient, economical, and attractive.

By modernizing your present kitchen, you are making a permanent investment with no maintenance costs—an investment which will increase the resale value of your home. And you are also making an investment which will save time and work for many years to come.

I would be pleased to show you any of the installations I have made and to have you talk with my customers who know the conscientious service I give.

May I submit a design and estimate for your kitchen without cost or obligation on your part? I'd like to call for an appointment within the next few days to tell you about the joys of having no dishes to wash, no garbage to be collected, and no weary miles to walk in your kitchen.

Sincerely yours,

Dear Mr. Zentgraf:

"Sculpture is very easy," said a famous sculptor. "All you do is take a block of marble and chisel off all the stone you don't want."

That's a good description of the way we can serve you as management consultants. For fifteen years, we've been aiding industry by cutting off the inefficiency and red tape that management doesn't want.

The enclosed brochure describes the many ways we can serve you—from expert time and motion studies to personnel evaluation plans. You'll be interested in the comments from our clients on pages 24–26.

Your signature on the enclosed card is all that's needed for you to arrange an interview at your convenience and, of course, at no obligation.

Sincerely yours,

Dear Bashful Customer:

You've
Earned

10¢	Is it worth 10 cents a line to you to read this letter?
20¢	We'll gladly pay that amount—but only if you read
30¢	the entire letter. We are so sure you will that we
40¢	have enclosed our check for $2.50 in full payment!
50¢	Now, we reason this way: you really are a valued
60¢	customer. But lately you haven't been in even to say
70¢	"Howdy." We want you to come back—want to see you
80¢	often—want you to reopen your account. It is better
90¢	for us to have a dependable old customer on our books than
$1.00	an unknown new one, and, as it would cost us all of $2.50 to
$1.10	open a new account, we would rather pass this amount on to you.
$1.20	So we say, "Here is a $2.50 check on the house." Come in
$1.30	and select anything you wish, to the value of $25.00 or more
$1.40	from our extensive stocks of nationally advertised clothing
$1.50	and shoes for the entire family—or do your early gift
$1.60	shopping for such things as diamonds, watches, silverware,
$1.70	radios. Pay NOT ONE CENT down. Your check is worth
$1.80	$2.50 off the total of your purchases of $25.00 or more.
$1.90	We are passing this amount on to you as a saving—
$2.00	and it will come in mighty handy just now, won't it?
$2.10	YOU BET IT WILL!
$2.20	DID YOU SAY, "I'LL BE IN TOMORROW"?
$2.30	Cordially yours,
$2.40	Bill Henry
$2.50	Henry's Store

Dear Mr. Myers:

Early this morning the white mists were lifting their curtains to reveal the blue-green Catskills in the distance.

Your summer home is at its loveliest now. Haven't you longed for those blueberries that line the winding paths around the hotel? Or for that view of the soft haze around High Point? Your four weeks at the Mountain View last summer must hold a cherished place in your memory.

Why not store up more memories to gladden your future? You'll go back to work more fit, more efficient, if you get away from it all for a while.

Mountain View offers you the same rates as last year, and if you want us to, we'll reserve the same room. Why not wire your reservation to us today?

Sincerely yours,

EXERCISES

1. Write a sales letter which would be effective in getting new subscribers to your favorite magazine.

2. You are offering a new correspondence service to businessmen, designed to sell for $5 a month or $50 a year. It will include specific suggestions for improving letters, examples of the best letters of the previous months, and actual correction of letters submitted. To get new subscribers to this service, you are sending out a sales letter offering a three-months subscription for $10. Write the letter.

3. Use a magazine advertisement for a novelty or an expensive product as the source for the facts to be used in a sales letter on the same product.

4. You are sending a sales letter *to housewives* for a new automatic oil-burning heater. Construct a letter which would appeal to this group.

5. Write a letter which a business school might use to get applicants for a secretarial course.

6. As proprietor of the Beaver Dam Club, Vernorville, New York, you are writing a sales letter to prospective guests. Your club is located in the beautiful Catskill Mountains only 90 miles from New York City, and it offers all kinds of sports as well as the opportunity for rest. Compose a letter that might appropriately be sent to professional men in New York City.

7. You are sales manager for a department store which sells only on a cash basis and passes on to customers the savings effected by the elimination of all the details of credit and collection. Your slogan is "No one owes a cent to Blank's." Write an appropriate letter to be sent on the first of the month with this slogan as its opening words and stress the fact that your customers save 6 per cent through this policy of cash buying.

8. Criticize any errors in the following sales letter designed to sell dealers space in a buyers' guide and convention:

Gentlemen:

We are not only disappointed but greatly concerned over our failure to receive your order for an advertisement in this year's Buyer's Guide.

We have sent you three letters to date, but it really appears as if they have not reached you, although they have not been returned to us.

Our coming convention and display of products at the Hotel Green, March 25–27, has been publicized since last November among our 1,100 members of the Sheet Metal Association. Your customers in this association will certainly be surprised at your failure to take space in either our Buyer's Guide or at the convention.

Our guide goes to press on February 15. If we don't hear from you before Febuary 10, we shall be forced to conclude that you aren't interested.

Sincerely yours,

9. Write a sales letter to members of the incoming students at your school telling them that you have been appointed the campus agent for Acme Portable Typewriters. Among other advantages of your product, stress the fact that it may be obtained with mathematical symbols on the keyboard and that this will be most useful in the two years of mathematics required at your school.

10. Write a letter to go to the mailing list of your local photographic society offering your new exposure meter on a 10-day trial basis. Your meter costs $5 less than other exposure meters and is guaranteed for five years against defective workmanship or materials.

11. As junior member of the sales force of the Superior Insulating Corporation, you have been assigned a small village of 3,500 inhabitants as a trial territory. Write an advance sales letter to the property owners in the village announcing the opening of your office in June and pointing out that if insulation is installed during the summer months, you can offer a 10 per cent discount.

12. Write a sales letter for a product using facts and slogans taken from advertisements in an issue of a widely circulated magazine.

13. You and two other graduates of your school have just organized the Complete Business Writing Service. Your service will prepare letters, reports, charts, booklets for any kind of business. Write a sales letter to be sent to a selected list of executives.

14. You have been appointed campus agent for the Collegiate Sportcoat Company which specializes in sport coats with college, fraternity, or other appropriate insignia sewed on the pocket. The coats are well tailored, of excellent quality material, and are available in green, brown, or tan. The price for a single coat is $25, but for orders of more than 10 with the same insignia, the price is $22. Write a sales letter to the leaders of the various organizations in your school to get a minimum order of 10 coats from each group.

15. Rewrite the following sales letter:

Dear Mrs. Cole:

You are probably aware that we have purchased a large number of surplus army and navy items. Right now we have on hand thousands of all-wool blankets of the same fine quality used by the navy during the war.

These blankets are brand-new and could not be duplicated for less than $15.00 in today's market. Because of our vast buying power, we are able to offer these blankets at the remarkable price of $10.95 each. They simply must be seen to be appreciated; each blanket has "U. S. Navy" stamped on it, showing they are genuine.

We must dispose of this merchandise before July 1, when we move to a new location. Hurry down and get one while they last, or, if you prefer, mail your check with the enclosed order blank and the blanket will be delivered to your home. Act now while the supply lasts.

Sincerely yours,

16. Write a sales letter for Photo Service which specializes in taking pictures of children in their homes. The charge is $10 for six 8 by 10 inch pictures to be selected from three different proofs. Use as the occasion for the letter the fact that Father's Day is one month from the date of the mailing.

17. Choose a product or service which you have used for some time and write a sales letter for it.

18. Select an advertisement which achieves conviction through the use of samples, trial offers, statistics, or testimonials, and write a sales letter based upon the advertising material.

19. Your community forum has arranged three six-week courses, meeting two hours each week, on Better Speaking, Great Books of Today, and Painting for Fun. This is a nonprofit community project; the $5 fee for each course will pay for the lecturers. As secretary for the group, write a letter that might be sent to a selected list of 250 people.

20. Write the rest of the sales letters for which these are the first paragraphs:

  a. You are driving down the road at 55 miles an hour when suddenly—Bang! Your front tire blows out. You'll wish then that you had our new blowout-proof tires.

  b. For your reading pleasure, we've just published a new *Omnibus for Mystery Fans* with 1,200 pages by the world's greatest writers of mystery and detective fiction.

  c. Now that you've bought that lovely new home, you are going to become interested in the shrubbery, the lawn, and the landscaping that form its setting. For 25 years we have been aiding home owners in this community with just such problems.

  d. Ever forget an appointment?
  You *can't* with the new Blank Memopad on your desk!

CHAPTER XI

The Application Letter

No letter the individual may write has greater potential for affecting his entire life than the letter of application. Despite this importance, few applicants have a clear conception of the conditions their letters face and of their function. And while the ups and downs of the business cycle directly affect the possibilities of employment, it is important for every individual to possess the ability to write an effective letter of application as part of his kit of tools. He may never have to use it, but this ability is excellent insurance against stormy economic weather and as a means of improving one's position.

Only the good letter can survive the competition for jobs even in prosperous times. Normally, a help-wanted advertisement in an urban newspaper for a position with a moderate salary will bring hundreds of letters in response. The advertiser can hardly be expected to read all of these carefully. His technique can be imagined—a glance through all the letters, a small pile of perhaps ten or twenty kept on his desk, the others tossed into his wastepaper basket. Then he reads the ten or twenty good letters carefully and selects five or ten whose writers will be interviewed.

For the job seeker who can write a good letter of application, the one hopeful fact in a situation like the one just described is that so few letters out of the hundreds received will really be effective. Hence, the odds affecting the chances of a good letter are not one out of, let us say, five hundred applicants but actually one out of ten or twenty good letters.

All of this discussion is, of course, based upon the assumption that the job seekers possess the essential qualifications to fill the position for which they apply. It should not be necessary to say that even the best letter will not get a job for an unqualified applicant; yet a surprisingly large number of persons seem to believe that by a lucky break they can get jobs for which they are not trained. Theirs are the first letters to be thrown away. Every job seeker will avoid wasted time and effort by not applying for positions for which he is only partially or not at all fitted. But if we may now assume that the applicant does have the proper qualifications for the job, how can he write the sort of letter that stays out of the wastepaper basket?

First, as has already been indicated, he ought to have a realistic conception of the sort of competition his letter will meet. Second, he must remember that the purpose of his letter is to get an interview, for few desirable positions are obtained directly by letter. The application letter is the opening step in the campaign to get a job. If it fulfills its purpose, there will be successive steps in the form of interviews, investigations of references, and closer scrutiny of qualifications; if the letter is weak, the campaign ends there. The success of the letter can be measured solely by whether the interview is granted. Third, the job seeker will do well to think of his application as a sales letter; instead of selling a product, it sells his services. The same sales principles and technique should be used as were discussed in Chapter X on Sales Letters. In the application letter, however, the writer has much greater difficulty in getting an objective point of view of himself than of some product.

Since this gift of seeing ourselves as others see us is not to be acquired overnight, the applicant will profit by showing his letter to his friends or his teachers to find out whether his self-analysis coincides with their opinions of him. Outside assistance of this sort is invaluable, provided the letter writer makes it plain that he wants constructive criticism rather than flattery. He should ask himself, "What qualifications do I have which would make me useful to a prospective employer?" To avoid the indulgence or complacence that many of us use in analyzing ourselves, he should call on the objective advice of friends or teachers in checking his answer to this question.

THE YOU ATTITUDE IN THE APPLICATION LETTER

The need for the you attitude has been stressed throughout our discussion of every type of letter thus far. Nowhere is it more difficult to obtain than in the application letter; this difficulty originates from a fundamental difference in point of view between the applicant and the prospective employer.

Since this is the most personal business letter he will ever compose, the writer's thoughts run in terms of "how badly *I* need work" or "how intensely *I* dislike my present job" or "how much *I* would like to work for a company like yours." The prospective employer cares little or nothing about such wishes; he hopes to obtain the services of an individual who may be useful or profitable to him. His function is not to give out jobs but to make money. His criterion is, "What does this writer offer which will prove useful or profitable to me?" He can, therefore, pay little attention to the applicant's likes or dislikes.

The you attitude in the application letter consists of taking the prospective employer's viewpoint and writing in terms designed to appeal to it. Remember that "what I have to offer you" is far more appealing to an employer than "what have you got for me?" The successful writer must forget *his* hopes, *his* desires, *his* dislikes —not an easy thing to do—and show his reader what personal qualities or education or experience he has that will make him a valuable employee. His letter must appeal to the self-interest of the employer by showing him what real service the applicant can render.

THE THEORY OF THE APPLICATION LETTER

We have already mentioned the similarity between the letter of application and the sales letter and the need for the objective viewpoint on the part of the job seeker. In theory, the applicant's letter should be arranged to attract attention, awaken desire, offer conviction, and stimulate action just as the sales letter does. In practice, a few minor modifications must be made. For instance, the task of attracting attention cannot be accomplished very effectively by catchy slogans or humorous stories in the application letter; nor can the applicant use the same glowing terms to describe himself that the sales writer uses for his product unless the applicant wants to be accused of excessive conceit. These are, however, but minor differences; the following analysis shows how the general principles of the sales letter may be translated into terms useful to the applicant:

1. *Attention.* Although humorous stories or catchy lines are occasionally used, the best way to attract the employer's attention is by a general statement of the service the applicant can render.

2. *Desire.* A more detailed statement of the qualities referred to in the opening paragraph, phrased in terms of how they may be of specific use to the prospective employer, constitutes the most effective method of creating desire.

3. *Conviction.* References are the usual way by which conviction is gained in the application letter; they are, in effect, the external evidence brought in to vouch for the truth of the applicant's statements. Samples of work done or statements of specific accomplishments that can be backed up by references may also be used.

4. *Action.* Since the desired action is usually an interview, the letter should close by suggesting an interview at the employer's convenience. Make it easy for him to grant the request by enclosing a self-addressed post card or mentioning a telephone number at which the applicant may be reached.

THE FORM OF THE LETTER

The specific problem which every applicant faces in arranging his letter is this: "How can I write a letter which is complete enough to include all the necessary details about myself and yet is sufficiently brief to get the reader to finish it?" The very practical objection may be raised that the letter which follows the above analysis in detail is far too long. To list all the details of one's education, business experience, personal qualities, and references' names and addresses may require at least a page and a half of tiresome detail in which the applicant's more important qualifications might be lost. Formerly, letters of application followed this outline through to the bitter end; but such letters are now considered old-fashioned and cluttered. The modern letter of application must be both readable and complete. To meet this standard, it usually contains two parts:

1. A comparatively brief letter of three or four paragraphs featuring the best qualifications of the applicant. This gives the job seeker an opportunity to emphasize whatever characteristics he wishes to.

2. A personal record sheet which gives all the necessary details about his education, experience, personal qualities, and references. This permits a complete statement of his entire career. Such a sheet can be headed "Personal Record," "Personal History," "Data Sheet," "Background," or "Autobiographical Sketch."

The advantages of this form of application are fourfold. First, it enables the applicant to feature, in a letter short enough to be readable, those qualities which best fit him for the specific position for which he is applying. Second, he can convey a far greater amount of information about himself in a readable form in this combination of letter and personal record. Third, this form of application is adaptable. Once a satisfactory personal record sheet is drawn up, it can be used over and over again; the letter to accompany it may be varied to meet the specific employment situation. Fourth, the personal record sheet presents in a concise form, which can be filed easily, all the details about an applicant and how he may be reached. Hence, it remains as a ready reminder of the job seeker's qualifications and availability if a vacancy does occur. These advantages suffice to make the combination of letter and personal record sheet the most effective technique of seeking employment by mail; the applicant who wishes to make the best presentation of himself will certainly use it.

A SPECIAL WORD TO STUDENTS

Obviously, what students should stress in their application letters and personal records is their education. The two extremes to be avoided, according to personnel men, are apologies for lack of experience, on the one hand, or assuming that the world is the college graduate's oyster, on the other. When approached without either undue humility or boundless conceit, your education is properly the feature of both your letter and personal record sheet.

Questions that a prospective employer might be interested in having you answer regarding your school or college education are:

What specific courses have you had which might be of value in the work for which you are applying? (But don't give the impression that you now know all the answers!)

How did you get along with your fellow students? (Don't express your own opinion on this subject; if you've been elected to offices or membership in organizations, the personnel man can draw his own conclusions.)

How were your grades? (Mention the third of your class you were in or what scholastic honorary societies you belonged to. If you were in the lowest third of your class, a golden silence is probably the best policy!)

What activities did you participate in? (Many employers prefer a person with broad interests in student organizations, like glee clubs, publications, and debating, to membership in Phi Beta Kappa. If you are both Phi Beta Kappa and Big Man on the Campus, you have all the answers to the old argument of whether studies or activities are the most important side of college life—but you'd better not sound as if you are now ready to inherit the earth because of these accomplishments.)

Did you earn any part of your school expenses?

Did you work during your summer vacations? If so, this may be listed under "Experience" on your personal record sheet. Be sure to include a description of the type of work you did.

These questions should suggest the way in which the detailed presentation of your educational experience should be approached. On pages 219, 220, and 221 examples of record sheets and an accompanying letter are shown. The personal record of Robert C. Cartwright on pages 219 and 220 is shown primarily as a guide for school and college students who must stress their educational preparation rather than their working experience.

THE LETTER TO ACCOMPANY THE PERSONAL RECORD

This letter is used as a device to feature the job seeker's best qualifications. It follows the structure of the sales letter, but it leaves the details to be filled in by the personal record sheet. Its contents should include:

1. A direct opening statement of why the applicant's training or education or experience may be profitable to the prospective employer

2. A short paragraph amplifying this opening statement or stressing other qualifications that might appeal to the reader's interests
3. A reference to the fact that complete details about the applicant are contained on the enclosed personal record
4. A request for an interview

The Opening Paragraph

Beginning the application letter is probably the most difficult part of the whole technique, as the hundreds of thousands can testify who have told their teachers, "If I could only get this letter started, the rest would be easy." Ideally, the opening paragraph should be direct; it should have the you attitude; it should feature the applicant's best quality. One of the simplest ways of attaining these qualities is by a summary beginning:

This is to request your consideration of my qualifications for a position with your company.

My seven years in the credit department of the Blank Company qualify me for a position as your credit manager.

Two years at Blank Business School have given me a training in business administration which should be useful to you.

Because of my three years' experience as a salesman for the White Company, I feel that I can qualify for the sales position which you advertised in this morning's *Boston Herald.*

My five years' experience in the collection department of the Black Company makes me confident that I can solve your collection problems as you want them solved.

Four years of college at the University of Michigan plus two summers of work with the Brown and Brown Company have given me a knowledge of the theory and practical application of engineering problems.

Although such beginnings are not too original, they will arouse the interest of an employer who is seeking applicants. From the writer's standpoint, these summary beginnings make the transition to the second paragraph very simple because it logically should give further details about the education or experience referred to in the opening paragraph. Furthermore, the summary beginning avoids the possibility of using such negative, colorless, or completely useless openings as:

No you attitude, trite, colorless	I should like to be considered as an applicant for a position as clerk with your firm.
Don't bother telling him such trivial details	I happened to be reading the *Washington Star* and saw your advertisement for a secretary
Don't tell him what is really his own business	Now that business is again aggressively pushing sales, you are undoubtedly adding to your staff. I should like you to consider my qualifications.

Applicants are usually too much concerned with the introductory section of their letters and, consequently, spend so much time in introducing themselves that they lose the reader's interest before the preliminaries are concluded. A good test of an introductory paragraph is to read the letter without it; if something important is omitted from the letter with such a reading, the opening paragraph is important and says something direct; the three opening paragraphs above, like the various pests in Gilbert and Sullivan, "never would be missed."

Another effective way to begin, if you have the person's permission, is the "name beginning," which mentions some business associate, friend, or customer of the prospective employer.

Mr. James Johnson of your advertising department has told me that you will soon need another secretary. My college education and three years as a private secretary in a legal firm should merit your consideration.

Mr. J. J. Moore has suggested that I might be well qualified for sales work in your International Division because of my command of four languages and my background of travel abroad.

The ultimate value of such beginnings depends almost entirely on the name used; but the fact that a friend, business associate, or customer is mentioned will invariably win consideration for this type of letter.

A third method of opening is by a question intended to challenge the reader's attention. While this type of beginning sounds rather abrupt, it has the desirable effect of forcing the applicant to plunge into the middle of his most salable qualities without any preliminaries or introduction.

Can your sales force write letters which get a minimum of 5 per cent returns? I have done that consistently and with a more highly specialized product than yours.

Can your stenographers take dictation at the rate of 120 words a minute? I can—and I am eager to prove that such speed does not lessen my accuracy.

Could you use a general utility infielder? A man who could fill in at any of the positions on your staff and relieve you of the worries and delays caused by absences of personnel?

The applicant who uses this question beginning should first be absolutely certain that his qualifications *do* answer the question which he himself raises; otherwise, his letter accomplishes nothing.

The Middle Paragraphs

The middle paragraphs of the application letter offer no great difficulty. They contain detailed statements which amplify the featured quality of the first paragraph. Specific educational experiences or personal qualifications or the names of products sold should be given as proof that the statement of the first paragraph rests on a solid foundation of fact. A mention should always be made that the enclosed personal record sheet gives complete information.

The Closing Paragraph

The closing paragraph must strongly suggest something for the prospective employer to do. Since the applicant usually wants an interview, his final paragraph ought to make it easy for the prospective employer to grant one. The following closes are effective:

May I have 15 minutes in which to substantiate these statements and to answer your questions? You may call me at Garfield 6680.

May I have an interview? The enclosed self-addressed post card will tell me when I may see you at your convenience.
(This letter encloses a stamped and addressed post card on which the prospective employer merely fills in the date and time when he can most conveniently see the applicant.)

Although I have gone into considerable detail in this letter, there are probably questions that you still want answered. May I come in for an interview? You may reach me at the address or telephone number given at the top of my personal record sheet.

May I show you actual examples of my work? Just sign the enclosed card and I shall call for an appointment at your convenience.

Notice how much stronger the above paragraphs are in motivating action than the following timid or colorless endings which the applicant should avoid:

I trust that you will grant me an interview.

I shall hope to hear from you soon.

If you feel that I may be of use to your organization, please let me come in for an interview.

How should the letter close when the prospective employer is at considerable distance from the applicant? This situation is always a difficult one to which there seems no completely correct solution. The job seeker cannot very gracefully suggest that he come 600 miles to interview the prospective employer. While a few employers would welcome so tangible an expression of interest in their company, the great majority feel that it places too much responsibility on them. They fear that the applicant is likely to conclude that since he is not deterred from coming, he certainly must have excellent prospects of getting a job. The ideal way is for the applicant to be invited for an interview or, barring that, to suggest a means by which the interview can be arranged without too much difficulty. The following closes may suggest methods of handling such a situation:

I shall be in New York from December 22 to January 3. Would it be convenient to talk to any of your staff there concerning the possibility of employment?
(This is obviously a student making good use of his Christmas vacation.)

Is it possible that you or some member of your staff will be in this vicinity within the next month? A telegram to me, collect, will bring me to see you at your convenience.

I shall be in Wilmington on May 4 and 5. May I see you on one of those days?
(It is altogether possible that the applicant's sole reason for being in Wilmington is the chance of getting this job, but it is usually better not to tell the employer this. Many an applicant has obtained a job through being willing to take a five- or six-hundred-mile trip to "Wilmington" on his own responsibility.)

You or your associates will undoubtedly be in _____ (name of the nearest large city) during the next few months. When you are there, may I have the opportunity of seeing you?

Does a representative of your company plan to visit this school? If so, I should be grateful for an opportunity to talk with him.

If none of the above can be adapted to the applicant's needs, he can always close by saying:

I hope that my qualifications will merit your consideration.

This would ordinarily be a very weak conclusion when an interview is desired or when the company is within easy reach. But when the applicant and prospective employer are hundreds or even thousands of miles apart, such a close may prove effective because it leaves the next move up to the employer. If he is indeed interested in the writer's qualifications, he can probably make some specific suggestion as to how they may meet.

The following letters show how some of these suggestions may be incorporated into complete applications accompanied by personal record sheets:

Mr. D. J. Wright, President
The William C. Bryan Company
3190 West Canal Street
Boston, Massachusetts

Dear Mr. Wright:

Could you use a dependable secretary?

During the past two years I have been with Jennings and Sessions, Inc., of this city. Because our office was small, I performed many different duties; this gave me an excellent understanding of the routine of an office.

I can take shorthand, operate a switchboard, type rapidly and accurately, act as a receptionist, and write letters dealing with routine situations. The enclosed personal record will give you complete details about my education and personal qualifications.

May I come in to see you at your convenience?

Sincerely yours,

Dear Mr. Stevens:

My ten years' experience as a salesman for the Green Wholesale Grocery Company should qualify me for a position as sales manager with your company.

I have traveled in western Massachusetts for the past six years, and my wide acquaintance among grocers and food buyers in that section should be valuable to you in marketing the new line of Premex Foods which you are introducing. My record as a salesman has been excellent, as my references will show; as a sales manager, I could use my own experience in training personnel rapidly but efficiently.

As the enclosed personal record indicates, I am a college graduate and have taken several graduate courses in Marketing and Sales Organization. I am widely known among businessmen in this city, since I have been active in many civic and fraternal organizations.

May I have an interview to substantiate these statements and to answer your questions? You may reach me at Main 4137.

Sincerely yours,

THE PERSONAL RECORD SHEET

Perhaps the greatest advantage of the personal record sheet is that it can be adapted to any individual's needs or experience. Certain general characteristics are, however, invariably the same. Centered at the top of the sheet are the name and address of the applicant; in the upper left-hand corner the telephone number or a small photograph of the job seeker. The information included in the sheet is usually arranged under the headings: education, experience, personal details, and references. Thus, the fixed parts of such a record look like this:

	Personal Record of	
Telephone	John Smith	August 22, 1953
Elmira 1246	12 Main Street	
	Elmira, New York	

Education

Experience

Personal Details

References

No pains should be spared to make the personal record sheet pleasing in appearance by keeping it well-balanced and un-crowded. The headings may be made to stand out by capitalizing all the letters or by underlining in either black or red type. The order of parts should be arranged to fit the applicant. If his accompanying letter stresses his experience, that should be placed first on the personal record. Many job seekers list their business experience in reverse order on the sound theory that a prospective employer is chiefly interested in what the applicant has done most recently. Since the material on the personal record sheet need not be expressed in complete sentences, there is room for great detail and for attractive spacing. Dates of educational and business experience ought always to be given, and wherever possible no gaps in the applicant's record should be left unaccounted for. The following sample shows the way the material under education and experience might be arranged:

Education

| 1940–1943 | Cleveland Heights High School; graduated June, 1943. |
| 1943–1947 | Oberlin College; Bachelor of Arts degree, June, 1947. |

Experience

January, 1950, to present	Employed as copywriter for the Blank Company. My duties include writing copy for electrical appliances and soliciting new accounts.
June, 1948, to January, 1950	Employed as reporter on the *Cleveland Heights Journal;* this was a temporary position which I took for the journalistic experience it offered. I acted as proofreader and general news reporter during the leave of absence of a regular member of the staff.
June, 1947, to June, 1948	Employed as proofreader in my father's print shop. This job offered the chance to learn general problems of the printing business. My duties consisted of helping out in any department where extra help was needed; this gave me the opportunity to see all the operations of the printing business in some perspective.

As in the above example, it is best under Experience to tell not merely the title of the job but to specify as exactly as possible what its duties were. Don't merely say clerk, salesman, or chemical engineer, but describe what the specific duties of these positions were.

The Personal Details heading is regarded as a miscellaneous section containing anything not classifiable under the other headings. There is no general agreement among personnel men and prospective employers as to just what should be included, but from the job seeker's viewpoint it is better to aim at completeness than to run the risk of furnishing an inadequate picture of his interests and characteristics. Hence, the listing ought to include statements concerning the applicant's age, height, weight, state of health, marital status, number and ages of children if any, nationality, church affiliation, and any interests or hobbies which might give the employer a clearer conception of the applicant's character. This personal material can be arranged in almost any fashion to suit the individual's needs. He may save space by arranging it as follows:

Personal Details

Age, 25; height, 6 feet, 1 inch; weight, 185 pounds; health, excellent; unmarried; American; veteran, USNR; Methodist; hobbies—photography and stamp collecting; sports—tennis and golf.

Or if the personal record sheet seems to have too little material on it, the personal details may be listed this way:

Personal Details

Age 25	Nationality ....American
Height ....6 ft. 1 in.	Veteran ....USNR
Weight ....185 lb.	Church ....Methodist
Health ....Excellent	Hobbies ....Photography,
Marital Status ....Unmarried	stamp collecting
	Sports ....Tennis, golf

Under References are placed the names and addresses of at least three people who can testify to the applicant's business experience, education, or character. Common courtesy requires that the consent of the individual used as a reference should be obtained *in advance* of the actual application. The full title and complete address of each reference ought always to be given; where the references are local, their telephone numbers may also be listed like this:

References

The following men have agreed to act as my references:

Mr. James Dwyer, President
The Blank Company
2034 Market Street
Newark, New Jersey   Telephone: Essex 2-3267

Professor Arthur Wright
Department of Physics
Rutgers University
New Brunswick, New Jersey   Telephone: New Brunswick 2-0200

Mr. Arthur Smith, Attorney
326 Main Street
East Orange, New Jersey   Telephone: Orange 3-6913

The example on page 221 shows how a well-organized personal record sheet looks and the material it may include.

The following personal record sheet and accompanying letter are a guide for students who must stress their education, emphasizing specific courses and school activities.

Personal Record
of
Robert C. Cartwright
271 College Street
Lafayette, Indiana

EVergreen 3926   May 15, 1953

EDUCATION

1943–47   George Washington High School, Eastport, New York. Graduated, June, 1947.

1949–53   Purdue University. I expect to receive my degree of Bachelor of Science in Metallurgical Engineering in June, 1953.

                Major Courses Studied
                        Fundamentals of Metallurgy
                        Metallurgy of Iron and Steel
                        Ferrous Alloys
                        Nonferrous Alloys

                Other Courses That Would Prove Useful in This Position
                        Fundamentals of Writing
                        Creative Writing
                        The History of Science
                        Psychology

                Activities in College
                        Glee Club—three years
                        Student paper—three years
                        Speakers Bureau—two years
                        Member of Tau Beta Pi and Blue Key

                Scholastic Record
At present I am in the upper third of my class scholastically; during my first two years I earned approximately half of my college expenses working in the bookstore and library.

EXPERIENCE

1947–49   I served for 21 months in the U.S. Army and was honorably discharged in July, 1949.

1950   June to September—During my summer vacation, I worked as a counselor at the Lakeside Boys Camp, Clifton, Michigan, where I had the chief responsibility for 24 boys, ages 12–15.

PERSONAL DETAILS

Age, 27; height, 6 feet, 1 inch; weight, 185 pounds; health, excellent; unmarried; member, Presbyterian church; hobbies—singing, writing, and photography.

REFERENCES

Professor Kenneth H. Dewitt
Head of the Department of Metallurgy
Purdue University
Lafayette, Indiana

Dr. James C. Struthers, Director
Lakeside Boys' Camp
Clifton, Michigan

Mr. William E. Knight, Principal
George Washington High School
Eastport, New York

To accompany this personal record, the student used this excellent letter with its effective "name beginning" and its closing paragraph aimed at getting an interview:

Dear Mr. Bateson:

Professor Kenneth H. Dewitt, head of the Department of Metallurgy, has informed me that your agency is looking for an engineering graduate with the ability to write about technical subjects for nontechnical readers.

My four years at Purdue have given me a thorough foundation in such fundamental sciences as physics, mathematics, and chemistry, in addition to specialized courses in metallurgy. I have also taken as many courses in English and psychology as possible with the expectation that I would enter the field of technical sales or editing following my graduation this June.

My enclosed personal record sheet will show that I have been interested in various extracurricular activities, which have given me useful experience. May I come in for an interview at your convenience? You may reach me at the address or telephone number given at the top of my personal record.

Sincerely yours,

Robert C. Cartwright

Robert C. Cartwright

[EXAMPLE OF A PERSONAL RECORD SHEET]

Personal Record
of

LOckhart 2-0392   Chester C. Parsons   November 6, 1953
6710 Parkwood Place
St. Louis, Missouri

EDUCATION

1943–1947   Beaumont High School;
graduated June, 1947

1947–1949   Central Business Institute
Business Administration Course;
graduated June, 1949

EXPERIENCE

January, 1951   Employed as an assistant to the chief engineer
to present   of the American Food Corporation, St. Louis,
Missouri. My duties included compiling reports for the chief engineer on production in
the various departments. I also made time-study analyses of production methods.

June, 1949,   Worked as a traffic rate clerk for the Con-
to January 1,   tinental Engineering Company of Pittsburgh,
1951   Pennsylvania. In this position I started as
an assistant in the traffic department and
later prepared and filed claims for
overcharges.

PERSONAL DETAILS Age, 25; height, 5 feet, 9 inches; weight, 165
pounds; health, excellent; married, no children; American; church, Episcopalian; hobbies,
photography, amateur radio, stamp collecting;
sports, tennis, bowling, and swimming.

REFERENCES   Mr. Ernest G. Blankenburg
Central Business Institute
St. Louis, Missouri

Mr. H. L. Judson, Personnel Manager
Continental Engineering Company
3926 Seventh Avenue
Pittsburgh, Pennsylvania

Mr. H. C. Williams, Chief Engineer
American Food Corporation
2241 Euclid Avenue
St. Louis, Missouri

THINGS TO AVOID IN THE CAMPAIGN FOR A JOB

Because of inexperience or ignorance of the job-seeking technique, writers frequently do their cause more harm than good by the appeals that they make in their letters. The following list of "don'ts" for application letters should help you avoid such pitfalls.

Don't appeal to the employer's sympathy. Even if a position is obtained by such a method—and that rarely happens—the conditions of employment will probably be highly unsatisfactory since the employer will always feel that he is doing the applicant a favor by granting employment. Don't say, "I need this job very badly because I must support my family"; try to get the position because you can be useful, not because you are to be pitied.

Don't discuss salary in the application letter; leave that to the interview. Advertisements often use the unfair technique of demanding that the applicant "state the salary desired"; the best answer is to suggest that salary be discussed in the interview, unless you are willing to be hired as a bargain because you will work for less than any of the other applicants.

Don't be afraid to use the pronoun "I" in your application. Since the letter is personal, "I" will be used rather more frequently than in other kinds of letters; don't try to avoid it by using "the writer," "the undersigned," or similar circumlocutions. What should be avoided is a conceited and aggressive air in the letter; a quiet tone of confidence in one's own ability is the ideal.

Don't stress dissatisfaction with your present position. If a change is desirable because no chance of advancement is offered, that is a legitimate reason which will be borne out by references. But personal dislikes or grievances should not be put into writing; if necessary, they can be explained in the interview. Employers are afraid of "the drifter" who goes from one job to another because of imagined grievances.

Don't express a lot of opinions in the application letter; particularly avoid expressing opinions about yourself. The facts of the applicant's career should speak for themselves in the letter; let the references give the opinions.

Don't waste time telling the employer a great many things he already knows. The best part of the application letter is wasted when the applicant begins with such statements as:

Because you are an advertising man, you certainly realize the value of a broad background of education. You must know, too, that a knowledge of the principles of correct English is invaluable in writing copy.

Don't apologize for applying for work. Every employer respects your honest attempt to find the position for which you are suited. No apology is expected, and none should be made because it weakens the whole letter.

ONE LETTER MORE

Let us suppose that the job seeker is in that blissful state of having worked long and well over his letter and personal record and that his labors have had their reward in an interview. Is there anything he can do but sit and wait? If he wants the satisfaction of knowing that he has done everything possible in his job-seeking campaign, he will write one more letter—called the follow-up letter. This is a very brief note of perhaps two or three sentences to be mailed to the prospective employer the day after the interview. It thanks him for his courtesy in granting the interview, it may refer to something that was said in the interview—a good device for recalling the applicant to the employer's mind—and it expresses the hope that the qualifications of the job seeker will receive favorable consideration.

Dear Mr. Moore:

I appreciate your kindness in granting me an interview yesterday. Your explanation of the problems faced by the automotive industry was very helpful to me. I hope that my past experience may entitle me to favorable consideration because the problems which you mentioned aroused my interest and I should like to aid in solving them.

Sincerely yours,

Why write such a letter? Isn't the tedious process of compiling personal record sheets and of writing the application enough? About 90 per cent of the applicants, by actual test, will think that it is—and will stop there. The 10 per cent who go on to this last step will have given an *extra* demonstration of their interest in doing everything possible to get the job. As such, it is well worth doing—and the applicant can end his follow-up letter with the

inward satisfaction that he has utilized the best technique of trying to get the position he wants.

EXERCISES

1. Write an application letter and personal record which you might use
in answer to one of the following advertisements from recent issues of
magazines, newspapers, and trade journals:

   a. Young man with college or business school education, as assistant
   to personnel manager to assist in planning and carrying out training and employment program for large department store. Retail
   experience desirable but not essential. Exceptional opportunity for
   right person. Y 34 Herald Tribune.

   b. Publicity man or woman, versatile, able to write and make newspaper contacts in handling public relations for rapidly growing
   technical institute. Previous experience not as essential as good
   personality and ability to write. X 79134 Times.

   c. Recent graduates between ages of 20 and 25 to represent large
   utility company in its negotiations with customers. Good starting
   salary; ideal working conditions—vacation with pay, all legal holidays observed. Write Box 4932, Boston, Mass.

   d. Assistant to executive—young, ambitious, capable of handling large
   volume of detail work to relieve busy executive. At least two years
   of education above high school. Low starting salary but opportunity for rapid advancement for the right man. TR 91 Herald
   Tribune.

   e. Opportunity for young business school or college men in sales with
   leading plastic manufacturer. Excellent future and earning possibilities for men who complete our training program. Write, stating
   all facts, education, experience, and salary required. P.O. Box
   2719, Philadelphia, Pa.

   f. Secretary wanted for vice-president of an advertising agency. Must
   be able to take dictation rapidly and accurately; possess good personality and the ability to get along well with other people. Good
   salary. Reply to P.O. Box 37194, New York 23, N.Y.

   g. Junior executive for mining company located in Bolivia. Single.
   Three-year contract. Salary $3,700 a year; transportation paid. Will
   consider recent graduate in engineering or business administration.
   Spanish an asset. X 79421.

   h. Secretary to vice-president; college or business school graduate
   with pleasing personality. Splendid opportunity for woman with
   initiative. Reply by typewritten letter to John Smithson and Bros.,
   86 Liberty Street.

   i. Attention college graduates in Psychology! Position open as a staff
   aide in a psychiatric institution in the East. Low starting salary,
   but to those interested in applied psychology, this position gives

experience that cannot be duplicated. Ideal experience for future teachers of psychology or anyone going into industrial testing work. Apply giving full details, Y 7956, this magazine.

j. Secretary to author. Young college or business school graduate, typing, shorthand. No previous experience desired; I prefer to train my own! Interesting work, chance to travel; some research experience desirable. Write giving full details, Box 941, Saturday Review of Literature.

2. Mr. John Devine, a friend of your father, has told you that a position in a certain department of the Novelty Manufacturing Company will soon be available. Mr. Devine is the sales manager for this company and believes that you are qualified for the position. Write a letter to Mr. Frank Anders, Personnel Manager, applying for the position.

3. For your term paper in a course in business organization, you made a survey of the methods, markets, and future possibilities of six of America's largest food-marketing organizations. You have decided to attempt to obtain employment with one of these companies following your graduation next month. Write a letter of application which could be sent to all six companies.

4. Yesterday you had an interview with Mr. E. J. Conroy, Assistant to the Personnel Director, Standard Products Company. The future possibilities of the company, as Mr. Conroy outlined them to you, seemed very attractive, and you are most interested in obtaining employment with this company. Write an appropriate follow-up letter to Mr. Conroy.

5. You are very anxious to find employment with a certain company in California. The nearest branch office of this company is in New York City, 650 miles from your home. Write your application to the central office in California with the object of being interviewed in the New York office.

6. What changes would you suggest in the following letter?

Dear Sir:

I should like very much to have you consider me for a position in your advertising department which a friend of mine who works for your company has told me will be available next month.

Although I have not had much experience in advertising, I have taken such courses in college as would best prepare me to do work along these lines. My major in college was English and I have also taken a lot of psychology, which some people think should be useful.

Although I realize that advertising men such as you do not regard work on college papers as very valuable, the writer has spent three years on the business staff of our paper and was elected business manager in the senior year. The details of my record are enclosed.

I shall hope to hear from you in the event there is an opening with your company.

Sincerely yours,

7. Criticize these opening paragraphs from application letters:
   a. You state in your ad in this morning's *Herald Tribune* that you need a salesman familiar with electrical appliances. Without question, I am the man you've been looking for.
   b. I regret taking up your time this way because I know that you are a very busy man. The fact is that I need work badly, and I've been hoping that you might help me.
   c. As a personnel man, you certainly know how hard it is to find good sales correspondents. You must have learned that years are required to develop an employee who can write letters which bring results. That's why I want you to look over my qualifications.
   d. If you happen to be adding any new men to your college training group, I would appreciate it greatly if you would be so kind as to consider my qualifications.
   e. I saw your advertisement for a young business-school graduate in this morning's *News,* and, as I read it, I realized that I had many of the qualifications you want. And so I am making this application for the position.

8. What changes would you recommend in these closing paragraphs from application letters?
   a. I must apologize for having taken so much of your time with this letter, but you probably know how difficult it is for inexperienced young people to get started in business. And, of course, the only way for us to get started is by writing letters. I hope you will write me and tell me to come in to see you.
   b. After looking over my qualifications, I am sure that you will want to talk to me. I can come in any time you say. Thanking you in advance for the interview, I am
   c. If you are hiring new men now, I do hope you will let me talk to you. Or if you don't need anyone now, would you please keep my letter on file in the event that you may need someone in the future?
   d. In this letter, I've outlined the reasons why I need work so badly. If you will give me a chance to talk with you, I can tell you about these reasons in greater detail. May I have an interview?
   e. Thanking you in advance for the consideration that you have given in reading this letter, the writer hopes to hear from you soon.

9. The following letter was sent by an experienced secretary to the presidents of fifteen companies. What would your reaction be if you received it? Would you grant an interview?

Dear Mr. Smith:

Are you looking for a person

. . . who has had college courses in Business Correspondence, English, mathematics, French, German, biology, shorthand, and typing?

. . . who has a secretarial background supplemented by considerable practice in industrial dictation, transcribing, and filing?

. . . who is interested in fostering good morale among associates by trying
to see things from their point of view?

. . . who has initiative and enthusiasm and will carry an assignment
through to completion?

. . . who has supplemented her knowledge of a subject by further study
when beginning a new position?

If these are questions you have been thinking about, you may find the answers on the next page, which gives my complete record and references.

Will you please write me at 2021 Blank Street, Centerville 6, or call me at
5-3129 at my expense, giving the time I may talk with you about how I
may assist you? So that you may be the judge, I shall welcome an opportunity to demonstrate my qualifications.

Yours very truly,

10. You have been offered positions in two different companies—A and
B—and have finally made up your mind to accept the offer of Company A,
because it gives you the opportunity to take a special six-months training
course. Yet there is a possibility that some time in the future you may wish
to seek employment with Company B, which is engaged in the same general line of business. Write a tactful letter declining Company B's offer.

11. Two months ago you had an interview with Mr. J. C. Day of the
General Supply Company. He outlined a position which seemed very attractive in both salary and future possibilities but said that it would be at
least six weeks before he could give a definite answer. You now have another offer to which you must give an answer in 10 days. You would prefer
the position with the General Supply Company, but if that does not mate-
rialize, you want to accept the other offer. Write an appropriate letter to
Mr. Day.

12. Criticize the following letters:

a. Dear Mr. West:

As I sat in your office during our interview yesterday, I certainly
realized what a busy man you are. It seemed to me that the
whole organization revolved around you because so many people
were waiting to see you and your telephone rang so often.

That's why I hope you will give favorable consideration to my
application for a position as your secretary because I thrive on
hard work, and I like to be where there are lots of people and
plenty of activity.

Sincerely yours,

b. Dear Mr. Hayden:

You'll probably be needing some assistance during the summer months because I know a lot of your employees go on vacation in July and August.

I have had two years of commercial training at James Madison High School, and now I'm very much interested in getting practical office experience. I can file, type, take dictation, and I have had a little experience in operating a switchboard.

Mr. Charles Byrnes in your company suggested that I write to you, and I hope that you will let me hear from you soon.

Very truly yours,

c. Dear Mr. Ellis:

I think you'll agree that I'm unusual because:

I completed a four-year college course in three years.

I had three short stories published in national magazines while I was an undergraduate.

My major interest was in dramatics and I was president of the Thespian Society.

Now, I'm interested in working for your advertising agency because:

I like to write.
Meeting people is my forte.
I know that you can use original ideas, and I have them.

You'll find all the details on the enclosed personal record. May I have an interview?

Sincerely yours,

d. Dear Mr. Barrett:

Let's look at my record!

Five years of successful sales in a tough territory
Three years as manager of The Johnston, White, and Williams Mfg. Company
Two and a half years with my present employer

These positions are all explained on the attached personal record sheet; you will notice that I have given every one of my previous employers as references because they will all vouch for me.

The fact of the matter is that I must leave New York because of my son's health. I don't want to be separated from my family, so I am willing to accept a big sacrifice in salary to settle in the Southwest.

I know that you will probably be coming to the annual sales convention next month. May I see you then?

Sincerely yours,

"The horror of that moment," the King went on, *"I shall never, never forget!"*
"You will, though," the Queen said, *"if you don't make a memorandum of it."*

Lewis Carroll, *Through the Looking Glass*

CHAPTER XII

Writing the Memorandum

In modern business, the exchange of ideas, information, and policies *within* the organization is a vitally important function. In essence, this function is carried on by what we may properly think of as "internal letters," in contrast to the letters previously discussed in this book which go to readers *outside* the organization. In this vital exchange of information, ideas, and policies, the memorandum, or, as it is sometimes called, the interoffice letter or intraorganization report, plays three salient roles:

1. It maintains a flow of information *across* the levels or ranks of an organization, as when an employee in one department sends a memorandum to his counterpart in another department or office.
2. It conveys information and policy procedure both *up* and *down* within the organization, as when a subordinate writes a memorandum to a superior or when a vice-president notifies his staff of a policy change or sends information on to his subordinates.
3. It serves as a reminder, as Lewis Carroll points out, and maintains a permanent record of discussions, meetings, activities, changes, procedures, or policies.

These three functions clearly show why the earmark of most successful organizations is their ability to maintain a continuous flow of information both horizontally and vertically; for no business of any size or complexity can long survive in an atmosphere of not letting "thy left hand know what thy right hand doeth." Confusion, inconsistency, and misunderstanding inevitably result when channels of internal communication are unclear or inexact.

The importance of the memorandum to the organization is matched by its significance to the individual's career. The ability to write clear, concise, readable memorandums stands high on the list of qualifications that make successful careers in business. It is no exaggeration, to paraphrase an old saying, that in modern business one is known by the memorandums he writes. Anyone meeting today's topflight executives is bound to be impressed by certain abilities which most of them have in common—the ability to sum up a situation, to reduce it to its essential terms, and to express it concisely—abilities which unquestionably contributed to these executives' success.

Unfortunately, students and novices in business frequently start their careers with an erroneous idea that the way to "impress the boss" is to write long-winded, noncommittal memos on the theory that a lengthy, involved, and detailed discussion is "more impressive" or "shows the amount of work done" better than a concise memorandum. Usually, the exact opposite is true—and, usually, the executive knows it. In their memos, inexperienced writers should keep three "don'ts" in mind—don't pad just to impress your reader; don't hedge just to make him think you've considered all the factors in the situation; and don't use ambiguous and roundabout expressions just to escape responsibility. A psychologist would doubtless have an interesting time interpreting these faults in terms of insecurity or a quest for status; for our purposes, however, we need only point to the fact that the successful executive, who is presumably secure, doesn't really need to "impress" anybody in his writing, can say "yes" or "no" without hedging, and has to take responsibility—and that beginners would do well to follow his example within the limits of their own responsibilities.

Beyond all else, *the standards set for writing memos and internal correspondence should be just as high as the standards set for communicating with those outside the company*. Many companies and individuals operate on the fallacious assumption that a kind of double standard exists. The important letter to a customer must be written and revised scrupulously until it is perfect, but the memorandum to John Jones, two floors up, can be dashed off without too much thought and with little care. This double standard produces unsatisfactory results. In the first place, it assumes that John Jones's time isn't very important and that no harm will be done if he has to spend a half-hour figuring out what you mean. But since John Jones's time is paid for by your company and since he may be passing judgment on you as employee on the basis of your memo, this assumption is both inefficient for the company and harmful to the writer. In the second place, every competent writer knows that he must constantly hold himself to the highest standards of proficiency in *everything* he writes or else all his writing suffers. Differentiating between the quality of external and internal correspondence is, therefore, as unsatisfactory as attempting to speak good English five days a week and using sloppy, careless language on week ends. The net effect must necessarily be a lowering of over-all standards; for just as economists have Gresham's law of the tendency of bad money to drive out good currency, good business writers have the law that carelessness in one medium of expression tends to replace high standards in another.

An interesting example of this truth occurred when one company, in a misguided drive for efficiency, instructed its salesmen to cut all "unnecessary" subjects and words from their memorandums. Two weeks later, this telegraphic style looked as if it would effect great savings:

Visited Jones in Atlanta. Described new line and got first order for spring suits. In interview tried to interest him in expanding stock but no success. Will follow up in three weeks but little hope for more now.

Three months later, a review of salesmen's correspondence showed them writing to customers in the same style:

Thanks for order. Goods are being shipped tomorrow. Notify if not received by Monday. Will visit Canton first of next month and look forward to seeing you.

Needless to say, the company returned to a single standard for all its communications.

The essence of written communication in any form involves three factors—*the reader, the writer,* and *the information or ideas to be conveyed.* Since the primary responsibility for bridging the gap between reader and writer always rests with the writer, the following analysis of these three factors is intended to show the writer's responsibility to his reader, to himself as a conveyor of ideas, and to his material.

The Reader

Generally speaking, writers of memorandums have the great advantage of knowing their readers personally since they work for the same company. To capitalize on this by taking the reader's point of view, the writer of a memorandum should ask himself the following questions about his reader. (And if the memo goes to more than one reader, the same questions should be raised about the group of readers.)

1. How much does he know concerning the situation I am writing about?
2. How much will he understand?
3. How does he want material presented to him?

At first glance, these may seem derogatory comments about the reader's intelligence. Actually, these questions focus squarely on the ultimate aim of all writing—the reader's understanding. By thinking through to the answers, the writer of a memorandum can avoid the worst faults of intraorganization writing:

1. *Assuming that the reader knows all the background on the subject covered in the memorandum.* The complexity and specialization of modern business often make such background impossible. Frequently executives tell employees to "send me a memo on that" *because* they want more background to make a decision; just as frequently they ask for memos from a large number of employees and do not expect to remember exactly who is doing what. When a reader asks "What on earth is this all about?" the writer has failed. His first job is to tell his reader what it is about, to orient him, to remind him. Furthermore, because the memorandum goes to the files, it becomes a semipermanent record which should be understandable six months or two years after it was written. It is always better, therefore, to err on the side of telling your reader what he may already know than to risk the impression that you have started in the middle.

2. *Assuming that the reader will understand more than he actually can.* In a complex business where accountants may send reports to salesmanagers or engineers to personnel men, this assumption constitutes a major block in communication. If an accountant reports to the comptroller about "net cost accruals," "comparison of works controllable performance," and "unfavor-

able yield variance," he can probably be sure of being understood —but he'd also better make very sure that his memo isn't going to be sent on to the directors of purchasing, sales, and engineering. Keep the language of the memorandum suitable to the reader's understanding; as writer, you have the responsibility to make him understand.

3. *Assuming that you have the one best way of presenting material in the memo.* When the goal is effective communication, the reader is the boss; you should cater to his prejudices in memos wherever you can. Some readers insist on one-page memos; others want recommendations or conclusions presented at the outset; some cling to a preference for impersonal style. The point is that a memo is usually written for a specific person or group whom the writer knows or, at least, can find out about. Present the material in the form the person or group prefers—they usually have good reasons for wanting it that way.

The Writer

From this analysis of the reader, we can readily list the obligations you have as a writer to:

1. Provide the background of facts necessary to bring your reader up-to-date
2. Tell him what your memorandum is about and how it is organized
3. Write clearly and in language he will understand
4. Present the memo in the form and style which he prefers or which company policy prescribes

The Material

Drawing an analogy from industry, we can think of the "raw material" of a memorandum as a kind of inert mass of facts, ideas, opinions, and attitudes. To transform this raw material into the finished product, the writer must process it by imposing a pattern on it, by rejecting irrelevant material, and by following it through step by step. This is organization—the process by which the writer thinks his way through his material and arranges it in a logical, orderly plan. In this process, the writer must do three things:

1. Decide on the central idea or main purpose of the memorandum.
2. Subordinate every fact or idea to this central idea or main purpose and show how these facts or ideas are related logically to the central theme.
3. Reject any material which is superfluous, irrelevant, or unnecessary for the reader's understanding of the central idea.

We can illustrate this process best by a specific example, which occurs frequently in business. Suppose that your superior has sent you to New York to attend a three-day meeting on the problems of modern management and has asked you to send him a memo about the meetings when you return. You could conceivably begin your memorandum this way:

As you requested, I attended the three-day meetings in New York on "The Problems of Modern Management."

After a rather rough flight which got me there 45 minutes late, I tried to get a room at the hotel where the meetings were held but there was apparently a mix-up in reservations. I then had to spend another hour locating a room and finally arrived at the meeting at the end of the president's address of welcome. Incidentally, a friend told me later that I hadn't missed anything.

On Monday morning, I heard talks on "The Obligations of Modern Management" and "Changing Concepts of Today's Executive." That afternoon, I heard an excellent presentation by Mr. Fred W. Becker on a specific program for "Evaluating and Preparing Tomorrow's Executive" which the Blank Company has carried on during the past year. This program consists of . . . .

Ridiculous? Not at all; this memorandum typifies too much of present writing with its irrelevant detail and rambling style. Above all else, it follows the thoughtless pattern, if indeed it can be called a pattern, of mere time sequence. The result is a tiresome, detailed, blow-by-blow account which irks the reader and makes him lose patience.

Suppose, instead, that the writer of the memo had asked himself two questions:

1. What does my supervisor want to learn from my visit to the meetings?
2. How can I best tell him?

From such thinking, he could probably draw two conclusions—the supervisor wants to know what the writer learned that might be useful to his company and wants him to sort out all the information so that it will be presented in readable form to stress only the essentials. Elementary as it seems, this is the essence of good organization. The result might be a memorandum which starts this way:

This report is intended to summarize those meetings on "The Problems of Modern Management" which I thought were especially applicable to our own problems. Of all the discussions listed on the attached program, the following three seemed worth consideration since they concern problems which we have been thinking about:

1. Mr. Fred W. Becker of the Blank Company described his company's experience with a one-year training program to select and prepare personnel for executive responsibilities. This company has spent almost two years developing a method of evaluating management personnel; they now have an elaborate rating sheet by which every member of management is rated by (a) his immediate superior, (b) two members of the executive staff, and (c) five subordinates. At my request, Mr. Becker will send you a copy of this rating sheet which I think might help us to develop one of our own.

Notice what has been accomplished in about the same number of words as the first example used for mere rambling. This writer tells his reader the following things:

1. What the memo concerns (a report on the meetings)
2. The method of selection (information most applicable to the organization's problems)
3. The method of rejection (the attached program gives all the unimportant details)
4. The organization (three meetings are described in detail because they are most useful to the reader)

Following logically through to the central theme of what the supervisor wants to learn from the employee's convention attendance, the employee would almost inevitably end such a memo with a paragraph like this:

In general, I found the meetings interesting and informative. I believe that the three discussions I have summarized were sufficiently valuable to justify the entire trip. On the basis of my experience, I would certainly recommend that our company be represented at next year's convention in Dallas. I would suggest that if it is possible we send two representatives to that meeting—one from our department and one from the finance and accounting division, who would have a background for understanding the rather technical discussions of tax structures, depreciation, and cost analysis. The extra benefits derived from having two representatives would, in my judgment, far outweigh the added expense.

To point up what was said earlier concerning the importance of memo writing in the individual's career, imagine yourself as the supervisor receiving both the memos discussed. Which writer would you send to next year's conference? And which one has the qualities that lead to advancement? The fact that the answer is so obvious clearly shows the importance of organizing material from the reader's point of view and boiling it all down in terms that he can understand.

THE FORM OF THE MEMORANDUM

Most companies have developed specific printed forms for their memos in an attempt to reduce all details to a standard pattern. The ultimate purpose of any such form should be to help the writer get on with his message as soon as possible and to place at the top of the first page, where it is readily accessible in the files, all the information about who wrote it, to whom it was sent, when it was written, and what was its subject. These topics should be arranged for maximum efficiency in typing and easy reading, as in the following typical example:

THE BLANK ELECTRIC COMPANY

MEMORANDUM   PAGE NO. 1

TO Members of   FROM   C. W. Black DATE May 17, 1953
   Management Committee PHONE 757
                         SUBJECT Advanced Management Program

The individual elements of such a form will, of course, depend on the size, diversity, and location of the business. Companies with plants or buildings in various places usually have "Location" or "Plant" or "Building" in place of the phone extension. Businesses with a large number of offices in the same building frequently include "Room" or "Office" or "Department" under "To" and "From" so that internal mail can be delivered easily. Small concerns often reduce the elements to "To," "From," "Subject," and "Date." Practice varies considerably on whether titles are used, either as part of the printed form or the typed information; for example, the use of such titles as

TO: Mr. Florent E. Virden, Director of Personnel

FROM: Mr. Charles W. Black, Manager of Personnel Evaluation

should be cut to a minimum unless a very good reason exists for their use. Generally speaking, the larger the company, the more information is needed; but even here, every element on the memo form should be carefully scrutinized to see whether it is absolutely necessary. In an attempt to take care of every contingency, some companies have developed such cumbersome memo forms that they defeat the main purpose of having such forms printed—namely, to reduce details to a standardized form, easily typed, read, and filed. The classic four W's, which a good newspaper reporter should answer in his lead, still constitute the best guide for material to be included on a memo form—Who? What? When? Where?

WRITING THE MEMORANDUM

We have already analyzed the interrelated factors in writing the memorandum as they affect the reader, the writer, and the material. One other factor directly bears on memo writing—time. The great majority of memos are undoubtedly written under conditions that add up to instructions to "do this right away." The department head, the section chief, or the top executive usually couches his directions in such terms as, "Send out a reminder of that meeting tomorrow," or "Give me a memo on last month's employment figures so that I can have them for today's conference," or "Let me have a summary of the meeting I missed before we discuss it tomorrow." As a matter of fact, it is precisely because the memo is so well adapted to such urgent conditions that business has made it such an important medium of exchange.

This pressure of time allows no opportunity for "fancy" writing or prolonged revision. The reader usually wants information, recommendations, or background material concisely stated in plain language. Certain patterns of thought, which the writer can quickly impose on his material are, therefore, very useful in writing memos quickly.

Probably the most widely used pattern for the memorandum is:

1. Telling your reader what you are going to do and how you are going to do it
2. Doing what you said you were going to do in the way you told him you would
3. Summing up what you have done or drawing conclusions or making recommendations on the basis of what you have said

This device, used by all good writers and speakers—remember how the preacher after his introductory statement usually announces the three points of his sermon and sums them up at the end?—is merely a functional statement of the introduction, body, and conclusion technique you learned in school as the main headings of an outline. A memo written in this pattern is easy to follow and has a definite movement forward toward its summary, conclusion, or recommendations. It is, therefore, ideally suited to answering requests for memos which "give me your recommendations on that situation in the sales office" or "let me have a summary of that analysis you made of office equipment."

A second pattern for memos is time sequence, or narration; here, events are followed through from first to most recent. In too many instances, this pattern is used merely because it is an easy way out for the writer, which is exactly what is wrong with the blow-by-blow account of the convention on page 235. On the other hand, it offers a very logical way of presenting material when you are asked to "give me some background material on why we located our branch office at Centerville two years ago" or to "list the points covered in that sales conference yesterday."

A third pattern develops the logical connection between cause and effect. Sometimes the effect is known and the memo writer is asked to present an analysis of what produced it when he is requested to "send me a memo on why our sales fell off last month in the Los Angeles office." Sometimes the cause is known and the possible effect or effects must be inferred, as when he is asked to submit a memo on "how much salary expense was saved by our introducing mechanized bookkeeping equipment."

In addition to the over-all pattern, the memo writer can help his reader by breaking material up into small units with appropriate headings. This is particularly helpful in long memos. In shorter memos, he should *list* items which can logically be grouped together, taking care that the items in the list are given in parallel form. Notice how illogical the third item is in the following excerpt from a memo because it violates this principle:

In his statement before the committee, Mr. Green urged that we do three things:

1. Use mechanical equipment for all routine operations
2. Stress the need for better service at lower cost with all our employees at their quarterly meetings
3. Assurance to all plant employees that the company has a highly organized safety program

The same general qualities that mark all good business writing characterize the effective memorandum—short sentences, short paragraphs, concise nontechnical expressions, and a readable tone of "here's what it's all about." Notice how the following memos illustrate these characteristics.

Examples of Short Memorandums

Memorandum Giving Information

This will remind you that we agreed in our last management meeting to extend our discussions for three additional sessions. We have now scheduled these as follows:

March 27—Speaker: Professor Ernest Dale, Columbia University
          Subject: "Organization"
April 24—Speaker: Mr. Arch Potter, Reed, Barton, and Stow, Inc.
          Subject: "Management Compensation"
May 21—Speaker: Mr. Karl Rudolph, Doane and Smith
          Subject: "Financial Structure and Interpretation"

All sessions will start at 9:30 A.M. in Conference Room C. If you *cannot* attend any of these meetings, please let me know before March 20.

Memorandum Giving Policy and Procedure

As you know, the Company has designated certain organizations in which we will pay one-half the membership fees. To assure uniform procedure in all departments, we request that you follow these instructions:

1. Each employee wishing to join or renew membership in such an organization should first obtain the approval of his department head.
2. The employee will then make his own arrangements for joining, pay the full amount of the fees, and obtain a receipt showing the amount and the period covered.

3. He will then prepare a petty-expense voucher, Form H-3, for one-half the amount of the fees.
4. His department head will then sign the voucher, which the employee may take to the Cashier's Office, Room 107, to receive his check for reimbursement.

If you have any questions about our policy or procedure in this matter, I will be glad to discuss them with you. We, of course, want to be as generous as possible in helping employees with these memberships; at the same time, I urge you to scrutinize each application carefully to see that it will be of practical benefit to the Company.

Memorandum Asking for Recommendations

During the last two months, we have had approximately 3,000 requests for the pamphlet "A Giant Conserves His Resources," which we issued for our twenty-fifth anniversary. I should like your recommendation as to whether we should reissue this pamphlet which is out of print.

Factors to Consider

Mr. C. M. Eckman has reported the following facts which I hope you will consider carefully in your recommendation:

1. The cost of reprinting 5,000 copies is approximately $2,250.
2. An analysis of the requests we now have shows that 1,731 came from high-school and college students, 339 from other industries, and 891 from individuals.
3. Our previous printing of 10,000 copies was sent to all shareholders, employees, and key industrial and educational leaders in the area we serve.
4. Pages 12–15 of the pamphlet should probably be revised since we now have more up-to-date sales figures and more accurate analyses of costs.

Recommendations

Since I am sending this request to 47 members of management, I will greatly appreciate your making your recommendation in the form of answers to the following questions so that we may tabulate the results easily:

1. Do you think we should reprint 5,000 copies of the pamphlet?
2. What, in your opinion, was the chief value of this publication?
3. Could it be improved in any way to get across our message that modern industry is interested in conserving natural resources?

May I have your answers by May 21?

Example of a Long Memorandum

This memo covers the general characteristics our company should aim at in our audit reports. It results from a two-week survey by the procedures group at the request of Mr. C. F. Smith, Controller.

Importance and Scope of Audit Reports

Since our audit reports are the principal means of recording our work, they greatly influence the judgments made about our activities and our personnel. Furthermore, they go to people who have many demands on their time and who are primarily interested in results.

For these readers, audit reports should be short, concise, and factual. Usually they should include the following:

1. What was covered in the audit
2. What was revealed that should be called to the manager's attention
3. What is the effect of the variance, if there is one
4. What you recommend to correct the situation

While we do not want reports which follow a rigid pattern, we can reduce both writing and reading time by following these topics.

General Arrangement and Organization

Audit reports should generally include:

1. A letter of transmittal which serves as a guide to tell the reader what really significant information the report contains.
2. The main section of the report covering the scope, findings, and recommendations.
3. The schedules and exhibits which present documentary evidence to support a finding or a recommendation. In the Quarterly Audit Reports, this should be labeled "Exhibit Section" with the exhibits clearly separated into three classifications:

   a. Information furnished the previous month to all managers who will read the report
   b. Material previously furnished to some, but not all, district supervisors
   c. Material which the auditor creates and which does not duplicate previous monthly reports

As a general guide, we should limit material to what is necessary for a complete understanding of the audit, being careful always to include enough to avoid any possible misinterpretation.

Review with Local Management Personnel

Wherever possible, discuss your findings with the local management *before* you prepare the final report. This review is intended to do three things:

1. Assure the examining auditor that his data and opinions are correct and factual.
2. Minimize any feeling in the local office that the audit is an undercover operation.
3. Provide the local manager with advance information on the report so

that he can take corrective action immediately or recommend changes which lie outside his authority.

Analysis of Present Reports

Our survey covering the entire Auditing Division showed that we can improve reports by:

1. Putting all facts in a general context. For instance, if the auditor says, "Ten errors were discovered," it is difficult for the reader to evaluate the situation. How many items were examined? What was the ratio of errors? Is this ratio within our generally accepted standards or is it too high?
2. Making all statements clear-cut and forthright. Many comments in our present reports seem to hedge. They force the reader to read between the lines. Where an honest difference of opinion exists between the auditor and local manager, say so clearly. If possible, give the reasons for both opinions so that the reader can pass factual judgment rather than guessing.
3. Ending with a definite conclusion. When everything reviewed complies with established policies, say so. If you believe policies should be changed, say so, giving your reasons and the benefits which may result from the change.

Conclusion

Our sole aim is to make our audit reports effective instruments for telling management whether action is needed, and, if so, what action should be taken. Remember that you write for readers who dislike technical terms, detailed analyses, and repetitious statements. Give them adequate information for making judgments; present your recommendations clearly; revise your report thoroughly. By doing so, you can help us make our reports an effective management tool.

EXERCISES

1. Write a memorandum to answer the following request from your department head: "I have noticed that memos submitted to me come in a variety of styles and forms. Will you set up standards that you would recommend for us to follow and attach a sample of a memo form which we could have printed?"

2. You have been asked to send your supervisor a memo summing up the discussion in a meeting which he could not attend. Using any class discussion or meeting you have recently attended as your subject matter, write a one-page memorandum to answer this request.

3. Your employer has assigned you to analyze all the carbon copies of correspondence sent out by your company during one week. You have

analyzed this correspondence very carefully and found four major faults: excessive wordiness, a large number of trite expressions, slovenly typing with crowded margins and careless spelling, and a variety of letter forms. You now believe that a training program for typists and dictators is needed and, above all, that the company letterhead, listing the 46 branch offices, should be changed to improve the appearance of the company's letters. In giving you this assignment, your boss said, "I looked over a lot of our letters last week, and they seemed pretty good to me. But I'd like to know if you'd make any changes, so give me your recommendations."

4. Prepare a memorandum to go over your supervisor's signature to all employees calling attention to the policy that "all company personnel are expected to be at work promptly at 9:00 A.M. Habitual tardiness will result in discharge." This memorandum is intended to serve as a warning to members of the sales department, where there has been increasing tardiness within the past week. While you yourself prefer a personalized style, you know your supervisor will not accept anything but a very impersonal method of writing.

5. Using some situation within your school or business which you think should be changed, write a memorandum to your superior describing the situation and recommending specific changes.

6. Because of a last minute emergency, all your office employees must be called on to work on Memorial Day. Factory employees, on the other hand, will have a holiday since the production of goods is running far ahead of the office records, and the management of the company is using Memorial Day as a means of reducing this lag. Company policy, as set forth in the "Procedures Manual," does not permit overtime pay for office workers. Write a memorandum, which will be issued over the signature of the Director of Personnel, explaining this situation and informing all office workers that if the lag in office work is corrected by July 4, they will be given a two-day holiday at that time.

7. Your company will pay one-half the tuition for courses taken in local evening schools so long as "such courses are of direct benefit to the employee's work." Recently a number of employees have requested half-tuition refunds for such courses as folk dancing, elementary oil painting, and music appreciation. Write a memo stating the intent of the original policy and giving specific illustrations where it may be properly applied and where it does not apply.

8. The Employees Association, of which you are the secretary, has built up a fund of almost $3,000 from various projects over the past three years. Among the suggestions for spending the money, which were made by the board of governors at their last meeting, were to hold a formal dance with a "big name" orchestra, to set up a scholarship fund for children of employees, to invest the money as a permanent source of income to defray minor expenses, and to purchase books and magazines for the employees' reading room. The board of governors has asked you to prepare a memorandum to be sent to all members to get their opinions on possible

policies for using this fund and specific projects for which it could be used. Write the memorandum.

9. Prepare a memorandum for your boss, who told you, "I'm getting worried about the amount of time our people are spending in the 'coffee hour.' It seems to me that this thing is getting out of hand. Send me a memo telling me what you think we should do."

10. Using material that is familiar to you, write a brief memorandum
   a. To announce a meeting
   b. To explain a course of action
   c. To explain a problem and to offer possible solutions which may be considered in a meeting
   d. To announce the appointment of a man from outside your organization to an important job within your company
   e. To report to your supervisor on a meeting you have attended
   f. To remind someone that an action must be taken before a deadline
   g. To survey the opinions of a group concerning a policy or action
   h. To report your business or educational activities for one week
   i. To recommend that a specific action or policy should be changed
   j. To sum up the merits or faults of a book on which your supervisor has asked for a one-page memo

Index